D1535357

The Age of Afflue.

The Age of Affluence
1951–1964

edited by

VERNON BOGDANOR
Fellow and Tutor of Brasenose College, Oxford

and

ROBERT SKIDELSKY
Research Fellow, British Academy

MACMILLAN

First published 1970 by
MACMILLAN AND CO LTD
London and Basingstoke
Associated companies in New York Toronto
Dublin Melbourne Johannesburg and Madras

SBN (boards) 333 09267 8
(paper) 333 11520 1

Printed in Great Britain by
RICHARD CLAY (THE CHAUCER PRESS) LTD
Bungay, Suffolk

Contents

5

Preface

WE have not aimed in this book at producing a comprehensive or final view of the years from 1951 to 1964. This, in any case, would be impossible. What we have tried to do is to draw together some of the crucial episodes of the period; most of the chapters are reflections on the twin themes of affluence and illusion.

We should like to thank Mr Philip Williams for his help and encouragement at all stages in the preparation of this book.

V.B.
R.S.

Introduction

TEN years ago it was possible, and indeed usual, to look back on the 1950s as an age of prosperity and achievement. This was certainly the verdict of the electorate which in 1959 returned a Conservative Government to power with a handsome majority, for the third time running. Today we are more likely to remember the whole period as an age of illusion, of missed opportunities, with Macmillan as the magician whose wonderful act kept us too long distracted from reality. Each generation, it seems, rewrites history in the light of its own experiences, and what has altered the verdict on the 1950s has been the experience of the troubles of the 1960s, which stem in part at least from the neglect of the earlier decade. Already by 1964 the appeal of the slogan 'Thirteen Wasted Years' was strong enough to give Labour a tiny majority; in the years following it has been confirmed almost as the conventional wisdom. What the verdict will be in ten years' time it is difficult to say. Perhaps the period of Conservative rule will be looked upon as the last period of quiet before the storm, rather like the Edwardian age which in some respects it resembles. In that case its tranquillity will come to be valued more highly than its omissions.

The illusion with the most profound consequences was the economic one. In his book *The Affluent Society* (1958), J. K. Galbraith intended to sketch an outline of a developed society which had in large part solved the problem of production, and could concentrate its energies on other things. The class struggle was obsolete; so also were the ideologies which sought to justify it. Politics would no longer involve large general choices but disagreement over more limited and piecemeal issues.

7

Uncritical transference of Galbraith's thesis into the British context helped obscure the fact that Britain had not, in fact, solved its economic problems. The optimism of the early 1950s is, however, perfectly understandable. From 1952 to 1955 Britain benefited from the very rapid growth of world trade in industrialised products, from the fall in world commodity prices and the consequent improvement in the terms of trade. The years 1952–5 were, as T. W. Hutchison has put it. 'ignorantly blissful years' in which *The Economist* could comment complacently, 'The miracle has happened . . . full employment without inflation' (June 1954). But this miracle was built upon temporary and fortuitous circumstances. From 1955, Britain was bedevilled by a series of sterling crises which gradually forced upon the attention of politicians problems they wished to avoid.

It is now possible to see that for Britain the years 1951–64 were neither a period of continuous and uninterrupted expansion as the Conservatives would have us believe, nor the 'Thirteen Wasted Years' of Labour mythology. They were, certainly, years during which genuine and important gains were made; but these gains gave Britain no more than a breathing-space during which she might have modernised her industrial structure and resolved the conflict between domestic expansion and her international obligations. The opportunity was not taken, however, and many of the political and economic difficulties facing Britain today bear witness to this failure.

In 1962 Dean Acheson said, 'Britain has lost an empire; she has not yet found a role.' After the Second World War, Churchill had insisted, in his famous doctrine of the 'three circles', that Britain could remain the closest ally of the United States and the head of the Commonwealth, as well as being a force in European affairs. The pressure of events soon showed, however, that these roles could not all be maintained simultaneously; a choice between them had to be made. But the failure to rethink her world role was as evident in diplomacy as in economics. Macmillan foresaw and expedited the final liquidation of Empire, but he had

8

few ideas about what to put in its place. The Commonwealth was certainly no substitute for Empire. For it
lacked the inner cohesion and loyalties of the 'white
dominions'. It represented, in Nicholas Mansergh's
phrase, little more than a 'balance of expediency'. The
special relationship with the United States was to remain the cornerstone of British policy. But without the
Empire, this relationship was bound to become increasingly one between master and servant, a reality
that could not be disguised by Macmillan's view that
Britain was to play Greece to America's Rome.

These illusions blinded Macmillan, as they did other
British politicians, to the far-reaching changes occur-
ring in Europe. It is a truism that during these years
Britain could have had the leadership of Europe for
the asking, had she been prepared to rethink her
traditional commitments. Instead, as de Gaulle saw it,
she sold her birthright for Polaris missiles, with the
Nassau Agreement of 1962. The imperial illusion remained although the Empire itself had gone; Britain
was to be a junior partner in the Pax Americana. The
rhetoric of the world role remained essential to the
Conservatives, who still saw themselves as an imperial
party; essential also to the Labour Party, whose moral
ambitions remained world-wide. These grandiose
schemes were entertained without any regard for
Britain's economic ability to sustain them; within two
years of Harold Wilson's accession to office they were
to collapse with ignominy. The Commonwealth had
become more insubstantial than ever, combining, as
one commentator put it in 1964, 'the maximum chance
of involvement, embarrassment, expense and humiliation with the minimum effect on the course of events'.
The Cuban missile crisis of 1962 made many question
the value of the 'special relationship'. For it seemed as
if Britain could, without being consulted in advance
by the United States, find herself involved in nuclear
war. Meanwhile Britain's military position East of
Suez was becoming untenable, and she had been excluded from Europe.

What is the explanation of these illusions? For we
are of course dealing not with one illusion but with

9

several, which reacted upon, and reinforced, each other. We are not here concerned with fundamental explanations, though if we were we should no doubt point to the desire for relaxation which inevitably follows periods of sustained effort such as the years 1940–51, and also to the psychological need to hide the facts of decline.

At the political level these psychological factors revealed themselves in consensus. In economics, as in foreign policy, consensus reigned. Consensus is, indeed, a fundamental idea in understanding the politics of the 1950s. It signified acceptance of the mixed economy and the Welfare State. From this point of view, it did entail a real humanising and civilising of the political battle. The Conservatives, as well as acquiescing in withdrawal from Empire, became genuinely attuned to the demands of a mass electorate. The Labour Party shed its unrealistic faith in nationalisation as a cure for all social ills. Consensus did ensure the emancipation of politics from the ghosts of the past; unfortunately it also imposed a moratorium on the raising of new and vital issues. For consensus also signified acceptance of traditional assumptions concerning Britain's political and economic role in the world. Thus real and important political choices came to be submerged in a generalised commitment to the objective of economic growth.

Economic growth was essential to the consensus. It enabled the Conservatives to offer for the first time a viable alternative to Socialism with their idea of a property-owning democracy. No one need be defeated in the class war because no war was being fought. Capitalism could provide affluence for the working class while at the same time preserving the gains of the well-to-do. This argument was given plausibility by the coincidence between the prosperity of the years 1952–5 5 and the Conservative policy of 'setting the people free'.

For the Labour Party, on the other hand, growth seemed to promise victory to the working class in the class struggle without the necessity of having to do battle with capitalism. Redistribution could be financed from the proceeds of growth without hurting the better off. Harold Wilson was to argue that the development of science alone would make the case for Socialism overwhelming, for planning would more than ever be required to prevent the abuses of technology, and to harness scientific possibilities to public needs. In this up-to-date version of Fabianism, the imperatives of national efficiency would inevitably produce Socialism without the need for class conflict.

This nebulous ideology of growth was particularly appropriate to the changing social structure of Britain in the 1950s. Consensus was the natural product of a lessening class antagonism, which in turn reflected a seeming trend towards embourgeoisement. New groupings of skilled and scientific workers complicated the traditional picture of British society. Polarisation between worker and management was dissolving into the subtler hierarchies of a world based upon 'status symbols', as measured by consumer goods – badges of the new affluence. The tight electoral struggle made competition for this middle ground of 'white-collar' workers crucial, and neither party felt able to antagonise it with ideological appeals.

Indeed, one of the striking characteristics of the 1950s was the absence of any major intellectual challenges to the dominant political assumptions. The thinking of the party intellectuals – Crosland and Strachey on the Labour side, the Bow Group on the Conservative side – tended towards acceptance of the political and economic assumptions behind Britain's traditional world role. The reasons for this have already been explained. More surprising was the passivity of the universities. Here we can discern a process which received proper attention only in the 1960s, namely the increasingly active identification of a large and influential segment of the academic community with the forces supporting the *status quo*.

The reasons for this are various and can only be hinted at here. At the level of ideas, there was a genuine revulsion against the ideological thinking of the 1930s, which had undermined democratic institutions and produced the excesses of both Fascism and Communism. (The shock of McCarthyism had a similar effect in the United States.) At the same time there was a real belief that the post-Keynesian mixed economy provided for the first time the possibility of a good life for all its members. Marxism, the main dissenting ideology, was thus simultaneously discredited by both Stalinism and Keynesianism. Not only did it lead to violence and terror, but its predictions about the collapse of capitalism had not come true.

The political science taught and studied at the universities reflected these preoccupations. It aimed at studying political behaviour, rather than making political judgments. But in renouncing a critical or visionary role, the political scientists, by implication, aligned themselves with the *status quo*. Their concern was with describing and explaining how the political system worked rather than with suggesting alternatives and improvements. This became even more evident when leading political scientists became political commentators or pundits, explaining to the uninitiated, on television and in the 'quality' Press, the mechanics and rules of the electoral and Parliamentary game. In general, the academic analysis of politics reflected the general complacency and inertia of the 1950s and strengthened them. Certainly the universities were dead in the 1950s as centres of political ideas and discussion. They were unable therefore to challenge the conventional wisdom of the day.

It is against this background of academic conformism that such intellectual challenges as arose to the dominant orthodoxies must be viewed. We have said little or nothing about the Liberal Party, which despite some good ideas (e.g. on Europe) was too closely committed to the conventions of the political system to have much impact. Nor, unfortunately, have we much to say on the New Left, exiles from Communism, who were beginning to have an influence on the Labour Party in the last period of Gaitskell's leadership (their influence rapidly disappeared when Wilson took over). We are left with two major protest movements – the Angry Young Men, and the Campaign for Nuclear Disarmament.

The Campaign for Nuclear Disarmament was a protest against the immorality of defending the affluent society with nuclear weapons. Of what permanent significance were the social gains at home, if foreign affairs remained the domain of an unregenerate power politics based on nuclear calculation? In its moral absolutism, C.N.D. was in the great dissenting tradition in British foreign policy; nor were its methods of mass demonstration, marches and, at the extreme, civil disobedience anything new, although their reappearance at the end of a tranquil decade surprised and alarmed many commentators who considered that such methods had gone from political life for ever.

What was completely novel about C.N.D. was its clientele. It represented the first appearance of youth on the political stage. For the first time in British life the rebellion of the young against the old acquired a political dimension. The radical middle-class youth which thronged C.N.D. were products of an enlightened education, in whom personal and political inhibition seemed to find a simultaneous release. In contrast to them, the lumpenproletarian 'Teddy Boys' who had so alarmed respectable society in the mid-1950s seemed old-fashioned, bizarre – even, in retrospect, slightly comic. Yet both C.N.D. and the 'Teddy Boys', in their highly dissimilar ways, were a foretaste of the new power of youth to fascinate, alarm and disrupt adult society, as well as being early symptoms of an alienation from the meritocratic, technological goals of the affluent society. It was, above all, the arrival of youth on the political stage that marked the beginning of the end of consensus. For the passions and hopes of youth could not be attuned to the subdued modulations of the 1950s, marked as they were by a profound mistrust of popular movements of any kind. Indeed the failure to take account of the spiritual malaise which lay behind many of the demands of the young was a contributory cause of the 'student revolt' of the late 1960s.

In contrast to C.N.D., the Angry Young Men were radicals who had already been disillusioned. Despite the social revolution of the 1940s, life in the 1950s remained very much as it had always been. The social structure itself remained intact; society was still snobbish and acquisitive; the 'white-gloved hand' still waved from the carriage window. One of the paradoxical consequences of affluence and greater equality of opportunity was to narrow human life to the quest for goods, status, position. The more room at the top there was, the more energy was expended trying to get there. The Angries responded with anger rather than with reasoned argument; they had as little faith in the Marxist critique as anyone else at the time. In other words they accepted that the economic problem had been solved. Unlike the academics, though, they found life in the Affluent Society unsatisfying. Their philosophy boiled down to an expansion of human awareness, an upgrading of 'authentic' human feelings and experiences, at the expense of the more superficial ones offered by the consumer society.

Sociologically the movement was a product of the early days of the meritocracy, a revolt of the 'redbrick' universities against the Oxbridge establishment. It was during the 1950s that the phrase 'the Establishment' first came into use to denote the continued dominance of the old cliques. Yet, paradoxically the very fact of worldly success marked the ending of the movement's 'outsider' status and its absorption into the literary establishment. Like so many other forms of protest in Britain, the Angry Young Men became emasculated by winning speedy yet superficial acceptance. The collapse of the movement shows that in the 1950s and the early 1960s the Affluent Society was rich and secure enough to buy off its critics, to smother them with publicity, status and financial success, in a new variant of the age-old tactic of absorption practised so skilfully by the British governing classes.

Nevertheless there was a legacy; or more accurately, the Angry Young Men represented part of a wider concern with the quality of life and experience in an affluent society. A few politicians, such as Anthony Crosland in *The Future of Socialism* (1956), did, it is true, emphasise the connection between Socialism and the quality of life. But such concerns never occupied

14

the centre of the political stage, and their continued expression was left to the neo-Marxists of the New Left, and to the new and invigorating styles apparent in the world of popular culture. The basic question was a serious one, however uneven and diverse the treatment: of what value were the purely mechanical and institutional changes associated with affluence and the welfare state, unless they led to an enhanced quality of life and increased possibilities of self-development and self-realisation? This question was easy to ignore in the first flush of enthusiasm for the new society created by social engineering and Keynesian economics, and in a sense it has been overtaken by the economic problems of the 1960s which focused attention on more mundane concerns, equally ignored in the temporary euphoria of affluence. It is a question, nevertheless, to which it seems likely that the politics of the future will increasingly revert.

But the reopening of the debate on the larger questions of Britain's future, both domestic and international, belongs properly to the story of the 1960s. For in the 1950s the politics of consensus remained supreme. It was adequate in dealing with detailed problems within the agreed framework of the 'three circles' doctrine, but unable to call the framework itself into question, to choose between conflicting conceptions of Britain's proper role. The politics to which consensus gave rise was one which reacted to events, but it was not able to provide the imaginative understanding needed to confront the future. For this the inherited framework was inadequate. The traditional party battle increasingly gave rise to apathy during the 1950s as divisions between the parties came less and less to reflect divisions of opinion on the real issues of the day; and the assumptions of the party system prevented realistic debate. For during the 1950s it was gradually being discovered that the questions vital to Britain's future could not be discussed within the confines of the party system and the political conventions which surrounded it. These questions remained to plague Britain in the 1960s. The true achievement of the Age of Affluence was, in Anthony Hartley's words, to have liquidated the past, without having begun to build the future.

1 Mr Macmillan and the Edwardian Style

L. A. Siedentop

How familiar, and yet how puzzling, is Asquith's description of the 'effortless superiority' of Balliol men! For anyone who knows Balliol today, or has read its history in the past century, the most striking thing about the college is its emphasis on effort, on striving, emulation and achievement. Balliol has always seemed to stand out and protest against the languid irony of Oxford aestheticism. And yet the extremes do sometimes meet. There is no better example of this than Harold Macmillan.

Looking back, it is fascinating to see how such apparently contradictory qualities came to be joined in Macmillan. And it is instructive. For it sheds light not only on an unusually complicated man but on a class educated to the attitudes of easy imperial preponderance, and on a country beginning to lose confidence in itself.

Macmillan's appearance and manner, as they became known in the later 1950s, remain vividly in mind even now. The heavily hooded but wary eyes, the sagging jaw which suggested weariness, the toothiness, the shambling gait which contrasted so oddly with his controlled, precise and epigrammatic turn of phrase, the drawl in which wide-ranging historical observations and old-fashioned patriotic appeals were delivered, and, finally, the well-cut but rather ill-kempt clothes which went so well with the long but often dishevelled hair and moustache.

The langour, irony and careless elegance which helped to make up Macmillan's 'Edwardian' style hardly need to be emphasised. They were quickly recognised once he became Prime Minister, and the act of recognition seemed to make them more pronounced – leading to charges that he was a *poseur*, a mere actor. What does need to be emphasised about Harold Macmillan, on the other hand, is the hard-working and hard-headed professionalism which went hand in hand with his more flamboyant qualities. For Macmillan had a prodigious interest in power and a remarkable mastery of it. Indeed, his story is one of the persistent pursuit of power.

Less justly than almost any recent politician can Macmillan be called an amateur. From the moment he became really active in public affairs in the 1930s, Macmillan impressed those around him with his ambition, his attention to detail and his extreme competence. At all times some found that working with him was an unpleasant experience. Such people were disconcerted by the extent of his calculations, and alarmed by the strength of his will to succeed.

That is certainly how Lord Allen of Hurtwood reacted to Macmillan in 1936. Allen, Arthur (now Lord) Salter, Geoffrey Crowther, Macmillan and others had formed a non-partisan reformist group – 'The Next Five Years Group' – which believed that problems like unemployment and the need for industrial reorganisation made many traditional political issues obsolete. Early converts to Keynes's theory, they campaigned for government intervention in the economy and non-doctrinaire planning in the interests of efficiency and social harmony.[1]

Now Macmillan did not behave in the Next Five Years Group quite as he was expected to. He came to the Group with a reputation acquired during ten years in the House of Commons: the reputation of being a clever young Etonian publisher who was at heart rather donnish and unpractical. He had bored the House (as he himself confessed) with speeches which combined long recitals of facts about unemployment and production with unorthodox proposals for planning and unhappily contrived metaphors. Captain Macmillan was generally thought to be well-meaning and a trifle smug. He was regarded as a rebel rather than as a serious contender for power.[2]

But something happened to Macmillan shortly after he became active in the Group – something which revealed qualities previously unsuspected in him. By 1935 Macmillan was disillusioned with the domestic policies of the National Government, and in the next year he resigned the Whip in protest against Baldwin's decision to abandon sanctions against Italy. The result was that Macmillan's energies became concentrated on the activities of the Next Five Years Group, and it was not long before other members came to see just how seriously he took politics and how keenly he sought to acquire power.

By working through committees, Macmillan tried to join the Group with Lloyd George's followers in a Popular Front Movement. For he wanted the Group to influence events and not merely debate the shape of the future. He also wanted effective propaganda. When the Group decided to establish a journal, the *New Outlook*, Macmillan quickly brought it under his own control. Lord Allen wrote wearily in June 1936 that he was 'compelled now to see that much of the trouble during the last $2\frac{1}{2}$ months has been due to one man, Mr Macmillan, functioning on every committee and attempting the guidance of practically all our activities'.[3]

Nor was this an isolated episode in Macmillan's political career. If Lord Allen had looked back a few years he would have seen interesting portents. When Macmillan lost his seat at Stockton-on-Tees in the 1929 election, the frustrations of being 'out of the game' soon told on him. He began to complain that the traditional parties were out of touch with the needs of the country, and he became an occasional visitor to Sir Oswald Mosley's house in London.[4] Macmillan was undoubtedly attracted by the prospects of action that Mosley held out – by his willingness to question received ideas and to do something about the massive unemployment. But he was also tempted by Mosley's New Party as a more rapid way to power.

The best examples of Macmillan's pursuit of power, however, are to be found in the war years. The war marked the end of Macmillan's splendid but largely unavailing campaign on behalf of the unemployed. When Churchill made him Parliamentary Secretary to the Ministry of Supply under Herbert Morrison in 1940, Macmillan was at last able to harness his energies and apply his ideas with effect. His pre-war interest in economic organisation helped him to plan the elaborate machinery required for war production. Indeed, he was full of plans. No one was more struck by Macmillan's ambition than Morrison himself. In an often-quoted passage of his memoirs, Morrison says that 'in his loyalty to me, his [Macmillan's] advice for my advancement tended to occupy his mind to such an extent that I had to remind him that we had a war job to do and that personal careers were not important'.[5]

But it was in North Africa that Macmillan established beyond doubt his ability to acquire and use power. In December 1942 Churchill sent him to Eisenhower's headquarters as the British Minister Resident, a post which others had turned down as being too far removed from London and probably unimportant. Macmillan accepted it immediately, and then remade it in his own image. The second volume of his memoirs, *The Blast of War*, tells how he turned a secondary and precarious position (when Macmillan arrived in Algiers he was received with suspicion and hostility by the Americans) into nothing less than the overlordship of the Mediterranean theatre of war. Macmillan's extreme importance is often unwittingly revealed in American accounts of the North African and Italian campaigns, though more openly in Robert Murphy's *Diplomat among Warriors*. And the testimony of those on Macmillan's staff at the time, like John Wyndham (now Lord Egremont) and Richard Crossman, only reinforces the impression.

Macmillan's extraordinary achievement in the Second World War has not been widely appreciated. And that fact is interesting in itself. For it suggests how much more he was interested in the substance of power than in its mere form. Without drawing attention to himself or offending the *amour propre* of Eisenhower and his colleagues, Macmillan overcame the Americans' suspicions, gained their confidence and saw to it that the British had a part in making decisions. Indeed, he soon came to dominate many of those decisions. He did this by sheer ability to anticipate circumstances, careful planning, subtlety, persistence and patience.

It was Macmillan, for instance, who untied the horribly knotted problem of French leadership. Roosevelt loathed de Gaulle and tried to set up a French Government-in-exile led by someone else – first by Darlan and then (after his assassination) by Giraud. Churchill was more or less committed to de Gaulle's Free French, but sometimes wavered out of concern for Anglo-American relations. It fell to Macmillan to bring the bickering French factions together, which he did by constantly overcoming the doubts of Roosevelt and Giraud, while convincing de Gaulle that he had larger French interests at heart. For he saw – perhaps more clearly than de Gaulle himself – that de Gaulle could quickly assert his authority over a unified French Committee of National Liberation.

It would be difficult to exaggerate the extent of Macmillan's sway over Eisenhower and Murphy. At one moment he even succeeded in convincing Eisenhower that an order from Roosevelt to sack de Gaulle should be disregarded. Yet there was nothing very sinister in Macmillan's sway. It was the result of an intellectual mastery which won him the respect of colleagues and subordinates alike. Just as his examination of the problems of deflation and unemployment had enabled him to expound a new policy of planning (*The Middle Way*) in the pre-war years, so now his assessment of strategic questions and their political implications had a consistency and breadth which made criticism difficult. Macmillan saw how important it was for the future that a French Government which was not merely a creature of the Allies should emerge. He acted accordingly in North Africa. In the same way, after the conquest of Sicily and southern Italy in 1943–4 he decided that the most important thing was to give the Italians a chance to restore their own affairs. He therefore dismantled Allied Military Government as quickly as possible, and preferred to exercise control indirectly through an Italian administration.[6]

Beginning as Minister Resident in Algiers, Macmillan became Minister Resident for the Central

Mediterranean (December 1943) as well as Acting President of the Allied Commission in Italy (November 1944). He had made himself indispensable to the conduct of the Mediterranean war. First Eisenhower and then Generals Maitland Wilson and Alexander had come to depend upon his advice and his diplomatic skill. By the last year of the war, Macmillan writes: 'I found myself as a political Minister with four Ambassadors more or less responsible to me....'[7]

Macmillan did not acquire so much power without opposition. General Sir Alan Brooke, the C.I.G.S., was perhaps foremost among those who saw the extent of Macmillan's influence and had doubts about it. He particularly disliked the way Macmillan's close friendship with General Alexander reinforced his control over the conduct of the war in Italy and later in Greece. Brooke had opposed the appointment of Alexander as Supreme Commander in the Mediterranean for that reason, and when it was a fact he spoke to Alexander about the danger of his relying excessively on Macmillan.[8]

The end of the war in Europe and the 1945 election changed Macmillan's position completely. He even lost his seat, returning to the House only after a by-election at Bromley in November. The Churchill Government's defeat was a shattering blow for Macmillan, who had acquired so much power and who enjoyed its possession enormously. Unlike other senior Tories he had foreseen the defeat, but that did not lessen his chagrin. Indeed, the blow was probably made worse for him by the fact that he had boldly criticised his party's domestic policies before the war, and so could hardly now think himself in any way responsible for its débâcle.

Macmillan became gloomy. His ambitions were thwarted and his skills largely unused. Debating in the Commons had never been his strongest point, though he was a better, more partisan speaker after the war than before. The self-confidence bred by war-time success emerged as a patrician disdain for men without substance or tradition trying to direct the fortunes of the nation. Intentionally or not, he effectively dispelled his earlier reputation as an unpractical idealist and rebel. Only in his fitful enthusiasm for European unity did the earlier Macmillan emerge.

On Churchill's return to power in October 1951, Macmillan's energies found an outlet once again. He became Minister of Housing, and in that post quickly displayed the skill at planning and organisation which had made him so effective during the war. He put his Ministry on a war footing (*à la* Beaverbrook), and soon exceeded the target of 300,000 houses a year, becoming the undoubted success of the Government.[9] Macmillan entered the national limelight for the first time, but he was still a much less distinct figure than Churchill, Eden or Salisbury. And soon his energies were frustrated again. When Churchill made him Minister of Defence in October 1954, Macmillan discovered that he was not going to be able to run the Ministry as he thought best. For Churchill regarded defence as his own domain. It was probably not just a coincidence that at this time Macmillan began to insist that Churchill was no longer up to his job and ought to resign.[10]

Yet when Churchill did go in April 1955, Macmillan was not much better off. He became Foreign Secretary in Eden's Government at a time of considerable diplomatic activity. He attended the Summit at Geneva, signed the Austrian Peace Treaty at Vienna and visited the Middle East. But he quickly came to see that Eden had not relinquished control over foreign affairs – that to be Foreign Secretary was by now Eden's second nature. Once again Macmillan was not his own master. Once again his strong and persistent desire to direct affairs was frustrated.

The pattern of Macmillan's political life then reasserted itself. With his ambition frustrated and his most characteristic energies held in check, he became sombre and fustian, almost unwell. Although he was occupying a post that he had long aspired to, his fortunes were thought to be declining. There was even talk of his retirement. But Macmillan was rescued from this impasse late in 1955. Eden made important changes in his Government, and Macmillan became Chancellor of the Exchequer. In his new post Macmillan had virtually free rein, for Eden did not know very much about financial or economic matters. Macmillan began to show the same drive, the same willingness to experiment and interest in central planning that he had shown during the war and at the Ministry of Housing. He made the young Edward Boyle his Economic Secretary, and together they explored new policies largely undeterred by Tory orthodoxy. While he raised the Bank Rate and restricted credit to meet an inflationary crisis, Macmillan also levied higher taxes on profits and introduced Premium Bonds. His fortunes began to rise again.[11]

Macmillan only climbed to the top of the greasy pole as a result of the Suez crisis and Eden's serious illness. But he might have got there anyway. For Eden's limitations – always known to his closer colleagues – had become more widely appreciated in the party and country during the year of his premiership. Vanity, irritability, jealousy and indecision – the charges against Eden were more and more often repeated in the course of 1956. For the truth about the two men, Macmillan and Eden, was then becoming clear. The truth was, that Macmillan was the sort of man who was at his best only when he commanded or dominated; while Eden was at his best when he served as a deputy.

This conclusion was firmly established by the events of Suez. The qualities which Macmillan then exhibited – the willingness to take risks, the determination, the loyalty to colleagues, the stylish patriotic appeals, and, perhaps most important of all, the cool acceptance of unpleasant facts – these qualities won Harold Macmillan a commanding position in his party. Anthony Sampson is certainly right when he argues that Macmillan's support for the Suez expedition was of critical importance; had he as Chancellor opposed it, Eden could hardly have gone ahead. But this does not, as Sampson suggests, make it surprising that Macmillan was not tarred by the brush of Suez. For most Conservative M.P.s, Suez illustrated perfectly the difference between Macmillan's resolution and Eden's vacillation, between Macmillan's reliability and Butler's ironical side-stepping.

24

Nor was that all. The question of health completed the contrast between the contenders. Butler, the most likely heir, seemed unwell since the death of his wife. And whereas the need to provide leadership had obviously done much to undermine Eden's health, Macmillan's vitality and spirits seemed to suffer only when he was *deprived* of the opportunity to lead.

What an extraordinary contrast there is between the story of Macmillan's rise to power and the rather flamboyant style with which he exercised power as Prime Minister! It is that contrast – that near divorce between content and form – which strikes anyone contemplating Macmillan's career. What can account for it? What sort of man would behave in such a way? What light does an appreciation of Macmillan's personality throw on his premiership?

In a 1961 *Encounter* article, Henry Fairlie compares Macmillan to Walpole. He stresses Macmillan's close study of human nature and human failings, his reliance on personal relations, and his careful attention to the House of Commons as the only secure base of political power. But this is only a half-truth. It is perhaps more a clue to the way in which Macmillan saw himself than a final description of his political style. Fairlie emphasises how much Macmillan learned from reading Disraeli frequently. And Disraeli was indeed an important figure in Macmillan's life. But not quite in the way that Fairlie imagines. No one ever learned very much about human nature *in general* from reading Disraeli, but only about one bizarre, ambitious and imaginative man – what would now be called an 'outsider' in politics. And it was precisely this that would fascinate someone like Macmillan, who was also conscious of being clever, ambitious, but different from most of those playing the political game. As he himself has said, 'I learnt books before I learnt people.'[12]

Macmillan had more than one favourite novelist. He liked to read Trollope, for example, as well as Disraeli. And how symptomatic of the two sides of his personality these contrasting literary tastes are! For in Trollope is to be found the real world in large measure,

25

accurately and yet sympathetically presented. Disraeli, on the other hand, demonstrates the uses of style, the romantic possibilities of gesture, epigram and pose. Macmillan seemed to borrow from both. He was not someone to whom mastery of the real world came easily, or who moved about it naturally. Rather, he carefully learned about it (*pace* Trollope) and acquired the necessary skills. And one of the skills necessary for someone so acutely self-conscious and sensitive was a public style. It was that, as much as his admiration for Disraeli's ideas about binding the Two Nations together, that drew Macmillan to Dizzy. Like Dizzy, he had to create an elaborate role in order to be publicly effective.

The contemporary statesman who most nearly resembles Macmillan in this way is undoubtedly General de Gaulle. De Gaulle's cult of personality, his skilful cultivation of mystery and grandeur, is the policy of an introverted, intellectual and even awkward man – a man not unlike Harold Macmillan. Their styles are different, but their use of style is similar.

It is only necessary to look at Macmillan's memoirs to understand why he needed a public style – to see the shy, sensitive and reserved nature his public style served to buttress and protect. For the memoirs reveal the Emperor without his clothes. These volumes must shock readers who remember only the languid, insouciant and witty Prime Minister. The memoirs reveal another man altogether. They reveal an acutely self-conscious yet determined intellectual, a mind that painstakingly assembles facts and analyses issues with a view to action. Reading the memoirs makes it easier to understand the surprise and dismay which many of Macmillan's acquaintances felt when they first observed his new political style after the war. They could hardly connect that style with the conscientious, awkward and rather pompous Harold Macmillan they remembered from before the war.

Macmillan's memoirs are extremely impressive for what they reveal, but they are also strangely flat and colourless. They are the work of a man who finds it difficult to express his own feelings and reactions simply or directly. The memoirs are, in fact, remarkably impersonal. Perhaps that is why Macmillan chose to cast them in the form of a history of his own times. His impersonal tone and analytical habits perfectly suited such a project.

Two other qualities of Macmillan emerge from his memoirs: his detachment and his sentimentality. Not surprisingly, one quality is closely related to the other. Macmillan always leaves the onlooker with the impression that he finds personal relationships difficult and even hazardous things. It is certainly not unusual for the precocious and shy to feel that other people are threats. And here again Macmillan's comment – 'I learnt books before I learnt people' – rings very true. In such cases the feelings of sympathy and loyalty which do not find direct personal expression often become attached to groups and institutions instead. Just how far is this the case with Macmillan?

Macmillan brings to mind Guy Crouchback, the hero of Evelyn Waugh's Second World War trilogy. For Crouchback, a fastidious and honourable but very reserved man who had, moreover, become disillusioned with life, suddenly finds pleasure and fulfilment in regimental life. The overt, disciplined and secure companionship of such a group, its ceremonial aspect, afforded him a kind of relief or release. When Macmillan joined the Brigade of Guards in 1914, newly down from Oxford where he had (under Ronald Knox's influence) seriously considered becoming a convert to Rome, he seems to have had a similar experience. Balliol had already engaged some of his feelings, with the intellectual and aesthetic appeals of undergraduate life. But the Brigade brought him much more closely and simply into contact with other men, many of them from backgrounds very different from his own. Macmillan adored the Brigade of Guards.

And much later it remained true that the detached, unemotional Macmillan could be very moved by the spectacle of robust, disciplined men acting together. When he helped to review the Allied troops in Tunis at the end of the North African campaign (May 1943), he wrote:

Unlike the French and Americans the British were in drill, not battle, order – shorts, stockings and boots, battle blouses or shirts with short sleeves – no helmets (forage caps and berets). The helmet gives a soldier the look of a robot.... With the forage cap or beret you can see his face – his jolly honest, sunburnt, smiling English, Scottish or Irish face – relaxed now, not worn or harassed as men look in battle – and confident and proud. All these brown faces, these brown bare arms and knees, these swinging, striding, outstepping men – all marched magnificently.[13]

How different the simple enthusiasm of this description is from both the studied irony of Macmillan's public speeches and the impersonal prose of his memoirs!

Yet Macmillan's sentimentality was only the reverse side of his detachment. For he always remained the onlooker, and often described British institutions or practices as if he were a foreigner – or at least half foreign. There is, for example, an extraordinary passage in the memoirs where Macmillan describes one of his visits to General Alexander's headquarters (in Tunis):

It is rather like a large country house. You come to meals and otherwise attend to your own business. There is plenty of quiet amusement available – sight-seeing, bathing or just agreeable conversation with the other guests.... No fuss, no worry – and a great battle in progress! This is never referred to but is understood to be going on satisfactorily.... The conversation is the usual tone of educated (and there are some *very* well-educated) Englishmen – a little history, a little politics, a little banter, a little philosophy – all very lightly touched.... It is a strange and fascinating experience. Very occasionally, an officer comes in with a message for the 'Chief'. After pausing sufficiently out of politeness for the conversation in hand – the campaign of Belisarius, or the advantages of classical over Gothic architecture, or the right way to drive pheasants in flat country to show them well, or whatever it may be – General Alex. will ask permission to open his message, read it, put it into his pocket, continue the original discussion for a few more minutes and then, perhaps, if the message should call for any action, unobtrusively retire, as a man might leave his smoking-room or library after the ladies have gone to bed, to say a word to his butler, fetch a pipe or the like. I have never enjoyed so much the English capacity for restraint and understatement.[14]

Here Macmillan sounds like Henry James. This heightened sensitivity to institutions or practices – as if they were almost more real than the people who make and change them – is often a characteristic of people who feel (for whatever reason) markedly different from those around them.

And it is another characteristic of such people that when they wish to compete in the public forum, they are inclined to do so not so much directly or spontaneously as indirectly or obliquely. It is as if they lacked the thick skin or vitality needed for direct contact. And so they invest themselves with the mantle of the accepted practices of their day. Their success comes from the intelligence and ingenuity with which they use their cloak. But their weakness is that they are too closely tied to certain practices for their own identity.

Macmillan developed an elaborate public style, and he used it with great effect. Indeed, he was so successful that the policies of his administration and the life of the country came to be seen through the image he himself projected. What exactly was his style? How did he come to develop it? And why? These are fascinating questions. And they are important. For the answers throw light on the man, the Government and the country.

From childhood Harold Macmillan was shy and detached, so much so that he grew up to see English life as a sympathetic foreigner might see it. And that, of course, is the beginning of the answer. Probably the most important fact of Macmillan's life is that his mother was a strong-willed and formidable American.

The daughter of a country doctor in southern Indiana, Helen Belles was widowed before she was twenty, and left America in order to live and study in Paris. There she met Maurice Macmillan, a son of the founder of the publishing house, and shortly afterwards (1883) married him. Helen Macmillan's common sense, outspokenness and ambition were thrown into even sharper relief by her husband's quiet, retiring disposition. To these parents Harold Macmillan was born in 1894.

Helen Macmillan threw herself into English life with gusto. Her friends, rather than her husband's, quickly came to provide the background for Macmillan family life. And *her* friends were decidedly grander and more varied than had been usual with the Macmillans', whose concerns outside business had been religious and intellectual. Fascinated by the ease, splendour and hierarchy of late Victorian and Edwardian society, Helen Macmillan seems to have adjusted her sights accordingly. In 1906 she found a small estate in Sussex, Birch Grove, which became the new family seat.

Helen Macmillan undoubtedly saw her son as a future Prime Minister, and she did everything she could to smooth his progress. Even after he married Lady Dorothy Cavendish (daughter of the 9th Duke of Devonshire) in 1920, Macmillan remained unusually close to his mother. And he always made a point of acknowledging her importance in the shaping of his personality and career. 'No one who has not experienced it can realise the determination of an American mother defending one of her children.'[15]

In a curious way Harold Macmillan now stands out as an American's Englishman – the slight exaggeration of a type. Nor is it unlikely that a forceful and anglophile Victorian American should have had a mannered Edwardian son. Harold Macmillan's intense awareness of the Englishness of English ways, and his pleasure in them, are undoubtedly the best signs of his complicated origins.

Introverted and delicate, Macmillan seems to have been a lonely, unhappy schoolboy. Only afterwards did he begin to derive a particular satisfaction from some forms of social life. Belonging to a group, con-

30

sciously and almost deliberately, then seems to have provided a companionship and strength which he badly needed. This 'clubmanship' – horrid word! – is one of the patterns of his life. It emerged first when he was an undergraduate. The lonely Eton scholar found Oxford a revelation because he discovered kindred spirits there. Probably for the first time he became one of a set. It was a lively, well-read, aesthetic and no doubt slightly mannered set which looked for inspiration to Ronald Knox (who had already tutored Macmillan when he came away early from Eton.)[16] It was a set of young men who mingled sprightly conversation with Anglo-Catholic ritual and speculation.

As a Guardsman in the First World War, Macmillan found himself even more closely associated with other men. And it is tempting to conclude that this enforced suspension of some instinctive shyness or diffidence was enormously important for him. He emerged from the war more manly and secure. The warm, almost naïve feeling with which he later evoked the Brigade of Guards' discipline and camaraderie testifies to his gratitude.

Even after marriage and the buffetings of political life, Macmillan seems to have been happiest and most relaxed when surrounded by a small club-like circle of men. Within such circles – as in North Africa and once again in Downing Street – he expanded. He took his associates into his confidence, joked with them, relied upon them, praised them and enjoyed their devotion. The most unusual and important of his associates was John Wyndham, who was his private secretary throughout the war and rejoined him at No. 10 for the term of his premiership. Other members of Macmillan's staff in North Africa included Roger Makins and Harold Caccia, while as Premier his staff included Timothy Bligh and Philip de Zulueta.

Macmillan was always most effective when sustained by such an intimate circle. It is as if the elaborate public style and the private club-like circle were his helmet and buckler – the armour which a sensitive, vulnerable and yet highly ambitious man needed to protect himself from the world. But more importantly, these qualities of Macmillan – his Edwardian manner and his reliance on a private circle as the base for his political operations – had decisive effects on his administration. They account for some of its foremost characteristics.

Macmillan's public style fitted the England of the later 1950s like a glove. It is extraordinary how his rather emphatic rendering of traditional English ways gratified a nation which was beginning to be anxious about its future. For Suez had been a shock. The possibility of independent political action by Britain was now seen to be drastically curtailed. Despite the domestic prosperity, a serious crisis of confidence with political repercussions might soon have followed. But it was not to be – at least yet. Macmillan was made for the part, and played it impeccably.

Macmillan played the part of an English de Gaulle. He offered the country his own version of Gaullism. Like the General, he believed that change is not only made easier, but is more likely to be for the better if some national virtue or genius is respected. He believed, again like the General, that by repeatedly invoking the national character and embodying it rather extravagantly, a leader helps to create and sustain it. Both Macmillan and de Gaulle treated politics as if it were indeed an art rather than a science. Their actions imply that – within limits – style can create its own content and rhetoric its own substance.

Macmillan's Edwardianism could not have been better fashioned for the purpose. In a way it was the last authentic English style – the figure cut by patrician Englishmen when their country last unquestionably dominated the world. It was a style which carried with it the resonances of that domination. Macmillan understood this, and exploited the fact. Above all, he found it useful in his dealings with the United States.

Macmillan founded his Government's policy on close co-operation with the United States. In that fundamental respect, of course, his programme differed from General de Gaulle's. Macmillan's was a cultural rather than a political form of Gaullism. The difference was not simply due to war-time nostalgia or Macmillan's being half-American himself, but arose from his assessment of how power was distributed in the post-war world. And yet it is even more complicated than that.

Macmillan prided himself that he knew how to 'handle' Americans. It was a skill he had developed in North Africa during the war. And he was to refine it further as Prime Minister, of necessity. For when he became Prime Minister, relations with America posed a serious problem, not only because of Suez, but because Eden had succeeded in antagonising Dulles and Eisenhower. Now Macmillan clearly (and probably rightly) believed that he could have managed the American reaction to Suez more successfully than Eden.[17] But Macmillan, too, had something to learn from Suez. It was the first time he had seriously miscalculated American intentions. Macmillan learned that American politicians had come on since the war – that a decade of exercising world power had made American policy more consistent and tough. Nor had Macmillan met before an American politician quite as determined as Dulles. And under Dulles's tutelage, Eisenhower was less malleable.

Macmillan learned the lesson. He developed even further his method of working hard and persistently for certain ends while at the same time contriving to seem aloof or unconcerned – of influencing events without appearing to do so unduly. Perhaps Macmillan found the need to act in this way only too congenial. For such a method was really just an extension of his temperament.

He met with extraordinary success. In Bermuda, Washington, Delhi and elsewhere he re-established Britain's diplomatic position within a matter of months. It hardly seemed possible that leaders who had strongly disapproved of the Suez adventure should so soon be talking of their 'old and trusted ally', and that in the world at large anger and consternation should give way to a view of England as 'the wise old man of the West'. It would be churlish to underrate the achievement. Macmillan did succeed in calming the country and reassuring the world. By displaying as well as evoking supposedly traditional qualities of moderation, common sense and sang-froid, he did help – and this was the better half of his style – to create those qualities in the country. And he būilt upon them. His pursuit of compromise over Cyprus, a looser multi-racial Commonwealth, and *détente* (especially in the form of arms-control agreements) testify to that.

Macmillan seems to have drawn one lesson especially from Suez. If Britain had much less of the substance of power than before. it could still be a master of the forms of power. It could draw on diplomatic habits, long-established connections and accumulated prestige. It could mediate between East and West, between America and Europe, between the Afro-Asians and the older-established countries. In all of this an assured, patrician style might accomplish much. By drawing on qualities of civility, imagination and patience, a British Prime Minister might be able to sustain his country in a rather special position in the world. And the style would be equally useful at home. For it would enable him to combine political dependence on America with a healthy independence in other areas – with a resolute defence of established English ways of doing things and a search for authentic new ones. This is the theme of Macmillan's administration. This was his pro-American form of Gaullism. He as good as said: 'We do not pretend to be the same as you, but we are with you.'

How canny this judgment of Macmillan's was! People *are* often particularly impressed by qualities which they feel they do not possess themselves. And Macmillan's 'High Tory' style served him well with Presidents as different as Eisenhower and Kennedy. It is hardly surprising that Americans should be impressed by the qualities of a traditional leisured class. It would be much more surprising if they were impressed by a style built around efficiency, homeliness and sentimentality. Macmillan must have seen that for this reason the Tory Party had intrinsic advantages over the Labour Party when dealing with the United States. He made the most of them. Harold Wilson, whose modernising and technocratic style might seem a far more plausible *entrée* to Washington, did not succeed in Washington as Macmillan had done.

Yet it would be unfair to say that Macmillan used his style merely for partisan advantage or chiefly to sustain national pride. There was something about his calm, urbane and disillusioned style which seemed to dictate ends as well as means. That style seemed to preserve certain Renaissance attitudes (not for nothing had Macmillan done Classical Mods. at Oxford!) in a world torn between the demands of technology and of rival ideologies. At his best Macmillan conveyed a concern for privacy, a scepticism about public statements and public actions, a belief that life was good enough to make its peaceful continuance more important than national pride or even ideological victory. And it was in this guise that Macmillan had an important influence on the diplomatic climate of the later 1950s. Coming after the first rigours of the Cold War, at a time when Dulles's influence was declining and Khrushchev was making coy overtures to the West, Macmillan patiently sought to lead the world out of the 'twilight zone' between peace and war. He laid great stress on the importance of contacts, pressed at every opportunity for summit conferences, and, above all, sought agreements to limit armaments and stop nuclear testing. His visit to Moscow, his proposals for an arms zone in Central Europe, his spadework for the Paris summit meeting in 1960 – all these served not just his evident desire to be a world statesman, but the interests of *détente*.

Macmillan used his international position to teach that rational men (even if they were no longer gentlemen) should be able to talk together. They should be able to find some common interests, and build upon those rather than upon their disagreements. The alternative in a nuclear age was, he suggested, unthinkable. Perhaps the climax of Macmillan's efforts towards *détente* was his appearance before the General Assembly of the United Nations in September 1960. Quietly dissociating himself from Khrushchev and Eisenhower (both of whom sought to enlist the support of the newly independent nations), Macmillan called for an end to propaganda and the tiresome evangelism of the Cold War.

Although influence of the kind in question is very difficult to assess, Macmillan certainly helped to bring about a more temperate international climate. His efforts made it easier for Kennedy and others to follow in the same direction after 1960. Indeed, Macmillan constantly urged Kennedy to press for a test-ban treaty, and his influence was probably crucial in inducing the President finally to set aside the doubts and objections of his advisers. In the Disarmament Commission's meetings at Geneva the British were constantly dragging the Americans after them towards some agreement.[18] The nuclear test-ban treaty, signed in July 1963, is rightly considered the peak of Macmillan's diplomatic achievements. It is the area in which Macmillan's political style and the substance of his policy were wholly in accord.

Macmillan's style and his policy were not always so harmonious. Indeed, his grand diplomatic manner helped to mitigate, if not conceal, what was probably the most important policy of his administration in its early years – the retreat from Empire. This retreat from colonial responsibility after Suez was almost precipitate, and it raises one of the great questions about Macmillan's Government. Was this policy one of strength or weakness? Was it radical and calculated on Macmillan's part, or was it the sign of a loss of confidence which extended even to him? It is difficult to know. And in any case it is probably too early to judge the issues involved. There are powerful arguments on both sides. Lord Salisbury argued that a more gradual transition to self-government would not only serve the interests of the indigenous population in the long run, but that it would favour political stability by preventing dangerous power vacuums from developing. The examples of the Congo and Nigeria certainly lend weight to his case.

On the other hand, those like Macleod who favoured the rapid granting of independence to the colonies argued that it would not only prevent Britain's becoming horribly embroiled like France in Algeria, but would make it possible to preserve more economic and political links with the new countries in the long run. What did Macmillan think? There is much evidence that, although he recoiled from the idea of a liberal crusade, he had accepted the arguments in favour of rapidly winding up the Empire, irrespective of Suez. For one thing, during the Second World War he had had far more opportunity than most British politicians to see how rapidly the economic and military tide was running against Britain. Also, he had shown a clear preference in North Africa and Italy for co-operating with native administrations rather than ruling by force. And finally, his Commonwealth tour of 1956 did seem a genuine indication that he wanted to replace the traditional imperial ties with looser ones of co-operation.

Macmillan wanted to carry out a policy. But he did not want to lead a crusade. Not only did he have a temperamental dislike of anything so evangelical, he also realised that a crusade would make it more difficult to carry out the policy. His famous 'winds of change' speech is only the exception which proves the rule. For Macmillan intended that the speech, delivered before the South African Parliament early in 1960, should err on the side of moderation and caution. He did not mean it to be a declaration of war on *apartheid*. The first reactions to the speech bear that out. It was only after two or three days and the efforts of London journalists that an interpretation was put on the speech which astonished not only those who had heard it, but Macmillan himself. The ease with which he later took credit for the speech only proves his agility.

Macmillan's colonial policy was probably more deliberate and radical than is now usually allowed. The unconventional and intellectual Tory of the thirties can be glimpsed once again in it. Where Macmillan had changed was in his determination and ability to carry his party with him – *and* in his anxiety that a necessary and desirable though painful policy should not at the same time undermine the confidence of the nation. That is where Macmillan was so effective: his confident patrician manner suggested that imperial pride and strength remained; his close relations with Eisenhower and Kennedy suggested that Britain shared in America's power, that the civilised and subtle British were (as he often said) the Greeks in the new American Empire; his emphasis on the H-bomb and Britain's nuclear capacity suggested that militarily Britain remained a major power; and finally, his unashamed assertion that the country had 'never had it so good' suggested just that.

While reassuring the party and the country in this way, Macmillan dismantled the British Empire. The euphoria of the later 1950s – that second Edwardian summer – seemed to rise from the feeling that it was possible to have influence and power without the undue burden of imperial responsibility. Macmillan personally evoked and sustained that mood. It may have been his recognition that he was peculiarly fitted for such a task that had led him on more than one occasion before 1956 to remark to colleagues – only half in jest – that he alone could 'save' the country.

Macmillan revelled in the part of Prime Minister. And naturally enough. It must be especially satisfying for a reserved and lonely man to achieve his ambitions. But is was more than that with Macmillan. He was also highly imaginative. As Anthony Sampson says, after 1956 Macmillan seemed to see himself taking the lead in a romantic play about politics and high society. His performance seemed to give him pleasure as a spectator as well as an actor. And the pleasure he felt made him that much more effective. He became jauntier and less inhibited. His speeches were earthier and funnier – though some of the credit for that belongs to John Wyndham, his unusual assistant.[19] Indeed, Wyndham's influence on Macmillan is a fascinating subject. Macmillan had always admired Wyndham's wit, his dislike of cant and indifference to the usual proprieties. But it was as if Macmillan were no longer content as Prime Minister merely to admire these aristocratic qualities. He was tempted to imitate them. He had always needed to learn his parts, whether that of aesthete, Guardsman or politician, and he was still good at it. But with learning of that kind there always seems to

38

come slight exaggeration. Some of the phrases which would have sounded amusing and right from Wyndham, sounded corny and even vulgar when they came from Macmillan. Perhaps that is why 'They've never had it so good' caused him so much trouble.

Success and age changed Macmillan. Perhaps the intellectual boldness which had so impressed his war-time subordinates receded a little. Or was it simply that tastes which had always been latent now had freer sway? The confidence bred by success made his High Tory act a bit too real. Macmillan's fondness for the colour, gaiety and splendid backgrounds of upper-class life grew. And so did his impatience with other things. The shy intellectual who had overcome his self-consciousness and proved himself as a formidable man of action seemed to reserve a particular scorn for other intellectuals in politics, whether Butler, Gaitskell or Enoch Powell. Perhaps because, despite everything, Macmillan remained deeply inhibited and reserved, he preferred the company of spontaneous, uncautious, 'real' men, whether self-made like Marples or grandly bred like Wyndham.

Yet Macmillan did strike the right note for the later 1950s. England was in the mood for a second Edwardian summer. It did not seem to want analysis of the serious difficulties likely to arise from its altered position in the world. England seemed to want reassurance that it was still a society which supported leisure, wit, elegance and sheer pleasure – a society highly cultivated and confident enough not to fear vulgarity. Macmillan was cast in just such a mould. His image of himself seemed, at least briefly, to be the self-image of the nation. And in many ways how like the first Edwardian era this second of Macmillan's was! – aggressively prosperous, increasingly permissive, averting its eyes from unpleasant facts abroad (as if tired by moral effort), gay, whimsical and a little tawdry.

Perhaps it was the completeness of this act of recognition – between Macmillan and England – that obscured the other side of the Prime Minister's character. Both the admiration and hostility which Macmillan aroused had to do with his rather histrionic public side.

Neither reaction seemed to take much account of the qualities seen by his Cabinet colleagues or companions at No. 10. Yet the ambitious, intellectual Macmillan, the man long accustomed to analysing situations and assessing people with a view to some action – this side of the man was still predominant.[20] This Macmillan was delighted to have achieved his ambition, and absolutely determined to remain in the front seat. This Macmillan reduced the Labour Opposition to a state of near impotence, saw to it that he had no serious rivals within his own party, and remained Prime Minister longer than anyone since Asquith.

Beneath Macmillan's sometimes flippant, sometimes fustian mask, there was calculation, effort and – occasionally – great anxiety. Even at the peak of his success he found the discipline of politics a hard one. Macmillan was never a natural child of politics like Churchill or Bevan; nor could he consider it one job among others as Attlee perhaps did. The art of politics consumed Harold Macmillan. It filled his life. And this helped to make him both inordinately skilful and very vulnerable. It hardly comes as a surprise that Macmillan was often sick before making important speeches in the House. The amount of self-control he had to muster even in his heyday was prodigious. Little wonder that he struck some politicians he dealt with as remote and even inaccessible. Macmillan's apparent nonchalance should never be allowed to disguise the real effort that went into his premiership.

Once he had become Prime Minister, Macmillan was determined to remain so, despite the seemingly interim nature of his appointment after Suez. Within a few months of his taking office two important Tories were deposited by the side of the road. The first was Antony Head, who had been a successful Minister of Defence and was generally popular. In making up his Government, Macmillan simply dropped Head from the Cabinet, gave him a peerage, and later sent him out to Nigeria as High Commissioner. It was – on the surface – an odd fate for one of the most promising of the rather younger Tories. The next victim of

Macmillan's determination was Lord Salisbury. Of Macmillan's own age but previously his senior in the party (indeed, Macmillan had served under him in the Colonial Office in 1942), Salisbury was perhaps the only figure in Macmillan's first Cabinet who might have found it possible to challenge his authority. It would be absurd to say that Salisbury went for that reason (for the disagreement between them over colonial policy was genuine), but it made Macmillan much less reluctant to see him go.

The best proof of Macmillan's determination to be the complete master was his retention of Selwyn Lloyd as Foreign Secretary. Observers at home and abroad were astonished by the decision, not only because Lloyd's handling of the Suez adventure had been (from any point of view) inept, but because however loyal and amiable he might be, Lloyd was clearly second-rate. For Macmillan's purposes, however, the decision was a brilliant stroke. Lloyd's presence reassured an important section of the party. But not only that. By retaining Lloyd, Macmillan could conduct his own foreign policy and at the same time have in the post a man who could not conceivably threaten him as Prime Minister. It is hardly surprising that the discredited Lloyd remained Foreign Secretary for more than three years. And it is interesting to notice who became Foreign Secretary when Lloyd did go. For Macmillan's choice of Lord Home was not just a case of snobbery. Home was the sort of upright, candid man who would never lend himself to conspiracy against his leader. He was content to serve. And Macmillan, who understood the temptations of power only too well, appreciated that quality in Home, and knew how to use it.

Macmillan consolidated his power quickly and fairly smoothly. He then set about preserving it. The most important part of that lay in doing his own work thoroughly. He did. Macmillan was a conscientious, hard-working Prime Minister. More often than not the papers which were left for his perusal and comment last thing at night, would be ready for his staff first thing the next morning. He frequently spent mornings in bed because he found it easy to work there. His staff would come and go as if the bedroom were an office. And by all accounts Macmillan was superb as chairman of the Cabinet. He drew not only on his own considerable intellectual resources, but on enormous war-time experience with committees. He kept discussions to the point, exposed the real bones of contention, examined alternative policies, and usually found a ground for agreement. Macmillan's sharp, quick and disillusioned mind, which could only be glimpsed in his public style as through a glass darkly, was plain for all his Cabinet colleagues to see. He dominated them easily.

Yet Macmillan was not content with such domination. He wanted reinsurance that power, so hard to come by, should not slip easily from his hands. It is clear from the circumstances of his premiership that he took careful steps to see that no one should emerge as the leading contender for his post. He was probably sustained in this resolve by the genuine – and, it must be said, plausible – conviction that no one at hand could do the job as well as he. Keeping Butler down was not too difficult. Apart from Rab's constitutional lack of pugnacity, Macmillan knew that he could always rely on powerful elements in the party to oppose Butler. As for the able younger men in the Cabinet, Macmillan flirted with each, but moved on. He was a fickle patron. Macleod at the Colonial Office, Hailsham as party chairman and again as envoy to Moscow, Heath with the Common Market negotiations, Maudling as Chancellor – each felt briefly that gratifying warmth of his attention and approval, only to feel its absence after a while. Macmillan juggled, and deftly balanced the contenders. Or, as it was put for public consumption, 'no one seemed quite to emerge . . .'.

Macmillan's way of forestalling possible rivals within his party is interesting not only in itself, but as an example of his characteristic method as Prime Minister. The story suggests the *leitmotiv* of his administration: Macmillan had a very strong preference for oblique policies. He liked to achieve his ends indirectly. Of course, it could be argued that circumstances forced indirection on him. He could hardly

42

proclaim, for instance, that the Suez policy had to be reversed, and that Britain must accept the consequences of its defeat. But Macmillan's preference for indirection went far beyond that. It is hardly an exaggeration to say that the most important policies of his administration were camouflaged. The retreat from Empire was as stealthy as possible. He preferred to avoid direct conflict, and let the questions of principle take care of themselves. Macmillan's oblique methods were most dextrously applied in the break-up of the Central African Federation. His ambiguities, ruses and stalling reduced white Rhodesians – and especially Roy Welensky – to speechless rage. And what was true of Africa, was even truer of Europe. Macmillan's campaign to take Britain into the Common Market in 1961–2 was an extraordinary series of feints and diversions. In the deftest possible way he paraded major political decisions as inquiries into ways and means. He stifled controversy by making the Brussels negotiations seem essentially technical. By saying that the strategic decisions about entry were to be reserved, he largely succeeded in making his strategy look like mere tactics.

It could be argued that here again Macmillan had no choice. In the country there was a stunning lack of enthusiasm about British entry into Europe. There was little interest in the Common Market as an institution. The ties that mattered to most people were still those with the Commonwealth and the United States. Despite these major obstacles, Macmillan succeeded in carrying his party and the country to the point of application, and encountered remarkably little opposition on the way. But the longer negotiations went on, the less successful his oblique methods were. For the magnitude of the issues became clear, and Macmillan had not really tried to create a groundswell in favour of his policy.

It is highly unlikely that a more open and emotional campaign to gather support for Britain's entry into Europe would have affected the outcome of the negotiations. De Gaulle had very good reasons of his own for preferring that Britain remain outside the

Common Market. But such a campaign might have made his move more awkward and damaging to French interests. It might also have created a more hopeful, constructive mood at home at a time when the delights of Edwardianism were beginning to lose their hold on the British people.

Why did not Macmillan conduct a more open and direct campaign for membership of the Common Market? Undoubtedly he had hoped it would not be necessary for the success of the negotiations. But he must have taken account of the possibility that de Gaulle would somehow block them. Did he not see that, as the stout fighter for a new cause, he might, even if the first battle were a defeat, have gained much credit in the country? Admiring Churchill greatly, did he not realise that even Dunkirks have their use?

After 1960 those qualities of Macmillan which had previously contributed to his success, began to work against him. The languid style which had helped him to sustain a public role and been so timely, now seemed so deeply rooted that he could not bring himself to lead a crusade, however necessary. The shyness and detachment which had led him, oddly enough, to become a superb tactician and master of manipulation, now seemed to make it almost impossible for him to attack an issue directly. And finally, the strength of his determination to remain in power made him suddenly less willing to take risks. In the last years of his premiership a possessive, almost feline Macmillan – who had perhaps always been lurking in the background – came to the fore. This Macmillan disliked open clashes and clamour, and always sought a less abrasive way to achieve his ends.

Thus, Macmillan's Common Market policy was indirect in more than one respect. It was not just that he tried to manœuvre Britain into Europe without anyone knowing quite when or how it had happened. He also intended that membership of the Common Market should give a much needed fillip to Britain's economy. For by 1960 the economy was becoming a matter of concern. In the first few years of the Macmillan Government the relaxing of controls and growth of profits had induced a kind of boom. That boom, very much strengthened by the 1959 Budget which reduced the rate of income tax, helped to carry the Conservatives to a spectacular victory in the October election. Tory democracy seemed secure for the next decade at least. But then things began to go wrong. Exports did not rise enough, imports rose too much. Inflation was taking its toll. It was against this background that Macmillan decided to seek membership of the Common Market. The tariff walls rising around the Six seemed to be casting an ominous shadow across the Channel. At the same time Kennedy's election gave the West a new leader, and suggested that, if Britain wished to remain a world power, it had better find a stronger economic and political base.

Alas, by 1960 the Prime Minister had changed too much from the rebellious young back-bencher of the 1930s. He was no longer primarily interested in economic policy or industrial reorganisation. Age and success had wafted him into the empyrean of international diplomacy. How tempting it was for him, then, to decide that the best solution for Britain's economic troubles lay in joining the Common Market. That decision enabled him to concentrate on the area of policy he preferred, and it spared him excessive involvement in economic debates for which he now had less feeling. That decision may also have appealed to him because it accorded so well with his inclination to settle difficult matters obliquely. After all, foreign adventures had often served the domestic purposes of rulers in the past. Why should not the same be true in the new industrial age? But however tempting the Common Market policy may have been, it begged too many questions as the answer to British economic difficulties. In fact, the economic arguments for and against entry were quite evenly balanced; it was the political arguments which were less ambiguous. And even if the economic case for entry were taken as proved, there was likely to be an interim period of some years before the forces of the larger market began to affect the British economy. What of the economy before that? To say the least, Macmillan after the

1959 election did not seem anxious to make a direct attack on industrial problems the chief policy of his Government. But after the 1959 election and the waning of the boom, these were probably the most important problems he faced.

Even then Macmillan's apparent distaste for economic questions need not have proved fatal to him, but for one thing: Selwyn Lloyd hung around his neck like an albatross. Macmillan ought to have sacked Lloyd when making important changes in his Government in 1960. But apparently he could not bring himself to do so. Instead, while moving Lord Home to the Foreign Office, he made Lloyd Chancellor of the Exchequer. This was a disastrous move. For it meant that at a time when economic problems were coming to the fore and his own distaste for them had become marked, Macmillan had at the Treasury someone who was not really in command of the issues. Lloyd had been useful as Foreign Secretary precisely because Macmillan had wanted to run things himself. And it may be that it now suited Macmillan to have Lloyd at the Treasury because the Common Market and related matters were going to force a change of direction on his administration. He may well have wanted the same back-door control of the Treasury that he had enjoyed at the Foreign Office for three years. There Lloyd had been the ideal agent, for he was completely loyal. But if that was Macmillan's calculation, it was a bad one. The Treasury cannot be run like the Foreign Office. It was not possible simply to lay down the general lines of policy and intervene personally only when something of real interest came up. The Treasury requires close attention to trends, pressures and opportunities. By 1960 Macmillan no longer wanted to exercise close supervision over the details of economic and fiscal policy. No doubt he was still capable of such work if he had to do it. But he would rather not have to.

The appointment of Lloyd as Chancellor of the Exchequer marked the beginning of the end for Macmillan. Lloyd's first Budget in April 1961 did little to halt the build-up of inflationary pressures (in fact, he even reduced the rate of surtax), and he seemed to be caught completely by surprise when a few months later trade deficits shot up and devaluation rumours spread. In his famous summer mini-Budget, Lloyd was forced to make heavy use of the classic deflationary methods. In addition, he introduced the notorious pay pause, applying it in the first instance to – of all people – nurses! These measures gave rise to a sharp recession in the winter of 1961–2. By the spring Macmillan's Government was in trouble.

It is extraordinary that Macmillan should have made Lloyd his Chancellor. He must have anticipated the dismay the appointment created among M.P.s and other observers. Did Macmillan simply miscalculate the use he could make of Lloyd? It was probably not just that. The habit of obliqueness, of pursuing his ends indirectly, had grown upon Macmillan to such an extent that he could not now easily shake it off. He had become incredibly skilful at avoiding direct personal conflict when pursuing his ends. But the one area where this approach could not succeed was in the removal of his own colleagues. In 1960 Macmillan, fresh from his election victory and still widely applauded as 'Supermac', could easily have forced Lloyd into a nominal post or even dropped him from the Cabinet. Then his actions would have been interpreted as a sign of strength. But in 1962, with adverse by-elections and rumours of a plot against his leadership, Macmillan's sudden dropping of Lloyd and wholesale Cabinet purge were interpreted – rightly – as a sign of weakness.[21] He was seen to be the victim, rather than the master, of circumstances.

Macmillan evidently disliked and feared the sort of personal clash that might be involved in firing a colleague and friend. He was not 'a good butcher'. The shy, hypersensitive boy survived in the man's sensibility. His later life seems, if anything, to have intensified these qualities. Macmillan always appeared to flee from situations involving personal unpleasantness. Was it this compulsion which led him to pursue his ends in such elaborately indirect ways, and which sometimes invited the charge that he was devious? However that may be, the flamboyant style and subtle methods

47

which Macmillan had developed as a public figure did not after all make up a complete set of armour. The case of Selwyn Lloyd revealed his Achilles' heel.

Macmillan badly mismanaged the 1962 Cabinet purge. He was frightened, and moved as hastily and awkwardly as possible. In the harsh light of the purge Macmillan's Edwardian panache seemed to desert him, only to reveal his great shyness and his even greater determination to stay in power. Once such things are seen, they are not forgotten. Macmillan never looked the same again.

None the less, it seemed at first as if Macmillan might re-establish his position. He had brought some of the cleverer young Conservatives forward in the Cabinet reshuffle, and so reduced the frustration felt by many of the M.P.s first elected in 1959. Despite the widespread ill-will, the rumours of revolt, and the rise of Butler to the post of Deputy Premier, it was clear by the autumn of 1962 that Macmillan's juggling with potential rivals during more than five years had been successful. No one was in a position to threaten him. By the spring of 1963 it was also perfectly clear that Macmillan intended to lead the Conservatives into the next election.

But it was not to be. The first storm that broke over Macmillan's head was the Vassall case in September 1962. Vassall's espionage, with the help of the Krogers, had been disconcertingly successful, and his trial revealed a very serious breach in British security. As the public outcry gained momentum, there were rumours that Lord Carrington and Mr Galbraith, both Admiralty Ministers, were also implicated. Macmillan was at a serious disadvantage in the face of the newspaper demands for an investigation of the Ministers' activities and for their resignation. He was still smarting from the wounds of the Cabinet purge. The extreme distaste he had felt in firing Selwyn Lloyd made him more than reluctant to embark on another such episode. Macmillan's confidence had been damaged by the affair, and he felt vulnerable to charges of disloyalty and ruthlessness.

In fact, Galbraith resigned, and Macmillan initiated

a holding operation by setting up a Commission of Inquiry under Lord Radcliffe. But the work of that Commission, though it led to the exoneration of both Galbraith and Carrington, only seemed to demonstrate how strongly the tide was running against Macmillan. For the Commission was obliged to send several journalists to prison for refusal to reveal the sources of the information which had led to their charges. Macmillan thus alienated the Press in a way that was to prove disastrous the following year.

The long harsh winter of 1962–3 was almost an emblem of Macmillan's fortunes. And it seemed to end not in spring, but in a torrid love-affair. Rumours of scandal circulated throughout the early months of 1963, but it was only in June that John Profumo, the War Minister, admitted in a letter to the Prime Minister that he had deceived the House about his association with Christine Keeler. The indignation of the Press, still bitter about its treatment the previous year, knew no bounds. At the same time the Opposition were anxious to show that the Profumo case, like the Vassall case, revealed an unpardonable negligence of security – for Profumo's liaison with Keeler had brought him into the company of a Russian attaché, Captain Ivanov.

The initial suspicions that Macmillan must have been a party to Profumo's deception did not survive his candid, doleful speech to the House on 17 June. In that speech he confessed to ignorance. He had not been informed when the Security Agency had first received information about Profumo nearly two years before, nor had he known about the warning then given to Profumo. But Macmillan confessed to more than ignorance. He admitted too the extreme pain and distaste which personal matters of this sort caused him. Thus, when the allegations concerning Profumo had first reached him some months before, he preferred to have the Law Officers question Profumo rather than do it himself.

How utterly revealing Macmillan's confession was! The delicate, vulnerable side of his character, which the purge and the Vassall case had opened to the eyes

49

of Westminster, was now bared to the gaze of an entire nation. The Edwardian clubman was seen in a new light. For how could anyone who was noted as a clubman have heard so little of what was being said about Profumo in the clubs for months past? And who could doubt that a real Edwardian man of the world would have acted swiftly and without embarrassment to nip scandal in the bud?

The dismissal of Selwyn Lloyd, the Vassall case, and the Profumo affair, all these made up a tough, hard substance which could not be mined with Macmillan's usual tools. They were matters which resisted his subtle, oblique and, above all, impersonal methods. It is not surprising that after six years as Premier matters which were not amenable to his methods should have accumulated and suddenly caused him trouble. But even when troubled, Macmillan retained a dignity. His manner and scruples had that virtue. Even when diffident feelings of doubtful value to any politician were revealed, the style which he had raised around them affirmed something about politics. For Macmillan hated incursions of the state into private life, and saw what an obsession with security might bring in its wake. He did not come altogether badly out of the Profumo affair.

Once again after Profumo, Macmillan tried to restore his position. And once again he seemed at the point of success. He was helped by that sense of solidarity which is peculiar to the Tory animal in times of danger. But he was helped even more by his continued success in keeping down possible contenders for the leadership. The many rivals cancelled each other out. Yet while he could still rouse himself when the occasion required, Macmillan was not quite the man he had been. In Cabinet his powers of attention seemed weaker – or was he simply less interested in many questions? In any case, his intellectual domination was not so complete. Macmillan seemed older and lonelier. The events of the last year had hurt him where he was most vulnerable, and he must have known that, however deftly he parry it, the pressure on him to go would by the very nature of things tend to increase. In the course of his career Macmillan had more than once become almost unwell when his ambitions were frustrated. It is not impossible that the sudden illness which forced him to to resign in September 1963 was at least partly the result of the growing threats to his position. Being Prime Minister had been too great a fulfilment for Macmillan to be able to relinquish the post for any less compelling reason.

Macmillan did not go empty-handed. Looking back from Harold Wilson's Britain, it is already possible to see how deep an impression Macmillan made on the country. Few Prime Ministers can have given such a distinctive flavour to the period of their ascendancy.

What were the ingredients of Macmillan's success? And how did he contribute to the making of a second Edwardian age? Perhaps his first contribution was a lowering of the diplomatic temperature in the world. His persistent advocacy of negotiation and compromise helped to eliminate the nightmarish features of the Cold War. His insistence that national interests rather than ideological victories were the substance of diplomacy made for a return to almost pre-1914 'normalcy'. As Kennedy asserted, the test-ban treaty might not have been possible but for Macmillan.

Macmillan's grand diplomatic manner helped to make something else possible. It eased Britain's way out of Africa. By making it clear that Britain's position as a world power and mediator were not in question, Macmillan made the dismantling of Empire seem much less than a calamity. Instead of a trauma like French Algeria, Britain came away with only a nagging Rhodesian toothache. Macmillan's handling of the economy also contributed to the same end. With the country so blatantly prosperous, critics of Macmillan's policies tended to sound like cranks. Impelled by his pre-war fight against unemployment and industrial stagnation, Macmillan was always reluctant to adopt deflationary measures. Nor did he do so badly as his Labour critics have since contended. The accounts, visible and invisible, for the years of his premiership were not unsatisfactory. It was only after he left Downing Street that the Tories seemed to lose control. Macmillan's management of the economy was founded on the premise that the Tories *could* take more risks, as it was still basically *their* system. The fact that they were in charge itself meant that they were likely to enjoy the confidence of investors and be granted considerable latitude by foreign bankers.

Macmillan's Common Market policy is more difficult to assess. He did not succeed in taking Britain into Europe. He did succeed in alienating the Commonwealth by his negotiating methods. And it may well be that he gave to British policy a too rigid preference for the Common Market in its present form. None the less, he managed to reverse the traditional political attitudes of both the country and his party with a minimum of anguish and self-doubt. Perhaps that is why, in his usual oblique way, he exaggerated the economic as against the political importance of entry into the Common Market. There is no doubt that the political case weighed most heavily with him.

Macmillan's foremost achievement ought now to be clear. He postponed the crisis of confidence in post-imperial Britain. He gave the country a breathing-space and, more than that, a heady atmosphere in which to breathe. Macmillan's combination of pragmatic change and traditional ways made him a kind of British de Gaulle. No doubt it will long be argued whether national confidence *should* be preserved in such a way. But Macmillan *did* largely preserve that confidence. It is no accident that a younger generation in the 1960s, when it began to assert itself, found that Edwardian finery and insouciance provided suitable forms. Carnaby Street – and all of Young England – owes something to Harold Macmillan.

Notes

1. *The Next Five Years* (1935). See also Martin Gilbert, *Plough My Own Furrow* (1965) pp. 291–323. Anthony Sampson has seen the importance of this episode in Macmillan's early political career. His *Mac-*

millan: A Study in Ambiguity (1967) is a successful first statement of Macmillan's life. Sampson shows considerable feeling for his subject, but is prevented by his design from doing as much interpretation as he might have liked. The only other comparable work, Emrys Hughes's *Macmillan: Portrait of a Politician* (1962) is anecdotal and superficial.

2. James Johnstone, *A Hundred Commoners* (1931); for a typical reaction to Macmillan, see Robert Rhodes James, *Chips: Diaries of Sir Henry Channon* (1967) p. 69.

3. Quoted in Gilbert, *Plough My Own Furrow*, p. 317.

4. Oswald Mosley, *My Life* (1968) p. 273. Also Harold Nicolson, *Diaries and Letters, 1930–1939* (1966) pp. 61, 76; Harold Macmillan, *Winds of Change, 1914–1939* (1966) p. 267.

5. Herbert Morrison, *An Autobiography* (1960) p. 300.

6. Harold Macmillan, *The Blast of War* (1967) pp. 452–61, 469–72.

7. Ibid., p. 566.

8. Arthur Bryant, *Triumph in the West* (1959) p. 396. Because Macmillan's authority in the Mediterranean was *de facto* rather than titular, he maintained it only through constant effort. He was much helped in this by his unusually able staff.

9. Macmillan later called his three years as Minister of Housing 'in many ways the happiest and the most rewarding of my time as a Minister'. See *Tides of Fortune* (1969) p. 373.

10. Lord Moran, *Winston Churchill: The Struggle for Survival* (1966) pp. 627–8.

11. Paradoxically, Macmillan had been extremely reluctant to move to the Treasury from the Foreign Office (on which he had set his hopes ever since his success in North Africa). His relations with Eden were never easy, and he suspected that Eden wanted to move him out of the way in order to have a more pliable colleague (Selwyn Lloyd in the event) at the F.O. While Macmillan in *Tides of Fortune* is at pains to acknowledge that Eden's concern about the build-up of infla-

tionary pressures may have contributed to his decision, his pride was none the less deeply hurt. That Eden had been wary of Macmillan's ambition and skill since dealing with him in North Africa is clear.

12. Anthony Sampson discovered this illuminating remark in the pages of *Queen*, 22 May 1963.

13. *The Blast of War*, p. 324.

14. Ibid., p. 370.

15. *Winds of Change*, p. 57.

16. Ronald Knox, *A Spiritual Aeneid* (1958) pp. 117–18. For an account of Macmillan's relationship with Knox, see Evelyn Waugh, *The Life of Ronald Knox* (1959).

17. This belief made him regret even more his transfer from the Foreign Office *before* Suez.

18. Sir Michael Wright, *Disarm and Verify* (1964) pp. 136–40.

19. See Lord Egremont's amusing *Wyndham and Children First* (1969) esp. pp. 160–95.

20. Not long after Suez, in February 1957, Nigel Nicolson wrote to his father: 'I must tell you about Harold Macmillan's speech to the 1922 Committee at the Savoy on Wednesday. It was superb. His whole speech turned upon the distinction between pride and vanity in the conduct of international relations, and there was not much doubt what he had in mind. . . . He said that the greatest moments in our history have not been those when we have conquered, but when we have led. You see the subtle change? I was delighted. I said to the Chief Whip as we were going out, "What a pity it is that now we have the most intelligent Prime Minister of the century, he has to conceal his intelligence from the public for fear that they will suspect it, and that only we, on such occasions as this, can be given the full quality of his mind." "Yes," said the Chief Whip. "Yes."' Harold Nicolson, *Diaries and Letters, 1945–1962* (1968) p. 331.

21. The Earl of Kilmuir, *Political Adventure* (1964) pp. 322–4.

2 Bread and Circuses? The Conservatives in Office, 1951–1964

Michael Pinto-Duschinsky

WERE they 'thirteen wasted years', a time of national stagnation and decline, or years of unprecedented progress? Seldom can national morale have fluctuated so violently. In the mid-fifties the new Conservative Government appeared to have succeeded beyond all previous expectations. Then came a sterling crisis and then there was Suez. By 1959 the mood of spendthrift optimism had returned, only to disappear amid the cynicism and the economic difficulties of the early sixties. Yet, at the beginning of a new decade, as the same old problems remain intensified, the years from 1951 to 1964 may come to be regarded once again with affection and nostalgia as a period of exceptional buoyancy. Who knows?

In the continuing debates about the condition of England, there has been an element of constancy. It has been realised throughout that the success of British foreign policy and social policy have been dependent on the establishment of an economy strong enough to support them. Consequently the central argument has quite rightly been concerned with the performance of the economy.

The list of Conservative achievements is outwardly impressive. From 1951 to 1964 there was uninterrupted full employment, while productivity increased faster than in any other period of comparable length in the twentieth century. In 1964 total production (measured at constant prices) was 40 per cent higher than in 1951. As a result of this growth, the nation was better housed, better educated and better cared for in old age. Conservative Governments had succeeded in fulfilling the pledge – which had appeared fancifully high when it was first made – to raise the rate of house-building to 300,000 units a year. By the time they went out of office one family in four was living in accommodation built while they were in power, and half the population was now living in owner-occupied housing, as against 25 per cent in 1951. A programme of school building had provided millions of places for the post-war 'bulge', and the number of schoolteachers had risen from 215,000 to 287,000, while the number of places at teachers' training colleges more than doubled. In 1951 only 22 per cent of the pupils at maintained schools stayed on voluntarily when they reached the legal school-leaving age of fifteen; by 1964 the proportion was 38 per cent. There was a threefold increase in the number of students following some course of further education or training, and a 60 per cent rise in the number of university places. Total expenditure on education rose from £381 million a year to £1,365 million.

There was a constant rise in pensions: the basic retirement pension, for example, had reached 67s 6d a week by 1964 and had 50 per cent more purchasing value than the 30s pension of 1951. The advance in the health service was more modest: although expenditure doubled, the increases were mostly consumed in higher costs. Nevertheless, there was a rise of 30 per cent in the number of hospital doctors, 18 per cent in the number of family doctors, and 40 per cent in nursing staff. During the same period the population had increased by only 7 per cent.

Newly acquired affluence was symbolised by a profusion of cars, television and other consumer durable goods. In 1951 there were only $2\frac{1}{4}$ million cars in Britain and 1 million television sets. By 1964 there were over 8 million cars and 13 million TV sets. There were twice as many telephones, and more refrigerators and washing machines. About 5 million people now went abroad for their holidays – a threefold increase since 1951. Average earnings had grown by 110 per cent, a rise of over 30 per cent in the average standard of living even allowing for inflated costs. This was a steadier and much faster increase than at any other time this century.

This performance becomes less impressive when it is compared with that of the other leading industrial nations. While the increase in total British production had been about 40 per cent, that of France had doubled, West Germany's and Italy's went up two and a half times, and Japanese production quadrupled. The decline in Britain's comparative exporting position was in direct proportion to that of her total production. From 1951 to 1962 there was a 29 per cent increase in British exports; the increases of France, West Germany, Italy and Japan were 86 per cent, 247 per cent, 259 per cent and 378 per cent respectively. Only Canada and the U.S.A. approached Britain's place at the bottom of the exporters' league table, with increases of 51 per cent and 33 per cent.

From 1951 to 1964 the cost of living in Britain rose by about 50 per cent – more than in any other major country with the exception of France. The balance of payments crises which threatened the economy almost every year from the mid-fifties onwards were the result as well as the further cause of the failure of production and exports to increase at a rate necessary to balance the growing consumption of home and imported goods. The economy appeared to become trapped in a vicious circle: crises in the balance of payments demanded deflation; deflation meant cuts and delays in investment and the under-utilisation of existing resources; this held back growth and thereby precipitated future sterling crises. The alarming feature of these recurrent difficulties was that they became much more serious as time went on. When the Conservatives were defeated in 1964, they left the country with the most dangerous sterling crisis since that which they had inherited from the previous Labour Government in 1951.

It is possible therefore to make two definite conclusions about the economy under the Tories. Using any major indicator of performance, the 1950s and the early 1960s were a great improvement on the years between the wars and on the showing of the Edwardian period. From 1921 to 1938 there was no year in which less than 9 per cent of the labour force was unemployed. In the slump of 1931–2 the figure exceeded 22 per cent, but even in the relatively prosperous years in the mid-twenties and the late thirties the figure was usually well above 10 per cent. It was thus widely feared in the early 1950s that mass unemployment would return as soon as war-time planning gave way again to a free-enterprise economy. These fears became obsolete as the decade proceeded. At no time between 1951 and 1964 did the annual rate of unemployment exceed 2 per cent. Unemployment – in its pre-war sense – appeared to be gone for ever, and by 1965 Andrew Shonfield, in *Modern Capitalism*, was able to talk of a 'new economic order ... that converted capitalism from the cataclysmic failure which it appeared to be in the 1930s into the great engine of prosperity of the post-war Western world'. The new economic order could also be seen in the greatly accelerated rate of economic growth. The complaints about Britain's comparatively slow growth have too often obscured the fact that in the years from 1951 to 1964 the British economy was growing faster than at any time since the peak of the Victorian era: annual growth rates of 2 per cent and 3 per cent are not as puny as they are sometimes made to appear.

Having said all this, it is necessary to restate the second conclusion: that Britain lagged behind almost all of her main industrial competitors, and that she failed to solve the problem of sterling. This resulted in an increasing lack of confidence (shared by foreigners and Britons alike) in the ability of the nation to extricate itself from such difficulties.

This leads to a further question: could Britain have done better? Were the troubles of the 1950s and 1960s the result of defective political management, or were they a consequence of deeper economic and social factors beyond governmental control? Though it is impossible to come to a satisfactory answer within the scope of this chapter, I want to suggest – rashly perhaps – that Britain could have made considerably more headway in the post-war period and that her failure is at least partly attributable to the shortcomings of Conservative Governments from 1951 to 1964. Certainly, their mistakes would have been less damaging if the underlying circumstances had been more favourable; and it is admittedly harsh to blame them for failing to diagnose situations which have become clearer only with the passage of time. Nevertheless, the case against the Conservative administrations is that they aggravated the underlying economic uncertainties by a policy of bread and circuses.

This is not intended as a criticism of the pursuit by the Conservatives of the ideals of prosperity and individual freedom. For what else should Governments exist but to provide well-being for the people they serve? By 'bread and circuses' is meant the sacrifice of policies desirable for the long-term well-being of a country in favour of over-lenient measures and temporary palliatives bringing in immediate political return. In fairness, a large share of the blame (and hence the question mark in the title) must be assigned to the political system, which produced such a close party battle in the 1950s, to the intellectuals and academics, who were unproductive in ideas or advice, and to the mass electorate, which refused to forgo its comforts while a solidly based prosperity was being created. Bread and circuses can be illustrated by two examples: the housing drive of the early fifties and the Budget of April 1955.

At the Conservative Party's annual conference held at Blackpool in October 1950, Miss Irene Dowling, a councillor from Clapham, proposed a motion on housing, deploring 'the slow rate of building' and urging 'the Conservative Party and H.M. Government to give private enterprise a freer hand'. It promised to be a typically rumbustious and vague conference debate. Miss Dowling complained that 'The Socialists believe in restrictions, controls, subsidised local authority building – the majority of houses to rent – and State buying of materials'. Mr Harmar Nicholls, M.P. for Peterborough, continued in the same ideological tone, urging the delegates to 'Free the building industry from its present shackles and extend private enterprise!'

During his speech, Mr Nicholls asked the Conservative leaders to accept a target of 300,000 houses a year when they returned to power. He was supported in this plea by Mr Stephen Minion (Liverpool, Edge Hill). At this point a representative (his name is not recorded) asked the Chairman to include the figure of 300,000 as an amendment to the motion, but he was ruled out of order by the Lady Chairman. The front-bench spokesman, Commander T. D. Galbraith, M.P., in his reply to the debate, accepted the figure that had been mentioned, but when the motion was called to the vote, the magical '300,000' was not included.

Uproar.

Hasty consultation on the platform.

Lord Woolton, the Party Chairman, then rose:

The Rt Hon. Lord Woolton, P.C.: This is magnificent. You want a figure of 300,000 put in. [Cries of 'Yes'.] Madam Chairman, I am sure that those of us on the platform here would be very glad indeed to have such a figure put in.

A representative: A minimum of 300,000....

(The motion, as amended, was carried with one dissentient.)

In this haphazard way, the Conservative commitment to build 300,000 houses a year was born. Had the party leaders been seriously embarrassed, they could have quietly shelved the proposal and omitted the specific pledge from their manifesto at the General Election of 1951. Even if the figure had been included, they could have given housing a low priority when they returned to office, and used the severe economic crisis as an excuse for leaving the target unfulfilled. Instead, the Ministry of Housing was one of the most important in the new Government. As its head, Churchill appointed a senior Minister, Harold Macmillan, assisted by 'an exceptionally brilliant engineer and organiser' called Ernest Marples. They went to work without delay. In 1951, the last year of Labour government, the total number of housing completions was 195,000. As the economic crisis and the shortage of materials intensified and continued into 1952, one might have expected the rate of house building to remain constant or to fall. But there were 240,000 housing completions during 1952; in 1953 Macmillan succeeded in passing the target of 300,000; by 1954, completions totalled 347,000.

The new Conservative Cabinet must have realised that by making housing a top priority they were delaying other urgent programmes. Although there were complex economic and social arguments for and against the housing drive, the decisive factor was political (one might even use the word 'ideological'). Tory leaders were convinced that home ownership eroded Socialist zeal and led to wider electoral support for the Conservative cause. The Socialist answer to the problem of the uneven distribution of property was common ownership. By contrast the Conservatives sought to defend the property system by giving as many people as possible a stake in it.

As early as 1946 a motion at the party conference called for the reformulation of party policy in a manner that would ensure victory at the next General Election. Anthony Eden's answer to the debate is indicative of the thinking of the leadership throughout the late forties:

This I believe we can say, that there is one single principle that will unite all the solutions that we shall seek and propound. There is one principle underlying our approach to all these problems, a principle on which we stand in fundamental opposition to Socialism. The object of Socialism is state ownership of all the means of production, distribution and exchange. Our objective is a nation-wide, property-owning democracy. These objectives are fundamentally opposed. Whereas the Socialist purpose is the concentration of ownership in the hands of the State, ours is the distribution of ownership over the widest practicable number of individuals.

Most of the post-war conference motions on housing emphasised the need to increase the number of houses for private purchase and to lower the proportion built by local authorities, and it was for this reason that the

Conservative Government concentrated on encouraging the production of houses by private builders and on raising the proportion of owner-occupied dwellings. When they came to power in 1951, the proportion of houses being built privately, was barely 12 per cent. In 1954 the proportion was 26 per cent, and it rose steadily through the fifties. In 1959, 56 per cent of the housing completions were private and the number of dwellings built for local authorities was half the peak figure reached in 1953.

Attempts are sometimes made to justify the housing drive on grounds of social and economic necessity. As the Conservative manifesto of 1951 (*The Conservative Faith*) stated: 'Housing is the first of the social services. It is also one of the keys to increased productivity.' I do not want to ignore the undoubted sincerity of many of the advocates of the housing policy of the early 1950s and their very real achievements, but I cannot help feeling that they generally stated their aims in misleading language. Had the Conservatives been concerned primarily with the removal of the *Cathy Come Home* conditions of postwar Britain, they would have given priority to slum clearance. But there was comparatively little effort to do this. Few of the houses that appeared in their neat rows during the 1950s were earmarked for the inhabitants of Stepney or the Gorbals. The housing programme benefited the upper echelons of the working class and the middle classes – Conservative voters or potential supporters. Indeed, it has been estimated that more slums were being created each year in the early 1950s by disrepair and dilapidation than were being removed by slum-clearance.

There were only two ways in which the problem of slum housing might have been solved, and neither was open to the Conservative Government in the climate of the fifties. It would have been possible to clear the slums by massive compulsory purchase, public building and the allocation of accommodation by the Government. But not even the Labour Party would have sanctioned the interference this would have required. Alternatively, rents could have been decontrolled much sooner and landlords given the freedom and incentive to improve their properties. Help could then have been directed by the Government to the sections of the community which could not afford to pay higher rents. The Conservatives did not dare to introduce such a policy as it would have involved rebates to those with the lowest incomes. The wounds of the 1930s had not sufficiently healed and the cry of 'means test' was too dangerous to permit a Right-wing programme of this kind. It was not until 1957 that the Government took the first significant step to relax its control over rented accommodation, and only in the 1960s that the party finally proposed methods by which housing subsidies would be directed to those in the greatest need.

It would be equally wrong to explain the housing drive under Macmillan on the ingenious ground that new construction aided the mobility of labour and thereby increased productivity. The accelerated rate of consumer building meant that less money and less labour was available for other types of investment more fundamental to the reconstruction of the economy, and that valuable dollars were being spent on the import of wood and construction materials. It is not coincidental that Britain's road-building programme lagged behind that of almost every other major industrialised nation, and that the average rate of industrial building from 1952 to 1954 was actually lower than in 1951.

We are used to hearing discussions of Soviet economic policy in terms of the conflict between the need for heavy capital investment and the desire for consumer goods. When there was a similar choice before Britain during this time, the requirements of industrial reconstruction were sacrificed too often. As the decade went on, it was inevitable that this neglect should lead to a slow growth in productivity. In 1958 Thomas Balogh published an article in *Oxford Economic Papers* which he had previously prepared for the Cohen Council on Prices, Productivity and Incomes. Balogh found that in the period from 1950 to 1956 German fixed investment (measured at constant prices) increased by over 100 per cent and investment in manufacturing increased even more steeply, while British investment rose in the same period by only 25 per cent and investment in manufacturing by 38 per cent. While these figures give a marginally distorted impression, as the German economic recovery started later than the British, the exaggeration is only slight. By the time Balogh was writing, German investment per capita in producers' durables had well overtaken British investment, yet British consumption was still some 25 per cent above the German level. The difference in the economic proprieties of the two countries could also be seen in the fact that from 1950 to 1954 the proportion of German industrial investment devoted to the key sector of metal engineering rose from 32 per cent to 56 per cent, whereas the corresponding growth in Britain was only from 37 per cent to 42 per cent.

The Conservatives came to power committed to show that the austerity of the late 1940s was a result of Socialist mismanagement and that they could govern in a manner far more efficient and materially advantageous to the mass of the population. From 1952 onwards they did this by the expedient of reducing taxes, making a bonfire of controls and by largely ignoring the burdens of investment required by a growing modern economy.

A striking instance of politics geared to immediate electoral advantage, and which, clearly prejudiced the national interest, is R. A. Butler's Budget of April 1955. In itself, it is a minor event in the troubled economic history of modern Britain; yet it is of great importance as it was the turning-point in the personal career of Mr Butler and in the whole post-war economy.

The two years preceding 1955 were a brief golden age: two years of stable prices, balance of payments surpluses and a rapid rate of growth; years which achieved a transfer from post-war restrictions and showed that a free capitalist system could work without creating mass unemployment. By the end of 1954, however, there were unmistakable signs of economic strain: a sharp rise in imports, aggravated by stock building; a weakening balance of payments; unemployment reduced to a level at which there were two vacancies for each person seeking work. At the same time the cost of living started rising again, and there was a worrying series of wage claims and major labour disputes. Accordingly, Bank Rate was raised by $\frac{1}{2}$ per cent in January 1955; in February there was a further rise of 1 per cent and Butler announced a mild series of hire-purchase restrictions. The unpublished economic forecast produced by the Treasury early in 1955 apparently emphasised the inflationary economic situation, and this would normally have led to a cautious Budget in April. There are conflicting accounts of the advice actually given by the Treasury to the Chancellor as Budget day approached. There is evidence that some Treasury officials at least overestimated the effectiveness of the February measures and took a rosy view of the situation quite unwarranted by the facts. Samuel Brittan, in his authoritative *The Treasury under the Tories*, attributes the 'real blame' for 'the 1955 blunder' to the Establishment wing of the official Treasury, with the connivance of the Bank of England:

Incredible though it may seem, it was just those elements that are normally most cautious about expanding production when there is unemployment and slack in the economy who egged on Mr Butler to a give-away Budget, and they did so at a time of overfull employment when extra summer spending would be sure to have the most inflationary possible effect.

The Treasury advice must be seen in its political context Churchill's resignation in April and the sudden announcement by Eden, the new Prime Minister, that there would be a General Election in May. It was in these circumstances that the Chancellor introduced his Budget, which included cuts in purchase tax and 6d. off income tax. The following month the Conservatives won the election comfortably. But they did not have long to enjoy their victory; within forty-eight hours the expected dock strike started. In June there was a further movement against the pound, and at the beginning of July the National Coal Board announced a rise of 18 per cent in the price of coal – the largest single increase ever. This measure was justified as deflationary on the curious ground that it would mop up excess demand – an argument which would of course mean that every single price rise could be called deflationary. In the same month Butler was forced to announce a number of restrictive measures: limits on credit, cuts in government spending overseas, cuts in investment in the nationalised industries, and the doubling of hire-purchase deposits.

Speculation against sterling continued. In September, Butler was compelled to abandon plans for making the pound fully convertible, and to announce further restrictions – this time a rise in interest rates for local authority loans.

In October, the unfortunate Chancellor found himself answering the acid comments of the constituency parties at the Conservative annual conference:

Last year I mentioned the possibility of doubling our standard of living in twenty-five years. That has not only been shown to be possible, but in some ways the manner in which we have galloped towards prosperity has shown how we can increase production and our standard of living. I use the word gallop, because in fact, we have gone a little too fast in this first year towards that objective. We have to put a curb or a bridle on the horse. I did not know that the horse would be quite so fiery and quite so excitable when it saw the oats of freedom for the first time.

A few days later he introduced an emergency Budget which took away much of the extra spending power he had handed out before the election five months previously, imposing further increases in purchase tax, an undistributed profits tax, higher postal charges, cuts

66

in housing subsidies and government building. It was Butler's last squeeze, for Macmillan became Chancellor in December and Butler was made Lord Privy Seal. The crisis continued and in February 1956 Bank Rate rose to $5\frac{1}{2}$ per cent and the restrictions were extended still further.

In his memoirs, Sir Anthony Eden defends the Budget of April 1955 with an argument that had been used at the time by Sir Winston Churchill, who wanted to lower the income tax by 1s. He maintains that the existence of a Budget surplus of £280 million for the previous financial year, 1954–5, justified the Conservatives in remitting half of this figure – about £140 million – in April 1955. This argument, which might have been understandable in the era of pre-Keynesian economic husbandry, is quite incomprehensible in the post-war world of management of overall demand. Nevertheless, a case – on grounds other than that put forward by Eden – can still be made out in Butler's favour. It is necessary to ignore the advantages of hindsight and consider how the situation appeared in the spring of 1955. It is too easy to forget that in the early 1950s memories of mass unemployment still outweighed fears of inflation. Also, it was seriously hoped that the lowering of the income tax would liberate a 'spirit of enterprise' and would thereby lead to a rapid increase in productivity which would counterbalance the inflationary effects of any increase in spending power.

It would be unjust, therefore, to represent the Budget of April 1955 as an act of cynical electioneering. But it would be wrong to ignore the element of politically motivated over-optimism which undoubtedly influenced the Prime Minister and some Treasury advisers. For the facts at the Government's disposal clearly indicated the need for extreme care. Not only were there all the normal signs of inflation – a weakening balance of payments, rising prices, growing quantities of unfilled vacancies, rising imports and rising consumer demand – but there were extra factors that should have made the Government especially cautious. In February the Chancellor of the Exchequer had instructed the Bank of England to support transferable sterling on the international money markets, which meant that from then on it would be *de facto* convertible. The move was designed to help the balance of payments by increasing confidence in the pound, and it was hoped that it would produce an inflow of gold and dollars into the reserves. But the policy inevitably involved large risks and made it imperative that no actions were taken which could weaken international confidence in the solidity of sterling at that particular time. Uncertainty about the terms of trade provided a further danger signal, and unsettled wage claims and the threatened strikes should have warned Butler that some dislocation of the economy and further wage rises were likely as the year went on. Furthermore, when he was preparing the Budget in April he must have known about the large increase in the price of coal, which had already been agreed but was announced only after the election.

All these factors should have made the Government particularly wary in the spring of 1955. Yet it chose this time for a give-away budget. Why?

The former reluctance of Governments to hold General Elections in May derived from their unwillingness to involve the Budget in the hurly-burly of electioneering. In 1950, for example, Attlee had held a General Election at the end of February rather than in May, when it would have been more advantageous, for this very reason. Eden's decision to have a snap election in May 1955 made the pressures against a severe Budget irresistible.

The 1955 blunder had far-reaching effects which could not have been predicted at the time. Had the inflationary strains been eased during 1955, it would probably have been possible to maintain the stability of prices and to continue to produce the growth rates that had been achieved in 1953 and 1954. Stop–go would in that case not have gained its momentum. As it was, the inflationary measures before the election of May 1955 made necessary the large cuts in the autumn and produced the stagnation of 1956.

It was not until 1958 that the economy fully recovered. The boom of 1958–60 was spectacular, but, like its predecessor, short-lived. There was widespread approval for the Budget of 1959. This included 9d off the income tax, 2d a pint off beer, cuts in purchase tax, the rintroduction of investment allowances and the repayment of £71 million of post-war credits. The boom was further encouraged by the sharp rise in the Government's own investment programme and by the general atmosphere of expansion and prosperity which was assiduously encouraged by Harold Macmillan and the public relations consultants of the Conservative organisation. As much of the 1959 refrigerator spree was spent on imported goods, the balance of payments understandably deteriorated after the election, and the next recession lasted until the upswing which preceded the election of 1964.

Why, then, did Conservative governments repeatedly ignore axioms of prudence for short-term, self-defeating expedients?

The answer can be found partly in the nature of the party struggle as it developed in the 1950s and 1960s. Despite the ultimate success of the Tories in retaining office for thirteen years, the political battle was desperately close throughout the whole period. From 1951 to 1955 the Conservatives ruled with a threadbare majority in Parliament – in the General Election of 1951 they had gained a smaller proportion of the total vote than Labour – and they did not expect to be returned to office for a second term.

No Government in modern history had previously been returned with an increased majority, and it was still thought that General Elections always produced a 'swing of the pendulum' against the party in power. As the Conservative majority was so small, this seemed to sentence them to defeat at the next election.

The Tory win in 1955 flew in the face of all modern precedent. But the declining economic situation and the failure of Eden to win the confidence of his followers led to a sharp and almost immediate slump in Conservative ratings in the opinion polls. A leading article in the *Daily Telegraph* on 3 January 1956 castigated the new government for its 'changes of mind . . .

half measures, and the postponement of decisions' and called for the 'smack of firm Government'. Eden was in such a panic that he issued a statement from Downing Street, denying that he had any intention of resigning (he had been in office no more than nine months at the time). Butler, already discredited but still heir apparent, hardly made matters easier by his back-handed assurance that he would 'support the Prime Minister in all his difficulties'.

All this happened before the Suez crisis. By the time Macmillan became Premier in January 1957, the defeat of the Conservatives seemed assured and Labour leaders were openly discussing the allocation of Ministries in their coming administration. The economic crisis worsened during 1957 and the Prime Minister had to deal with dissensions in the Cabinet on colonial and economic matters, which led to the resignation first of Lord Salisbury and then of the Chancellor, Peter Thorneycroft. It was not until the end of 1958 that the Conservatives regained their confidence in Parliament and overtook Labour in the polls.

After the third Tory victory in 1959 – a foregone conclusion only in retrospect – it seemed for the first time that the two-party system had ceased to function and that Labour was doomed to Opposition. It was at this period that the 'embourgeoisement thesis' was advanced to explain the repeated Conservative success. Books with such titles as *Must Labour Lose?* argued that as middle-class people voted predominantly for the Conservatives, and as the modernisation of the economy drew more people into the middle classes, the Conservative percentage of the vote was bound to increase.

These tracts were out of date almost as soon as they were published. Following the credit squeeze and the pay pause introduced in an emergency Budget in the summer of 1961, there was a dramatic reversal of public opinion; Labour forged ahead in the opinion polls, and by-elections confirmed the Conservative weakness, culminating in the spectacular loss of Orpington to the Liberals in the spring of 1962.

Throughout this period the party struggle was so

close that at any election from 1950 to 1964 a net swing of three votes in a hundred from the Conservatives would have given victory to the Labour Party (see Table 2.1). The opinion polls are also a good guide to the course of politics; apart from the two years from the spring of 1959 to the spring of 1961, Labour had an almost constant lead, the Conservatives being ahead for a total of less than two of their other eleven years of office.

The evenly matched electoral strength of the major parties was accompanied by a striking measure of agree-

Table 2.1

The Close Party Struggle, 1950–64

General Election results

	Total votes cast	Conservative	Labour
1950	100%	43·5%	46·1%
	28,772,671	12,502,567	13,266,592
1951	100%	48·0%	48·8%
	28,595,668	13,717,538	13,948,605
1955	100%	49·7%	46·4%
	26,760,493	13,311,936	12,404,970
1959	100%	49·4%	43·8%
	27,859,241	13,749,830	12,215,538
1964	100%	43·4%	44·1%
	27,655,374	12,001,396	12,205,814

ment between them on matters of policy. There was no major issue, from 1951 onwards, which produced a fundamental cleavage between the official policy of the Labour Party and that of the Conservatives.

In 1951 there were still widespread fears among the working classes that the return of Conservative government would bring with it the economic conditions of previous capitalist administrations in the 1930s; the middle classes regarded with equal distaste the prospect of further nationalisation and the continuation of Socialist restrictions. When the pollsters included in their questionnaires an item asking whether there was a 'great deal of difference' between the major parties,

71

the responses in the early 1950s indicated that the majority of the electorate thought that there was. These differences dissolved as the decade progressed. Conservative rule did not bring the return of mass unemployment. Nor did it mean the end of the National Health Service and the paraphernalia of the welfare state. Indeed there was a constant rise in pensions and a general extension of welfare. Churchill's new administration did not indulge in the orgy of denationalisation for which some of the die-hard Tories were hoping. Apart from the steel industry and road haulage, which were denationalised but kept under close public control, the Conservatives left the public sector untouched. Lord Moran reports that Beaverbrook used to tease Churchill for stealing the Socialists' clothes while they were bathing: 'Max harps on this. In his impish manner he pictures Winston discarding the laurel wreath of the great war leader for the cloth cap of Keir Hardie.'[1] Churchill himself acknowledged to Moran that he kept advising the party to make concessions: 'I have come to know the nation and what must be done to retain power.'[2]

The Labour Opposition played the consensus game with no less conviction and attempted to throw off their commitments to further nationalisation as gracefully as they were able. As a Left-wing writer, Ralph Miliband, correctly emphasises, Labour leaders were

> haunted by a composite image of the potential Labour voter as quintessentially *petit-bourgeois*, and therefore liable to be frightened off by a radical alternative to Conservatism.... It was in many ways extremely fortunate for the Labour leaders that the Conservative Government should have decided to denationalise steel and road transport. For however much they might be opposed to any serious extension of nationalisation, these leaders could hardly do less than pledge themselves to the renationalisation of either steel or road transport. This soon became the well-gnawed bone which the leadership threw back to the hungry activists, as a token of the leadership's belief in public ownership.[3]

72

The politics of the Centre also dominated foreign and colonial policy. Any signs of pacifism that the Labour Party might have shown in the 1930s disappeared while they were in office after the war. In 1948 they became the first British Government to introduce conscription in peace-time; they started to produce an atom bomb and initiated a huge rearmament programme at the outbreak of the Korean War. Conservative foreign policy and defence policy in the 1950s was no more than a continuation of what had gone before.

In 1951 it was perhaps reasonable to expect that the Conservatives would reverse the colonial policy of 'Socialist scuttle' when they returned to office. Churchill had himself been the leading die-hard over the Indian question in the 1930s. The Labour manifesto of 1951 drew a sharp contrast between the policies of the two parties: 'The Tory still thinks in terms of Victorian imperialism and Colonial exploitation. His reaction in a crisis is to threaten force.... He would have denied freedom to India, Pakistan, Ceylon and Burma.'

Throughout the 1950s, however, the Conservatives abandoned the path of Empire, substituting in its place 'Commonwealth development'. By 1964 they were able to claim that thirteen of the twenty countries in the new Commonwealth had achieved independence since they took office. The Labour propagandists bravely attempted to maintain that there was still a difference in the colonial policies of the two parties. According to their 1964 manifesto, in a section on 'The End of Colonialism',

> So long as they were in Opposition, the Conservatives denounced [the policy of independence] as Socialist Scuttle. Faced with responsibility, however, in 1951 they were compelled very largely to accept it.... How little they were able to transfer their faith in the new Commonwealth was shown when Harold Macmillan and Alec Douglas-Home both declared there was no future for Britain outside the Common Market.... The Labour Party is convinced that the first responsibility of a British Government is still for the Commonwealth.

Within three years, Harold Wilson applied for British membership of the Common Market.

The most vigorous political debates of the 1950s and 1960s were conducted independently of the party battle. The controversy between a Socialist economy and a mixed economy, between those who wanted an extension of state ownership and those who were generally satisfied with the position that had been reached by 1951, between those who favoured the Bomb and British participation in the Western Alliance and those who advocated unilateral disarmament – all these gave rise to a wider range of disagreement between the central core of the Labour Party and its Left wing than with their Conservative opponents. The conflict between the Bevanites and Labour Party leaders in the 1950s, and, to a lesser extent, the debates between the *laissez-faire* capitalists and the advocates of a 'mixed' economy in the Conservative Party in the 1960s, have provided the main substance of political discussion.

The two major parties, engaged as they were in a continued and inconclusive battle for votes, and unable to distinguish themselves – much as they sought to do so – by any fundamental differences of policy, sometimes failed to resist the temptation of engaging in a political auction, each outbidding the other in its appeal to the materialist instincts of the electorate (see Table 2.2). No party tactician could afford to ignore the speed and sensitivity with which the votes of the minority of the population uncommitted to either party swayed with the immediate economic situation. These floating voters showed repeatedly that they were unable to distinguish between lasting prosperity and that which was artificially and temporarily created for political purposes. In this way, the politics of consensus went hand in hand with the politics of bribery.

But the nature and alignment of the parties was by no means the only reason for the difficulties of these years. The affairs of the country would probably have been managed no better had they been delegated to the experts. Few of the mistakes of Conservative government would have been avoided by the employment of specialist advisers, who were often divided in their views and showed no greater foresight than the politicians. Before Butler, Eden and their Treasury officials are judged too harshly for 'the 1955 blunder', it should be remembered that their over-optimistic assessment of the economic situation was shared at the time by many professional economists. A few days before the Budget of April 1955, *The Economist* could declare that there were 'no grim furies looking on' and that the Chancellor might reasonably be tempted to give away up to half his

Table 2.2
Housing Pledges in Party Manifestos

Labour	Conservative
1951 We shall maintain the present rate of 200,000 new houses a year.	*1951* Housing is the first of the social services. . . Our target remains 300,000 houses a year.
1964 While we regard 400,000 houses as a reasonable target, we do not intend to have an election auction on housing figures.	*1964* Since 1951, houses have been built at an average rate of 300,000 houses a year. . . . Next year we shall reach our new target of 400,000.
1966 We intend to achieve a Government target of 500,000 houses by 1969–70.	*1966* [We shall] reach our target rate of 500,000 new homes a year by the end of 1968.

1954–5 surplus in the Budget, which is exactly what he proceeded to do. Similarly, the Conservative building drive was more often criticised by housing experts for consuming too small rather than too large a slice of national resources. Had they been more influential, the economy might well have been distorted even more.

The declining years of the Macmillan Government produced a stream of writing, magnifying Britain's troubles out of all proportion and arguing that they stemmed from 'dilettantism' (Thomas Balogh), 'the cult of amateurishness' (Arthur Koestler) and 'a mistaken veneration of old ideas' (Professor Brian Chapman). The implication that politics had suffered from ignoring intellectual or expert opinion does not bear close examination. The achievements of the university economists and professional advisers who were later employed by the Wilson administration was far from encouraging.

While the absence of major policy debates across party lines was an important feature of the Age of Affluence, it cannot be attributed to a conspiracy between the political leaders to sweep fundamental discussion under the carpet. They could not ignore the fact that the mass of the electorate was more directly concerned with the standard of living than with the abstract causes championed by small fringe groups at either end of the political spectrum. By 1953 any pretensions to a continuing imperial role were restricted to a diehard rump in the Conservative Party led by Captain Waterhouse and at the most forty Conservative M.P.s. When Churchill reluctantly accepted the 'policy of scuttle' from the Suez Canal base, the rebellion of the Suez Group of M.P.s failed because its backing in the party and electorate was so small. Sir Harry Legge-Bourke, who resigned the Conservative Whip in protest against the 'ignominious withdrawal', too often supported by the Conservatives, 'from Palestine, Burma, India, Persia, the Sudan and now Egypt', failed to ignite any spark of colonial fervour.

At the opposite pole there was little support for the Bevanite opposition in the 1950s to British participation in the Western Alliance. The Campaign for Nuclear Disarmament failed in the early 1960s as only one voter in seven shared the aims of the tens of thousands who marched each Easter from the nuclear base at Aldermaston to Trafalgar Square.

The absence of any serious debate about dismantling or extending the welfare state or about public ownership reflected in part the genuine satisfaction with the compromise between private freedom and public responsibility that was soon reached under Churchill's premiership. Before the 1959 election, only one Conservative in twenty and one Socialist in three favoured further nationalisation, but there was widespread

76

opposition to denationalisation and to any reduction in the social services.

The generation which came to maturity in the 1950s had been born in the Great War, schooled during the slump, conscripted in the Second World War and rationed for years afterwards. It had no inclination to forgo the security and comforts now within its grasp in the hope of long-term economic growth. The nation demanded the priority to consumption which the politicians willingly offered. Even during the final defection from the Conservatives, the electorate did not reject the pursuit of short-run materialist objectives, but only the Government's inability to achieve them to the extent it demanded.

It is said that Lord Poole, one of Macmillan's most astute and influential party managers, used to drive on a Saturday from his country home to nearby Watford. Here he observed the changing moods of the suburb by watching people shopping in the new supermarkets, enjoying the opportunities they had never had before, absorbed in the rickety world of hire-purchase, intent on becoming owners of a television or a cut-price (imported) washing machine. If these were their desires and what they demanded with their votes, is it fair to blame the Governments of Churchill, Eden, Macmillan and Home for providing them so generously?

Notes

1. Moran, *Winston Churchill: The Struggle for Survival* (1968 ed.) p. 517.
2. Ibid., p. 524.
3. R. Miliband, *Parliamentary Socialism* (1961) p. 339.

3 The Labour Party in Opposition, 1951–1964

Vernon Bogdanor

'You are going into first principles,' said the duke, much surprised.
'Give me then second principles,' replied his son, 'give me any.'

DISRAELI, *Tancred*

The masses have got damned lethargic after such long prosperity.

ENGELS, quoted in CROSLAND, *The Future of Socialism.*

THE years of affluence were years of disaster for the Labour Party. During the 1950s they lost seats in four successive General Elections and remained in Opposition for thirteen years, the longest period spent in Opposition by a major political party since the Reform Bill of 1832. What were the causes of these electoral defeats? Were they due, as some argued, to the failure of the Labour Party to adapt itself to contemporary circumstances, and to present a policy relevant to the 1950s rather than to the 1930s? Or, on the other hand, were they the result of too little adherence to principle, and too much pandering to the spirit of the times? Did the Labour Party suffer by failing to come to terms with affluence; or did it fail by surrendering its moral vision to a cynical materialism? Suggestions of this kind were bandied back and forth, from Right to Left, more and more frequently and with greater and greater vehemence as the decade unfolded. And even the election victory of 1964 did not settle the question. For the Left could claim that Clause 4 of the Labour Party Constitution was still in existence, pledging the party to the nationalisation of the means of production, distribution and exchange; while the Right could claim that

78

Harold Wilson had abandoned in practice the full-blooded Socialism which the Left demanded, even if he continued to use and to support the rhetoric.

A different suggestion, popular among market researchers and students of elections, was that the social trends brought about by affluence led inevitably to a decline in Labour support. Thus any radical party, whatever its political stance, was bound to face insuperable difficulties during a period of rapidly increasing national prosperity. The difficulty with this suggestion, of course, lies in the fact that the Labour Party *did* succeed in winning the 1964 election.

In fact, as I hope to show, both types of explanation – the sociological and the political – fall wide of the mark. The sociological explanation failed to show why the Labour Party did not succeed in counteracting the social forces working against them, and the political explanation does not reveal the reasons why both Left and Right were unable to create a radical agenda for the party.[1]

I. *Consolidation and the Bevanite Revolt*

In 1951 the Labour Party was surprisingly complacent about the Conservatives' return to power. The prevailing mood was one of relief – relief that the period of office on a narrow majority was now over; relief at the prospect of a united party in Opposition, rather than a divided one in office. But above all, there was a feeling of grim satisfaction that the Conservatives would now be revealed in their true colours as a reactionary party. For a party based upon financial and industrial capital would surely not put either full employment or the welfare state very high on its list of objectives. As the *New Statesman* put it just before the 1951 election: 'The industrialists who have contributed their millions to Lord Woolton's fund would at once demand their pound of flesh ... the suppressed resentments of the last six years would at once sweep away the mild Me-Tooism of Mr Butler and Mr Eden.'[2]

This would lead to an erosion of the hard-won gains

79

secured by the Labour Government. In particular, it would lead to the return of unemployment. For full employment could only be maintained through a system of economic controls. A Conservative Government, however, because of its free-enterprise ideology, would inevitably dismantle all controls. And, as Aneurin Bevan put it, at the 1952 Labour Party Conference: 'It is a fact, and even the Keynesians have to admit it, that there is no means of preventing unemployment in capitalist society.' Nor were these doubts confined to the Left. At the same conference, Mrs Braddock argued: 'whatever we try to do, there will be mass unemployment while a Tory Government is in power, since that is part of the capitalist system that the Tory Party stands for'. This assessment of events dictated the style of opposition of the Labour leadership until Attlee retired in December 1955. The posture of the leadership was essentially defensive: to preserve the Socialist gains of full employment and the welfare state, and to make clear to the voters how fragile these gains were, in face of the expected Conservative onslaught. This, combined with some natural 'swing of the pendulum', would soon suffice to replace a weak administration with a united Labour Government. There was therefore no cause for alarm at the temporary set-backs of 1950 and 1951. As the *Spectator* noted:

Ever since the Government took office the Opposition has confronted it as though any fool could see that this was an administration that must fall to pieces, because of its plain incompetence, whereupon the rule of the saints could begin anew.[3]

These tactics were, of course, based upon a complete misjudgment of the situation. The Conservative leaders did not yield their 'pound of flesh' to their hidden wealthy supporters, and the 'Me-Tooism' of Butler and Eden pervaded all the policies of the Conservative Government. Evelyn Waugh was able to lament that, after the vicissitudes of Socialism, when Britain had seemed to him like a country under enemy occupation, the Conservatives had not put the clock back by one minute. And, whether through luck or judgment, the Conservatives were able to remove economic controls and to manage the economy successfully. The years 1951 to 1955 were, in fact, the years in which Conservative freedom worked.

The Labour Party were thus left in the invidious position of having predicted doom in the face of clear economic progress; they were left as defenders of full employment and the welfare state when they did not seem to require defenders. By the election of 1955 they had no new or creative ideas to put before the elector- ate. Perhaps they were fortunate in losing only twenty- five seats in this election.

A more realistic attitude on the part of the Labour leadership would have shown them that their own in- ternal difficulties were far deeper than those which they claimed to perceive in their opponents. The Labour Party was rent by dissension after 1951, because it had completed the classical programme of British Socialism and was compelled to search for another. This programme, which had been carried to fruition by the post-war Labour Governments, was that embodied in the party constitution of 1918. This constitution, in- fluenced very greatly by the Webbs, placed nationalisa- tion at the centre of the party's domestic policy. Indeed the only reference to the domestic aims of the Labour Party lay in the famous Clause 4, which calls for 'the common ownership of the means of production, dis- tribution and exchange'. This was a policy upon which both Left and Right of the party could unite, what- ever their differences concerning tactics or the speed of advance towards the Socialist Commonwealth. Herbert Morrison, for example, generally regarded as being on the Right wing of the party, could write:

> The vision of one Minister alone socialising two big industries pleases me enormously.... Socialism for me is a policy for today and not for some indefinite day after tomorrow. ... The function of Labour Governments in the future will rather be to secure the socialisation of industry after industry....[4]

81

After 1945, therefore, the Labour Party translated its traditional proposals into practice by nationalising major public utilities and the steel industry. But with these traditional proposals exhausted, the problem remained as to what should be done next. Or, as the *New Statesman* put it in May 1949, 'The plain fact is that the Labour Party is reaching the end of the road which it first set itself to traverse in 1918. . . . What next?'

Further nationalisation did not look at all attractive. For it did not seem to have brought many of the advantages which had been claimed for it. The nationalised industries were not noticeably more efficient than those in private hands; nor did the salaries paid to the managers of these industries satisfy the egalitarian instincts of Socialists; while the bureaucratic structure of the industries, their relative freedom from control both by Parliament and by the workers within the industry, prevented them from being successful as extensions of democracy within the economic sphere.

For these reasons, both the Left and Right wings of the party were hesitant about further large-scale nationalisation of industry. But, given their Socialist beliefs, it was impossible for them to admit this. Nationalisation played a highly important role in holding the Labour Party together; for if the commitment to nationalisation was abandoned, what other principles could be found which would cement the party together so successfully?

The Left claimed that they wanted more nationalisation, to proceed at a faster rate, but they rejected the Morrisonian model of the public corporation, the basis of the post-war Labour Governments' nationalisation measures, without putting forward any constructive alternative. They spoke a great deal about workers' control, but were unable to present a plan showing how this could be made practicable, within the framework of large-scale industry. For these reasons the Left, led by Aneurin Bevan, tended to confine themselves to issues of foreign policy. They campaigned more eagerly against the SEATO pact and against German rearmament than for speedier nationalisation. On domestic affairs in general, the Bevanites were essentially uncreative. They had no new ideas to offer, and their continual call for new ideas acted merely as a substitute for their failure to produce any.

Thus, for all the sound and fury produced by the disputes between the Bevanites and the leadership, it is difficult to regard these disputes as contributing greatly to a solution of the intellectual problem facing Socialists. Bevanism was indeed a revolt against the older generation of Labour leaders and their remoteness from the aspirations of many party militants. But the revolt never became an articulate one. Policy differences on domestic issues were never clearly stated. The Bevanites, although they rejected the political strategy embodied in Morrison's call for 'consolidation', were never able to put an alternative strategy in its place. Thus the years 1951 to 1955 were not, contrary to appearances, years of great ideological ferment, years in which Socialist principles were being rethought, It was not until the Revisionists, led by Gaitskell and Crosland, came upon the scene that ideological differences came to the fore.

The Right also, after 1951, were unwilling to abandon the Fabian strategy. They did not want to say publicly that the model of the public corporation, which had been the basis of their own nationalisation measures, was no longer applicable. Nor was it worthwhile to overturn a useful piece of rhetoric which could be brought out to assuage the Left, fearful of 'betrayals'. Thus Morrison could answer criticism of his gradualist methods at the 1952 conference in the following way:

> Let me say this about nationalisation in general. I have said that we have not finished with it, and we must never say that we have finished with it until we have got the nationalisation of all the means of production, distribution and exchange. I cannot promise when that date will be reached.

The slogan of 'consolidation' adopted by Morrison for the 1950 election provided an admirable camouflage for the Right. For it implied that, before extensions of nationalisation could be seriously contemplated, the existing nationalised industries must be made to run more efficiently. How long this task would take, however, no one was able to tell. In the words of Emanuel Shinwell at the same conference:

> We have not abandoned any of our principles, nor any of our schemes nor any of our projects, but it is a question of prevailing conditions.
> In view of our achievements in the sphere of nationalisation ... it is desirable that we should bring these schemes to full fruition before we proceed to embark on a great many others.

In this way, the distaste which many Labour ex-ministers felt for further acts of nationalisation was concealed by the use of Socialist rhetoric. In theory, the Labour Party seemed to be committed to further steps along the Fabian road to Socialism. In practice, as Cole wrote, 'We have drifted into a position in which nobody feels any enthusiasm for further nationalisation.... There is, in fact, nothing much left to be done along the established lines.'[5]

The failure of both Left and Right to clarify the choices available after 1951 entailed a moratorium upon new ideas. The period 1951–5 was one in which the older theorists of Socialism – the Webbs, Shaw, Laski – were no longer on the scene, and no intellectual replacement had yet been found for them. This lack of ideas placed the Labour Party in a conservative position; there was no positive new theme to put before the electorate. The Labour Party was not able to discover the direction in which it wanted to travel. It remained intellectually exhausted by the experience of office.

The defensive posture adopted after 1951 suited Clement Attlee's style very well; it is no accident that different tactics were put forward as soon as he retired from the leadership. For Attlee's indispensability to the party consisted not in his being an originator of new ideas, but rather in his being a conciliator, perhaps the only man who could have held the 1945 Government together. He was therefore temperamentally sympathetic to the tactics of the Labour Party in opposition before 1955. The divisions within his own ranks and the intellectual vacuum within the party prevented Attlee from mounting a full-scale attack upon the Conservatives either in the House of Commons or during the election campaign. Defence of hard-won gains against suspected Tory attack, and consolidation of these gains, were all that the Labour Opposition had to offer.

II. *Revisionism*

The result of the 1955 election discredited Attlee's approach. It was clear that the defensive posture of the Labour Party would not lead to an automatic return to office. The lesson to be learned from the election defeat was, therefore, that a more aggressive and clear-cut challenge to the Conservatives was necessary. But what form was the attack to take? Was it to consist of a break with earlier policies, or should there be a return to the traditional faith? Obviously Right and Left would be divided on this issue. The policy of blurring issues, which had enabled Attlee to hold the party together, was now discredited and ideological differences would be brought out into the open. Nevertheless the period between the election of Hugh Gaitskell as leader in December 1955, and the General Election of October 1959, was the most peaceful of Labour's thirteen years in Opposition. The main reason for this was that Aneurin Bevan, the natural leader of the Left, made his peace with Gaitskell after the latter was elected to the leadership. At the Labour Party Conference of 1957, Bevan showed that he was tired of the long years of rebellion. As Shadow Foreign Secretary he argued, to the accompaniment of jeers and cat-calls from his erstwhile supporters, that to pass a motion calling for abandonment of the British hydrogen bomb would send the British Foreign Secretary 'naked into the conference chamber'.

By 1959, Bevan had become so mellowed as a result of the responsibilities of office in the Shadow Cabinet that Harold Macmillan could chide him in the House of Commons: 'I feel sorry for him as he gropes about abandoned by his old friends and colleagues – a shorn Samson surrounded by a bevy of prim and ageing Delilahs.'[6]

Deprived of its leader, the Left lost its main source of energy, for there was no one to take Bevan's place. The Left, therefore, did not attempt any 'rethinking'. Instead it contented itself with arguing that if only the Socialist message was blazoned forth loud and clear, un-committed voters would rally towards it. Frank Cousins's speech at the 1956 conference is typical:

> We have to go to the doors and tell the people our story, and it has to be a Socialist story ... Some of the people I represent would not agree with the critics who say that nationalisation, for instance, does not work. Some of them would say that it does work, and it has worked well.

This kind of response inevitably branded the appeal of the Left as a traditional one; it meant that all the creative thinking between 1955 and 1959 was done by the Right, and in particular by the Revisionists, men such as Anthony Crosland, Douglas Jay, Roy Jenkins and Denis Healey.[7] The Revisionists were closely associated with Hugh Gaitskell and are to be sharply distinguished from the traditional Right wing of the party, as represented by men such as Herbert Morrison. For they wanted to 'rethink' Socialist policies in the light of social and economic change, and not merely to 'reapply' traditional principles. They resented the dishonesty of pretending to support policies which were privately thought to be unattainable or impracticable. Unlike the Left and the traditional Right, they did not regard the completed programme of 1945–51 as a neces-sary model for future Labour Governments. Certainly this programme represented a valuable first stage. But now the important thing was to change direction, and not to continue along the same path. The Revisionists questioned the Fabian strategy of proceeding gradually towards a fully collectivised economy. For this strategy had been formulated in social and economic conditions

86

which no longer existed. The problems which the Fabian strategy had been formulated to solve had been largely dealt with by the reforms of the post-war Labour Governments. And therefore, as Crosland writes, 'The intellectual framework within which most pre-war Socialist discussion was conducted has been rendered obsolete.'[8]

Calls for the reformulation of Socialist doctrine had, of course, been heard even before the electoral defeats of 1950 and 1951, and in 1952 the *New Fabian Essays* had revealed many of the themes of Revisionist thought. But it was not until Crosland's *The Future of Socialism* in 1956 that these themes were fitted together into a coherent and systematic theory. Crosland's aims in this book, and in its sequel, *The Conservative Enemy* (1962), were extremely ambitious. For he was attempting to show the irrelevance of the traditional Socialist *analysis,* as well as replacing the traditional Fabian *strategy* of political advance.

First he had to show in what ways British society differed from the society attacked by the early Socialists. Then he had to show what new policies were necessary if the traditional aims of Socialists were to be achieved. In doing this, he would be bound to fall foul of the Left, who denied that anything had changed, and of the traditional Right who agreed that changes had occurred, but wished to spend their time 'consolidating' these changes:

> The trouble is that some of its [the Labour Party's] leaders are radical, but not contemporary – they are discontented, but with a society which no longer exists; while others are contemporary but not radical – they realise that the society has changed, but quite enjoy the present one.[9]

Crosland had little difficulty in showing that society had changed since the 1930s. It was clear that such social gains as full employment, the virtual abolition of primary poverty, and the welfare state owed nothing to the existence of the nationalised industries. And retention of these gains under Conservative rule showed that they were perfectly compatible with the existence of a large private sector in the economy. In fact, Britain no longer corresponded to a 'classically capitalist' society; the achievement of the Labour Governments had been to show that the worst evils of the unregulated market economy could be removed without a total transformation of society. Certainly Britain in the 1950s, though not Socialist, was very different from the society which the early Socialists had criticised. Thus the furious disagreements in the Labour Party reflected a genuine intellectual dilemma. For 'If this is not still capitalism, then what is Socialism now about? The Labour Party has not yet given a clear answer to this question.'[10]   And it was especially difficult to find the answer to this question, since 'the much-thumbed guide-books of the past must now be thrown away'.[11] There was no 'one orthodoxy to be consulted now for guidance about the future'.[12]

Nevertheless Crosland managed to isolate five aspirations common to most Socialist theorists. These aspirations were basically ethical; their aim was to transform men morally, and not merely to alter institutions. For 'the one single element common to all schools of thought has been the basic aspirations, the underlying moral values'.[13] Of the five aspirations, only two – the abolition of poverty, and the attainment of full employment – were economic in nature; the other Socialist objectives were a concern for social welfare, the desire for a sense of solidarity within the community, and, above all, the desire for equality.

The internal logic of Crosland's argument could not be faulted. Socialists had always held in common certain moral aims and aspirations. At one time it seemed as if these aims could only be achieved by collectivising society, by transforming capitalism into a society in which the major industries were owned by the state. But society was no longer classically capitalist, and some, though by no means all, of the traditional Socialist objectives had been achieved. Thus Crosland was implying that Socialism might be achieved without large-scale nationalisation. For if some of the objectives had been achieved within the mixed economy,

88

why should not others be achieved in this way also? Thus public ownership was not a necessary means to the end of Socialism; the mixed economy could be accepted as final. For, as Gaitskell had written:

> Anybody who thinks about it for a moment will agree that nationalisation ... must be treated as a means and not grouped with the ultimate aims ... The fact that it is nevertheless often treated as an end, as, indeed, more or less identical with Socialism, is because it has been regarded not as *a* means to achieve the ideals of Socialism but as the *only possible* means *which could not fail to produce the desired ends.*[14]

It was necessary, therefore, to discover new ways to achieve the traditional Socialist objectives. For the Revisionists, the central Socialist objective was equality. Crosland, in *New Fabian Essays*, had quoted with approval the statement of Professor Arthur Lewis that 'Socialism is about equality'. And equality could be achieved by fiscal and educational reforms within the framework of the mixed economy.

If, as the Revisionists argued, their proposals for reform followed directly from the ideals of the early Socialists, why did their suggestions meet with such opposition within the Labour Party? This opposition was not confined to the Left, but embraced the traditional Right, and in particular the leaders of some of the major trade unions. The division between the traditional Right and the Revisionists was piquantly shown at the 1957 conference when the policy pamphlet *Industry and Society*, embodying much of the thought of the Revisionists, was opposed by Morrison and Shinwell of the traditional Right. For in this debate, Shinwell called nationalisation 'the vital principle on which this party was founded'.

There was certainly some truth in Shinwell's contention; nationalisation was the vital principle upon which the Labour Party had been founded and had remained united. The Webbs, who had been mainly responsible for the constitution of 1918, were by no means excessively preoccupied with the moral issue of equality which Crosland had discerned as the core of Socialist thought. Indeed the Webbs had been adamant in their view that a Socialist society would still contain great inequalities between the workers in industry and the managerial and administrative class. Besides, the constitution of 1918 represented more than the commitment to a particular ethic. For Socialists, a political programme had to follow from an ideology, from a set of very general beliefs; only a theory and critique of the workings of society could show the main forces operating to prevent the attainment of well-being. For the Webbs, the main impediment was simply the private ownership of the means of production, distribution and exchange.

The Webbs had shared with Marx the belief that the fundamental character of a society was determined by its pattern of ownership. Common to Socialist thought had been the view that the ideal of human dignity could only be realised under a social system within which public ownership prevailed. Crosland, in showing that nationalisation was hardly relevant to the central ideals of Socialism, was attacking the central assumption of previous Socialist thought:

> Is it not then clear that the ownership of the means of production has ceased to be the key factor which imparts to a society its essential character? Either collectivism or private ownership is consistent with widely varying degrees of liberty, democracy, equality, exploitation, class-feeling, planning, workers' control and economic prosperity ... the pattern of ownership, although it may influence, is unlikely to *determine* the extent to which such goals are attained.... It therefore seems rather pointless to define and distinguish societies according to this one criterion.[15]

Crosland was showing that the theory of society embodied in Clause 4 of the constitution was no longer valid. And Clause 4 represented the only domestic objective to which members of the Labour Party seemed

90

necessarily committed. So, if this objective was removed, what was there which made the Labour Party Socialist? Could not the ethic of equality be accepted by any liberal or radical? Acceptance of the Revisionist argument would clearly intensify the struggle within the Labour Party. Hitherto the party had been united by its commitment to the ultimate goal of wholesale nationalisation. Within this framework, Left–Right disagreement could be fairly easily contained. For, provided the Utopia was a shared one, what did extra time spent in its attainment really matter?

The Revisionists, however, were proposing to tell the Left, not merely that large-scale nationalisation was to be put off for the immediate future, but that it was no longer essential to the aims which Socialists set themselves. In place of the tactical considerations advanced by the traditional Right, they produced arguments based upon doctrine. Thus the split between Left and Right would be worsened because they now wished to move forward in different directions. The Left wished to proceed towards a wholly socialised economy; the Right, although they did not wish to accept the present division between public and private ownership as final, nevertheless emphasised other reforms and accepted the permanence of the mixed economy.

The Left did not manage to oppose Revisionism with any critique as central and coherent as that of Crosland. They never succeeded in showing how future instalments of public ownership could be purged of the evils which the measures of 1945–51 had revealed. The nearest the Left came to an answer to Revisionism was in the work of Richard Crossman. Crossman was by no means an orthodox member of the Left. During the Attlee Governments he had been the most prominent critic of Ernest Bevin's foreign policy, and he had become a follower of Aneurin Bevan after Bevan's resignation from the Government in 1951. But he had never shared the pacifism of the traditional Left, and he was to oppose the C.N.D. campaign for unilateral disarmament and neutralism. Crossman clung to an independent position, criticising the defence policy of the leadership and the theory of

91

Revisionism. His writings well illustrate the confusions and bewilderment of the Left during the period of affluence.

Crossman started from the same position as Crosland, from a realisation that the Labour Party had lost its way. And he argued that the traditional Right's distrust of theory was mainly responsible for this. In the new situation in which it now found itself, new theories were necessary to replace the old orthodoxies. The Labour Party was suffering from

> a failure of the sense of direction which alone can unify and sustain a great political party. The Labour Party was unsure where it was going. The familiar landmarks on the road to Socialism had been left behind ... The Labour Party has lost its way not only because it lacks a map of the new country it is crossing, but because it thinks maps unnecessary for experienced travellers.[16]

Unfortunately, however, the outlines of Crossman's own map were somewhat blurred. He rejected, of course, the Morrisonian public board as a model for future acts of nationalisation:

> the proper way to counter public hostility to nationalisation is not to re-write Clause 4 but to admit frankly the dreadful mistakes made by the Attlee Government and then to work out precise proposals for decentralising their oligarchies and subjecting them to full public control.[17]

Such precise proposals were not to be found, however, in Crossman's writings, nor in the writings of any of his supporters on the Left. Indeed most of the proposals for altering the institutional framework of the nationalised industries came from the Revisionists. It was men such as Crosland and Gaitskell who put forward ideas of municipalisation and of 'competitive public enterprise', which involved an extension of public investment through the purchase of shares in private companies.[18]

Nor were Crossman's reasons for favouring a vast extension of socialisation convincing. His argument was based upon the chronic instability of the Affluent Society. This instability did not arise from the internal contradictions of the system, as in the classical Marxist analysis, but rather from without, from the successful competition of the Soviet bloc in the struggle for markets. Communist successes would, of course, be due to the inevitable superiority of the nationalised industries in the Communist countries:

> we can predict with mathematical certainty that, as long as the public sector of industry remains the minority sector throughout the Western world, we are bound to be defeated in every kind of peaceful competition with the Eastern bloc.[19]

The higher growth rate of the Communist countries was the central factor which the Revisionists had ignored:

> What is wrong with the Revisionists is that they misjudge altogether the times in which we are living, and in particular the stability and strength of the Affluent societies in which we have lived for under a decade. I am convinced that the kind of Keynesian-managed capitalism which has evolved since the war is intrinsically unable to sustain the competition with the Eastern bloc to which we are now committed.[20]

The logic of this argument was, no doubt, quite impeccable. What was lacking was any factual demonstration that Soviet competition really was such a significant threat to the Affluent Society, that the Soviet rate of growth was, in fact, likely to prove faster than that of the West. Crossman gave no evidence, statistical or otherwise, that this outcome would occur, let alone that it could be predicted with 'mathematical certainty'. And even granted the superiority of the Soviet rate of growth, the case for Socialism had still not been established. For it had to be shown that this growth was specifically due to the size of the public sector in the Communist countries. In fact, no positive connection of any kind has been established between the rate of growth in a developed economy and the size of its public sector.

Thus Crossman, like Bevan, failed to give direction to the sense of bewilderment existing on the Left during the years of affluence. Bevan's attack on the party leadership and Crossman's attack on Revisionism can be seen in retrospect as romantic and yet inchoate revolts. Bevan was reacting against the caution and unimaginativeness of a leadership which had lost touch with the idealism of the early Socialists. Crossman was reacting against the Revisionist conception of politics which seemed to him to accept too much of the trappings of the affluence of the Macmillan era. But both Bevan and Crossman were unable to give content to their frustrations; they were unable to put forward any convincing programme to replace the fading vision of the Fabians, or the new horizons of the Revisionists.

III. *Clause 4*

These disputes between the Revisionists and the Left remained purely on the theoretical level until after the Labour Party's third election defeat in 1959. This defeat was remarkable when considered against the background of the Conservative record over the previous four years. For the Suez débâcle had left the Conservatives almost totally demoralised. Sir Anthony Eden, the admired hero of 1955, had been shuffled embarrassingly off the Parliamentary stage, to be replaced by Harold Macmillan. And the failure of the Suez expedition was combined with growing economic difficulties. Before 1955, the economic situation had, on the whole, developed smoothly; but now the ominous signs of 'stop–go' had begun to appear, culminating in the sterling crisis of 1957 and a Bank Rate of 7 per cent.

But the Labour Party had failed to channel the resentment aroused by Suez into permanent support for Labour policies. Of the years between 1956 and 1959, Enoch Powell has written:

At no stage were the Opposition benches able to establish a decisive ascendancy over the Government

94

in morale and in debate, even when all the cards which a Government's opponents could possibly want had been thrust into their hands. This is the phenomenon which challenges analysis, all the more because in 1957 the Bevanite schism was healed on 'the road to Brighton pier'.[21]

It was inevitable, therefore, that the third election defeat would lead to renewed introspection in the Labour Party. Those whom Crosland called the 'Clause 4 Bourbons' again renewed their call for a Socialism loud and clear. The election had been lost because the evangelical zeal of the movement had been compromised by the timidity of the leadership. At the 1959 conference, called to discuss the meaning of the election defeat, Michael Foot argued that 'in order to win an election we have to change the mood of the people in this country, to open their eyes to what an evil and disgraceful and rotten society it is'. Frank Cousins produced the fantasy of 'five or six million people who are Socialist in embryo waiting for us to go out and harness them to the power machine we want to drive'. And Mrs Castle complained that 'our ethical reach was beyond the mental grasp of the average person'.

Serious discussion, however, revolved around Gaitskell's speech in which he proposed that Clause 4 of the party constitution be amended. Gaitskell based his argument not only on the theoretical analysis provided by the Revisionists, but also upon the findings of sociologists concerning the Labour Party's continuing loss of electoral support.

David Butler and Richard Rose concluded their study of the 1959 election by remarking: 'It is more than ever possible to speak of the Conservatives as the country's "normal" majority party.... The Labour Party ... now has to face the fact that its support is being eroded by age and by the impact of social change.'[22]

The Labour Party's position seemed to be threatened by three interconnected consequences of affluence. First, there was the great rise in real incomes, leading to an increase of 20 per cent in consumption per

95

head between 1951 and 1959. This contrasted remarkably with the austerity of the post-war Labour Governments when productive investment had been increased and consumption hardly at all. It seemed natural to many voters to argue that affluence reflected the priority given by the Conservatives to improving ordinary living standards. Secondly, this increase in consumption led many members of the working class to identify themselves with the middle classes. And a natural concomitant of this identification might be a weakening of the attachment of the working class to the Labour Party. This was clearest in the case of home-ownership. A man who owned his own house was more likely to vote Conservative than one who lived in a council house, or in rented accommodation. In 1959 almost one-half of the working-class supporters of the Labour Party lived in council houses. But as more and more voters were able to purchase their own houses, the swing away from Labour would be accentuated. For the Labour Party seemed associated with municipal housing rather than with the Conservatives' 'property-owning democracy'. Thirdly, automation and the drift to service industries and white-collar jobs were lessening the economic importance of manual labour. The force of class solidarity, which seemed so necessary to the Labour Party's electoral support, was weakening. The social changes of the 1950s seemed likely to lead to a permanent and continuing swing away from the Labour Party.

It is difficult now to recapture the atmosphere of the years between 1959 and 1961, when so many political commentators were arguing that the Labour Party, in its present form, would never again win a General Election.[23] Professor Samuel Beer, for example, wrote an article for the *Political Quarterly* in 1960 which he entitled 'Democratic One-Party Government for Britain?' And Professor Mackintosh, in a book written in 1961, argued that 'it is hard to escape the conclusion that the Labour Party is unlikely to return to power and that the government of the country will remain in the hands of the Conservatives for the foreseeable future'.[24]

96

Fear of the political consequences of inaction was therefore an additional weapon in the armoury of the Revisionists. They could now argue not only that traditional Socialism was politically irrelevant, but also that it was electorally damaging. This seemed to be one of the few occasions in politics when the demands of principle and of expediency coincided. For as Gaitskell argued in his conference speech of 1959:

> The stark fact is that this is the third General Election we have lost and the fourth in which we have lost seats. ... In the past the pendulum has always swung against the party in power after one or at most two periods of office. It has not been swinging in these last few years. ... What has caused this adverse trend? It is, I believe, a significant change in the economic and social background of politics.

He then instanced the 'changing character of the labour force' and the spread of consumer durables among the working classes, as the major changes in 'the economic and social background'. The Labour Party was seen increasingly as a party concerned with issues which had already been settled, and committed to a doctrinaire policy of nationalisation for its own sake:

> It is not that public ownership is condemned outright: people are discriminating and are quite prepared to say that certain publicly owned industries have been a success. ... But their attitude reveals the empiricism for which British people are renowned. They will judge each issue on its merits, and insofar as Labour appears to be doctrinaire on the subject of ownership, it saddles itself with a liability.

To make matters worse, the unfavourable 'image' of the Labour Party seemed most pronounced in the minds of young voters. Among the youngest group studied in a survey conducted by Mark Abrams[25] – those aged between eighteen and twenty-four – the intensity of the reaction against Labour seemed greatest. They seemed more likely than their elders to be indifferent to

97

nationalisation and to see the Labour Party as a purely working-class party. 'There is among young people today a complex of barely conscious Conservative sympathies which have still not yet fully expressed themselves in overt party affiliations.'[26]

This was indeed frightening for the Labour Party.

Gaitskell's one positive proposal to counteract these changes – the amendment of Clause 4 – might seem remarkably tame when considered alongside the prognostications made by the political market-researchers. But Gaitskell regarded Clause 4 as a symbol of the Labour Party's unwillingness to adapt. For although in practice more Revisionist than 'fundamentalist', the party often gave the voter the opposite impression. Was it not morally and intellectually more honest to amend Clause 4, and to risk the howls of rage and possible defections on the Left?

Moreover, Clause 4

lays us open to continual misrepresentation. It implies that common ownership is an end, whereas in fact, it is a means. It implies that the only precise object we have is nationalisation, whereas in fact we have many other Socialist objectives. It implies that we propose to nationalise everything, but do we? Everything? – the whole of light industry, the whole of agriculture, all the shops – every little pub and garage? Of course not. We have long ago come to accept, we know very well, for the foreseeable future, at least in some form, a mixed economy.

But this proved to be more a pious aspiration than a fact. Speaker after speaker rose to pour scorn on the acceptance of the mixed economy and to accuse Gaitskell of 'betraying Socialism'. Many argued that it was better for the party to remain in Opposition seemingly for ever rather than to compromise on its principles. Frank Cousins committed the ultimate fatuity of suggesting that the Labour Party ought not to want to win elections on 'Tory votes'.

The Revisionists were clearly surprised by the extent of the opposition to Gaitskell's proposal. Denis Healey

98

found it necessary to remind the conference that they were a political party seeking power to carry out their programme, not a Socialist Sunday school. Anthony Crosland later ruefully commented:

> It is surely depressing, and would be true of no other country in the world, that a proposal to re-write a forty-year-old constitution should arouse such acute suspicion and resentment, even amongst those who like to think of themselves as radical.[27]

Gradually however it became quite clear, as the conference proceeded, that the seemingly innocent proposal to amend Clause 4 would arouse overwhelming opposition and divide the party at every level. As Mr Benn Levy put it: 'We have heard two voices from the platform, Barbara Castle's and Hugh Gaitskell's. If there is any person in this hall who thought these two voices were speaking the same language, then he is very deaf indeed.'

Again the only coherent attack on Revisionism came from Crossman, and again the same perfect logic was combined with the same lack of evidential support. Crossman denied that the swing of the pendulum was a normal feature of British politics, and he therefore denied that drastic measures were required to make the Labour Party more palatable to the electorate. The voters would always, in normal times, prefer the Conservatives, who guaranteed affluence, to the Labour Party which seemed to threaten it. But when Crossman's *deus ex machina* – the economic triumph of the Soviet bloc – was introduced into the scheme, the way forward for Labour was clear. The way forward, in fact, consisted merely in waiting for the confidently predicted catastrophe which the Communist successes would cause. The occurrence of the catastrophe would, of course, lead voters to transfer their allegiance gratefully to the Labour Party which had courageously stood by its principles until these principles again became relevant. Crossman detected a forty-year cycle of radical Governments. In 1868 and 1906 Gladstone and Campbell-Bannerman had led the Liberals to victory;

99

Attlee had continued the cycle in 1945. It began to look as if poor Mr Gaitskell would have to wait until 1984.

Although Gaitskell's attempt to amend Clause 4 did not succeed, his failure owed little to Crossman's arguments. The Left defeated Gaitskell on this issue, because it was not alone. It was joined in an unholy alliance with elements of the traditional Right who were attached to Clause 4, not because they believed in wholesale nationalisation, but on grounds of sentiment. Harold Wilson, who opposed the Revisionists on this issue, argued that tampering with Clause 4 was like denying the authority of Genesis: 'We were being asked to take Genesis out of the Bible. You don't have to be a fundamentalist to say that Genesis is part of the Bible.'[28]

Just as one could be a Christian without believing in the literal truth of everything in Genesis, so also one could be a pragmatic Socialist without ceasing to regard Clause 4 as a respectable guide. But perhaps in this analogy Wilson revealed more of the theological origins of the opposition to Revisionism than he intended.

Many leading trade unionists agreed with Wilson's viewpoint. On the whole, they were less concerned with questions of ideology and doctrine than with securing election victories so that the working classes could benefit from social reforms. Drawing an analogy with their own organisations, they deduced that the most important precondition for electoral success was organisational unity. They had opposed the Left, less for doctrinal reasons, but because the Left, in making public disagreements within the party, was also splitting it, and stabbing the duly elected leaders of the party in the back. From this standpoint they were bound to oppose the attempt to remove Clause 4; for Gaitskell too could be regarded as an intellectual seeking to alter the traditional basis of the party. This would inevitably provoke disagreement and further damage Labour's electoral prospects.

Faced with the opposition of both the Left and the traditionalist Right, Gaitskell was forced to give way. Besides, he needed the support of the Right, and especially of the leaders of the large trade unions, for the more important struggle against unilateralism which was brewing. In July 1960 Gaitskell conceded defeat. For the National Executive of the Labour Party decided 'not to proceed with any amendment or addition to Clause Four of the Constitution'. At the conference of 1960, Gaitskell confessed:

it became obvious that there was throughout the Party and the Movement very strong feelings about this 1918 Constitution. It might be misleading to call them sentimental . . . but . . . we . . . felt bound to take note of the obvious feelings that existed.

Therefore

in view of the reaction, not only of people who would ordinarily be regarded as left-wing . . . but of many other people in the Movement who . . . would probably describe themselves as right-wing, we decided to drop the idea.

By the end of his life Gaitskell had, in effect, abandoned the attempt to alter the nature of the Labour Party. At the party conference of 1962 he broke with other leading Revisionists, when he led the Labour Party into opposition to the Common Market. His speech, with its curious reference to 'a thousand years of history', reconciled him to the Left as well as to the traditional and insular Right. Thus Gaitskell's period of leadership showed how difficult it was to modernise the Labour Party. For he found that he could maintain his position and defeat the unilateralists only by compromising with the most traditional elements in the party.

Gaitskell's attempt to amend Clause 4 has often been attacked as tactically unwise. Professor R. T. McKenzie, for example, wrote of the episode 'that it was one of the most maladroit operations in the modern history of party politics'.[29] Attlee, who had studiously avoided frontal assaults on the myths of the party, thought that Gaitskell was 'a little ill-advised'.[30]

Sam Watson, a trade union leader, who supported Gaitskell on most issues, felt that the attempt was 'misjudged and unnecessary'.[31] Professor Crick has argued that skilful political leadership could easily have compromised with the various elements of the party, by solemnly pledging its adherence to Clause 4 while in practice working out a programme of radical reform on Revisionist lines:

> For the Labour Party has found its support in all sorts of different places. It has never been a party of a single doctrine. And even if that single doctrine is called socialism (there are in fact many socialist doctrines), it should be obvious that this is only one part of the actual Labour movement.[32]

But these tactical arguments seem misconceived. A party is not merely a machine for fighting and winning elections. It has, in Britain at least, to provide the dynamic for government – in the case of the Labour Party the dynamic for radical government. For a party to be united in support of a radical agenda of politics, its members must possess similar instincts and preconceptions about its proper role in politics. This does not mean, of course, that all members of the party must be in agreement on every central item of policy. Indeed the nature of democratic politics implies that any governing party must be broad-based enough to be a coalition of ideas and interests. Certainly the Christian Democrats in Germany, the Gaullists in France and the Democrats in the United States do not possess total intellectual coherence. Nor do they even possess a single coherent party 'image'.

But the situation of the Labour Party was no longer like that of the Christian Democrats, the Gaullists or the Democrats. For the advent of Revisionism had destroyed the premisses upon which a coalition of ideas and interests could remain effective. It had done this by altering the nature of the disagreements between different elements of the Labour Party. Before the Revisionists, disagreements within the party were held together by a consensus of opinion on the ultimate aims of the party. Disagreements were therefore concerned more with tactics than with first principles. In the 1930s, for example, there had been quarrels over the desirability of extra-Parliamentary action to secure Socialism, or of a Popular Front with the Communist Party. In the 1950s, the Bevanites had implied that the party leadership was too cautious and timid. They had not suggested that it was travelling along the wrong road. Within the framework of agreement on ultimate aims, differences could, in the last resort, be accommodated, and the Labour Party could remain a pluralistic, yet viable, coalition.

The Revisionists, however, in questioning the ultimate aims of the party, had destroyed that basic agreement among the different sections of the party which made the coalition viable. For now the Labour Party was no longer merely a coalition; it was a coalition facing in two diametrically opposite directions. The majority of the party accepted the mixed economy, at least for the foreseeable future. They relied upon economic growth to secure radical reform. This required dependence upon private industry to increase production and exports. In this scheme of things, private industry was to be the motor of economic progress and radical reform. Another section of the party, however, was totally hostile to private industry, seeking to enclose it within more and more rigid controls with the ultimate aim of eliminating it altogether. It would rely upon state control and the growth potential of the nationalised industries to increase the wealth of the community. These two visions are totally inconsistent and incompatible. Even if skilful leadership can unite the party and make it an election-winning force, by mouthing the old slogans, such leadership is incapable of making the Labour Party an effective radical engine of government. For the continual necessity to pay homage to the old slogans inhibits new and creative thought upon the problems of the day.

IV. *Harold Wilson and the 'Scientific Revolution'*

By a supreme effort of will, Gaitskell attempted to rid the party of its traditionalist incubus and force it to face in a different direction. But the forces favouring the *status quo* proved too strong for him, and he died with the task still uncompleted. Despite appearances, the Labour Party was not essentially different from what it had been before the beginning of the Revisionist assault.

Gaitskell was succeeded by Harold Wilson, who reverted to a more traditional style of leadership. Wilson, as we have seen, regarded the Clause 4 dispute as an unnecessary one. He also saw no issue of principle involved against the unilateralists, since 'defence policy ... by the very nature of things changes from year to year and even from month to month'.[33] Wilson had therefore refused to support Gaitskell against the unilateralists, and had indeed stood against him for the leadership of the party in 1960. Wilson argued that, although not himself a unilateralist, he had a better chance of keeping the party united than a leader dedicated to 'fight, fight and fight again' against a conference decision.

Unity was Wilson's central theme. He argued that the Labour Party must 'unite on policy, not divide on theology'. He did not accept the view that it was necessary to change the ideological basis, and with it the whole nature of the Labour Party, in order to make it a radical engine of government. For if Socialists could reach agreement upon an immediate programme, then the doctrinal differences which Gaitskell had emphasised would not be relevant in the immediate future. Wilson could not believe that the rhetoric of Socialism would seriously inhibit effective action on the part of a Labour Government. Perhaps the failures of his administration in the years after 1964 offer an ironic comment upon this view.

Nevertheless, Wilson's style of leadership did succeed in the short run, both in uniting the Labour Party and in turning it into an election-winning party. By September 1963, only seven months after Wilson was elected leader, Henry Fairlie, the Conservative political commentator, could say: 'For the first time in twelve years, the Labour Party looks again like a great governing party. The struggle has been terrible; but now that it is over, we can see that the only casualties are the dead. In my view, this is a remarkable achievement.'[34]

The solvent of unity in the Labour Party was the 'scientific revolution'. Wilson, drawing upon ideas which had been developed under Gaitskell's leadership, made the slow pace of scientific and technological advance the basis of his attack upon the Conservatives. It was not the inhumanity and vulgarity of the Affluent Society which Wilson attacked, but rather the amateurism responsible for the low rate of economic growth in Britain. The theme of the scientific failure could be used to launch a general critique of British institutions. For the failure could be ascribed to the outmoded structure of British industry and to the deficiencies of the educational system. Above all, it would provide a splendid excuse for attacking the background and attitudes of the Conservatives under the 'grouse-moor' leadership of Sir Alec Douglas-Home.

Labour and the Scientific Revolution, a policy document prepared by the National Executive Committee of the party in 1963, summarised the measures necessary for obtaining scientific advance: 'A new deal for the scientist and technologist in higher education, a new status for scientists in Government, and a new role for Government-sponsored science in industrial development are three essential requirements for reviving the economy.' This programme, despite its modernistic colouring, seemed to contain enough material which was relevant to traditional Socialist aspirations to satisfy the Left. The 'new role for Government-sponsored science' could easily be interpreted to mean a large extension of public ownership. This had been noticed by James Callaghan at the 1963 conference: 'I say now that it is an astonishing thing – I do not think Aneurin Bevan would have been surprised – to see the way in which public ownership is coming back again into the field of consideration. . . .'

For the Right, on the other hand, the programme seemed to imply that the primitive techniques of nationalisation were being laid to rest, and that more sophisticated methods of controlling the economy would be applied. From the point of view of the Right, the theory of the 'scientific revolution' could be allied with Galbraith's criticism of the 'social imbalance' generated by the Affluent Society.

Galbraith had argued that the market economies of Eisenhower in the United States and Macmillan in Britain were inherently incapable of providing sufficient resources for social investment. The proceeds of economic growth would inevitably accrue to the private sector, while the public sector would remain starved of funds. This would create problems which could be solved only by a Government believing in large-scale intervention in the economy. For while more and more cars would be produced by private industry, less and less would be spent upon maintaining the roads on which they travelled. The health and education services would suffer, while private consumption continued to expand at an unprecedented rate. Thus, according to Galbraith, the Affluent Society, if not made subject to public control, would inevitably result in the neglect of social needs in favour of private wants. This analysis had always found much favour among the Revisionists. In his book *The Conservative Enemy*, Crosland had announced: 'I am ... wholeheartedly a Galbraith man.'[35]

The idea of the 'scientific revolution' thus succeeded, partly on account of its very imprecision and vagueness, in uniting the Labour Party. At the conference of 1963 there was the strange spectacle of Wilson's diagnosis receiving the universal plaudits of every section of the party. Mrs Judith Hart, a fundamentalist and unilateralist, felt that 'together scientists and Socialists can bring the dreams into reality'. Mrs Hart was followed by the Gaitskellite Dr Jeremy Bray, who argued that 'We have to form a partnership with science amplifying the freedom of ordinary people'. It was little wonder that Crossman, now an ardent supporter of Wilson's leadership, felt able to write:

The question forced upon us is how we can become the masters, not the slaves, of technological change. Directly this question was asked ... we realised that here was the new creative Socialist idea needed to reconcile the Revisionists of the Right with the Traditionalists of the Left: Harold Wilson succeeded where Hugh Gaitskell failed ....[36]

The idea of the scientific revolution also provided a relevant theme with which the Labour Party might hope to win the General Election. For the emphasis on science was just what was required to woo the marginal voter away from the Conservatives. The Labour Party was no longer appealing to the declining manual labour force, but rather to the expanding white-collar and professional sector. These were just the sections of the population whose allegiance had been given to the Conservatives in 1959. Thus Wilson had discovered a way of counteracting the 'long-term social changes' which had seemed to be working against the Labour Party, while at the same time uniting the party in a way that Gaitskell had never been able to do.

But these achievements were obtained only at the cost of the re-appearance of the weaknesses which had always been inherent in the structure and organisation of the Labour Party, and which Gaitskell had attempted to remove. The crucial weakness, in the short run, lay in the return to the traditional style of Labour leadership. Many Left-wingers failed to notice this; they were so impressed by the contrast between Wilson and the 'Right-wing' Gaitskell that they overlooked the similarities between Wilson's style of leadership and the methods of Attlee and Ramsay MacDonald in the past. For Attlee and MacDonald also had combined Socialist rhetoric with moderate and practical proposals. The Socialist rhetoric kept the Left-wing contented; the programme of moderate reform satisfied the Right. Despite the contemporary trappings, Wilson's leadership represented a return to the ancient tradition of ambiguity. Seen in this light, the commitment to Galbraith and to the scientific revolution represented merely an obscure and clouded vision which, however, possessed the essential tactical merit of uniting the party. In Wilson's hands, the thought of a Galbraith could be reduced to slogans. These slogans – planning, social justice, expansion – served not as stimulants to thought but as a substitute for it. Coherent and seriously thought-out policies would have run the risk of re-opening the doctrinal arguments. No one foresaw that the ambiguity which made a Labour Government possible also necessitated compromises which might emasculate its radicalism.

In terms of theory also, the changes initiated by Wilson were not as revolutionary as they at first appeared. The stress on technocracy and the essential role of a scientific and managerial elite was a return to a tradition which had been begun by the Fabians. They too had argued that Socialism was necessary in order to harness the abilities of gifted administrators, whose talents were not fully appreciated in an unregulated economy. Wilson echoed what the Fabians had called 'a policy of national efficiency', arguing that economic growth could only be secured when the strategic importance of the scientific and managerial elite was recognised.

One consequence of this approach was that the moral dynamic which lay behind former varieties of Socialism receded into the background. The Revisionists had attempted to underline the humane elements in Socialist thought; for them Socialism was 'about equality', or as Gaitskell, quoting G. D. H. Cole, had put it, 'a broad human movement on behalf of the bottom dog'. Wilson stressed not equality, but the necessity of giving higher rewards to the scientists and technologists who contributed so greatly to economic advance. From this point of view it was difficult to see that the 'scientific revolution'

has anything particular to do with the humanitarian socialism from which the Labour Party has usually drawn sustenance. The image presented at Scarborough of a Britain pulsing with dynamic energies where technologists and scientists will be valued at their proper financial worth is hardly that of a more just or a more humane society. It is a society of technocratic privilege, high salaries and early coronary thrombosis. . . .[37]

Nor was Socialism any longer the ideology of the manual working class, what George Lichtheim has called 'the intellectual expression of working-class sentiment'.[38] The appeal was mainly to workers by brain; the appeal to workers by hand became gradually muted. Thus the Labour Party had become a purely 'pragmatic' party – pragmatic was one of Wilson's favourite words. The party was to justify itself not by faith, but by works, and to be judged accordingly.

V. *The Erosion of Socialism*

When they came into office, Labour leaders were fond of speaking of the 'thirteen wasted years' of Conservative rule. It might have been more accurate, however, to characterise their own period in opposition in this way. For when the Labour Party came to power, it could be seen that it was not, in fact, committed to radical policies. The Labour Government deflated tenaciously to maintain the parity of the pound sterling. It failed to discover a foreign policy which made them independent of the United States. And it failed to deal successfully with the Rhodesian rebellion. The seeds of these failures were laid during the period of opposition.

The central failure of Labour thought in the 1950s was its failure to come to terms with economic problems. The Labour Government was not equipped to deal with the large balance of payments deficit which it inherited from the Conservatives, because it had not given sufficient thought to the role of the pound sterling in its economic strategy. For it was these financial barriers rather than the technological and scientific backwardness of British industry which were to prove the main block to raising the rate of economic growth and therefore to the success of Labour's other policies.

But curiously enough, both Revisionists of the Right and Fundamentalists of the Left had assumed that the main problems with which an incoming Labour Government would have to deal would not be economic.

The Revisionists had assumed that the Affluent Society could be indefinitely maintained, uninterrupted by economic crises. The central economic problems for traditional Socialists had been the abolition of primary poverty and the maintenance of full employment. Since the Affluent Society did away with large-scale poverty and secured full employment, the Revisionists assumed that likewise affluence solved *all* economic problems. Their view of the problems was dictated by their upbringing in traditional Socialist ideology. The economic problems which they had been taught to regard as making the case for Socialism seemed to have been solved. Therefore there were no economic problems left. It did not occur to them that problems of a different kind could arise in the economic sphere. Their traditional ideology was like a searchlight so rigid that it could focus only upon one particular set of problems.

Thus Crosland and the Revisionists failed to analyse the barriers to growth constituted by the balance of payments and the requirement to maintain the parity of the pound; nor did Revisionist literature deal with ways in which Britain's overseas commitments and the Sterling Area might impose constraints upon economic expansion.[39] Crosland, although setting out a list of radical reforms, whose achievement depended mainly upon securing a high rate of economic growth, could write in *The Future of Socialism*, in a chapter entitled 'How Much Do Economics Matter?':

The programme for economic growth ... should increasingly be overshadowed by the 'social' policies ... and we should not now judge a Labour Government's performance primarily by its record in the economic field. This may require a mental adjustment in many quarters on the Left. Traditionally, or at least since Marx, Socialist thought has been dominated by the economic problems posed by capitalism.... The pre-war reasons for a largely economic orientation are therefore steadily losing their relevance; and we can increasingly divert our energies into more fruitful and idealistic channels, and to fulfilling earlier and more fundamental Socialist aspirations.[40]

The Left shared this distaste for economics. They also assumed that the Affluent Society was impregnable from within, and, when threatened by Soviet advance, economic growth could easily be secured by policies of large-scale nationalisation.

Thus both wings of the Labour Party combined to misunderstand the nature of the problems which the Affluent Society would bring. And when practising politicians unite in misconceiving the problems which face them, it is natural to look for an underlying cause of this failure of perception.

The roots of this failure lie precisely in the ideological nature of the Labour Party. Throughout the 1950s the Left held on to the traditional ideology, attempting to give it a more modern 'image', and suggesting that it be applied more thoroughly. The Revisionists, in attacking the Left, seemed also to be attacking ideology. But in fact, they were only substituting one ideology for another. They wanted to bring the ideology of the party up to date, but they agreed with the Left that a successful reforming Government must be founded on a coherent social philosophy. In the *New Fabian Essays* it had been argued that the party needed not merely 'new expedients', 'new planks in an election programme', but rather a 'new analysis of the political, economic and social scene as a basis for reformulating Socialist principles'. The Revisionists dedicated themselves to providing this new social analysis, upon which alone effective political action could be based.

Samuel Beer is one of the few commentators upon the Labour Party to have perceived that the struggle was not one between ideologists and pragmatists, but rather between two competing ideologies. This struggle reflects what Beer calls the 'compulsive ideologism'[41] of the Labour Party. He argues that

> the contestants, whether fundamentalist or revisionist, agreed on a basic premise. All accepted the necessity for a social philosophy with programmatic consequences. The opposing sides were at swords' points with regard to their respective ideologies, but they were united in their ideologism.[42]

This ideologism can be seen at its most extreme in Crosland's suggestion that the reformation of Socialist doctrine, upon which successful policies depended, required one 'clearly to decide what precise meaning is to be attached to the word "Socialism" '.[43] This was the culmination of the ideological style of argument. Politics had become not a matter of appraising the merits of different policies, but rather an analysis of the meanings to be attached to a concept.

This fixation on ideology, which afflicted Revisionist and Fundamentalist alike, prevented them from appreciating the economic difficulties which would confront a Labour Government. The Labour Party spent its period in Opposition discussing the wrong problems. For they were not discussing the problems which an incoming Labour Government would face. They were discussing the problems which had been raised by the particular stage of historical evolution which the Labour movement had reached. The long arguments about whether the Labour Party should or should not 'accept' the mixed economy as a final resting-place were, in the last resort, irrelevant. For the argument was one dictated by the intellectual heritage of the party. It was not an argument about anything which a Labour Government would have to face during its period in office, except in the long run. And, as Keynes reminded us, in the long run we are all dead.

The 'ideologism' of the Labour Party thus prevented them from attaining the tactical flexibility necessary for the success of a radical or reforming Government. This was particularly the case in the field of economic policy, where their failure was most noticeable. For

112

their planning before 1964 had been based upon the Galbraithian assumption that they would be returned to power during a period of economic stagnation. Instead they assumed office at the height of a boom, and they inherited a large balance of payments deficit. They were, however, unable to make the adjustments in their thinking which would have enabled them to deal successfully with the problem.

More generally, it can be seen that the attitudes of the Labour Party prevented them from appreciating and making use of the stream of thought based upon the economic radicalism of Keynes. Keynesian policies would have dictated priority for growth over the balance of payments, and priority for full employment over the maintenance of the parity of the pound. Keynesian thought had been channelled into party politics by Lloyd George in the inter-war period, and was continued to some extent by Macmillan. Keynes's economic radicalism dictated a particular style of politics which proved to be beyond the comprehension of the Labour Party. For it regarded politics as a creative and improvisatory activity, an activity which looked at the real problems facing a society, rather than one which began from general theories about the nature of capitalism or the mixed economy, Macmillan was actually aware of the existence of Keynesian radicalism, and of the style of politics which it implied.[44] The Labour Party was not.

Thus the Labour Party failed to solve its problems while in Opposition. The Left failed to make a coherent and relevant case for nationalisation. The Revisionists failed to wean the party away from its traditional commitments. And those whose primary concern was to make the Labour Party an efficient and radical governing party failed to alter its doctrinal nature. It is difficult, however, to ascribe this failure to the actions of any particular individuals within the party. It was dictated by the contradictory nature of the tasks which faced the party. For it was required simultaneously to make itself into a radical engine of government by shedding the ideological baggage bequeathed by the Fabians, while also maintaining unity within its ranks. Before 1950 the problem had not existed, for most

Socialists could agree that the Fabian diagnosis was relevant to the problems which they faced. But during the 1950s realisation of the irrelevance of Fabianism by one wing of the party was combined with adherence by the other wing to traditional views. This meant that the two wings of the party were facing opposite directions.

Perhaps the fragmentation of Socialist ideology is in itself partly a reflection of the erosion of the social base of the Labour Party, the manual working class. For the Labour Party was formed to give expression to the sentiments of this class when it could be said to form a socio-economic interest, sufficiently united in its aims to provide a broad and coherent basis for a common policy. This policy would be genuinely radical in so far as it aimed at the emancipation of the working class. But with the weakening of class feeling, the social base of the Labour Party has become eroded. And with the erosion of the social base, the politics became eroded also. The Labour Party thus ceased to provide an agenda for radical change. On the central issues which faced it in office – on devaluation, on the maintenance of military bases East of Suez and on the Common Market – the Labour Party found itself divided. It could be held together only by the tactical skill and the political ambiguity of a Harold Wilson.

Notes

1. This chapter expands upon suggestions made by the author in 'The Ideology of Failure', *Encounter* (June 1968).

2. *New Statesman*, 22 September 1951.

3. *Spectator*, 14 March 1952.

4. Herbert Morrison, *Socialisation and Transport* (1933) p. 140.

5. *New Statesman*, 12 May 1951.

6. Quoted in Krug, *Aneurin Bevan: Cautious Rebel* (New York, 1961) p. 11.

7. John Strachey's *Contemporary Capitalism* (1956)

114

is in some ways the most profound work of British Socialist theory in this period. But although he supported them on central issues, Strachey cannot be regarded as being engaged in the same intellectual task as the Revisionists. For he was opposing Marxism, not revising the Fabians.

8. C. A. R. Crosland, *The Future of Socialism* (1956) p. 41.

9. C. A. R. Crosland, *The Conservative Enemy* (1962) p. 131.

10. Crosland, *The Future of Socialism*, p. 79.

11. Ibid.

12. Ibid., p. 87.

13. Ibid., p. 103.

14. Hugh Gaitskell, *Socialism and Nationalisation*, Fabian Tract No. 300 (1956).

15. Crosland, *The Future of Socialism*, pp. 74–5.

16. 'Towards a New Philosophy of Socialism', in *New Fabian Essays* (1952); *Planning for Freedom* (1965) p. 36.

17. 'The Clause Four Controversy', *Encounter* (April 1960), *Planning for Freedom*, p. 115.

18. These proposals were satirised by the *New Statesman* with the slogan 'Workers of the World Invest'.

19. R. H. S. Crossman, *Labour in the Affluent Society*, Fabian Tract No. 325 (1959); *Planning for Freedom*, p. 110.

20. Ibid.; *Planning for Freedom*, p. 111.

21. Enoch Powell, 'Labour in Opposition, 1951–1959', *Political Quarterly* (1959).

22. D. E. Butler and R. Rose, *The British General Election of 1959* (1960).

23. Often indeed they were the same commentators as those who asserted after the General Election of 1966 that Labour was now the natural 'majority party' and was in for a generation.

24. John P. Mackintosh, *The British Cabinet* (1961), p. 488.

25. Cf. M. Abrams and R. Rose, *Must Labour Lose?* (1960) chap. 4.

26. Ibid., p. 58.

27. Crosland, 'The Future of the Left', *Encounter* (March 1960); *The Conservative Enemy*, p. 120.

28. Radio interview reprinted in *The Listener*, 29 October 1964, and quoted in R. Rose, *Politics in England* (1965) p. 53.

29. R. T. McKenzie, *British Political Parties*, rev. ed. (1963) p. 607.

30. W. T. Rodgers (ed.) *Hugh Gaitskell* (1964) p. 151.

31. Ibid., p. 112.

32. Bernard Crick, *In Defence Of Politics*, rev. ed. (1964) pp. 137–8.

33. Quoted in McKenzie, *British Political Parties*, p. 621.

34. *Spectator*, 27 September 1963.

35. Crosland, *The Conservative Enemy*, p. 103.

36. Crossman, 'Scientists in Whitehall', *Encounter* (July 1964); reprinted in *Planning for Freedom*, p. 135.

37. *Spectator*, 11 October 1963.

38. G. Lichtheim, *Marxism in Modern France* (New York, 1966) p. 162.

39. Roy Jenkins is the only honourable exception. In his book *The Labour Case* (1959) there is a most effective analysis of Britain's international financial weakness. But this analysis was quickly forgotten in the excitement of the ideological dispute.

40. Crosland, *The Future of Socialism*, p. 517.

41. Samuel Beer, *Modern British Politics* (1965) p. 239.

42. Ibid., p. 234.

43. Crosland, *The Future of Socialism*, p. 100.

44. This can be seen from the first volume of his memoirs, *Winds of Change*.

4 Muddling Through: The Economy, 1951–1964

Peter Oppenheimer

AFTER more than three decades of turmoil and radical change, the 1950s and 1960s were a period of 'back to normal' in economic affairs. Of course it was not the same normal as before. The economic environment had been transformed, directly and indirectly, by two world wars, by the experience of mass unemployment, by the great Labour reforms of 1945–50 and by half a century of technological advance. The issues which policy-makers now had to face were once again marginal in character, posing no threat to the basic framework and stability of Britain's social order. Much more was expected of Governments than before 1914 or indeed 1939. But equally, Governments were now in a much better position to deliver the goods.

A summary treatment of economic policy in these years cannot devote very much attention to the comings and goings of Chancellors of the Exchequer, interesting and even relevant though these may be.[1] It is more important to appreciate the background factors which affected policy throughout the period, notably the Keynesian revolution, the new political impact of the working classes and the decline of Britain's world position, including the international role of sterling. Two further points of importance on a more technical plane are the size of the public sector and the legacy of twenty years of cheap money (1931–51). These historical and technical factors are discussed in Part I, and the performance of the U.K. economy under Conservative management in Part II.

I. *Background Factors*

The Keynesian revolution is aptly named. The practical repercussions of *The General Theory of Employment, Interest and Money* were both far-reaching and rapid.[2] Keynes's book was published in 1936. The Second World War began three years later, and by the end of hostilities in 1945 U.K. economic management, though still encrusted with war-time controls and rationing, was firmly established on a Keynesian footing. Primarily, this meant that the Government accepted responsibility for keeping aggregate monetary demand at a level just sufficient to ensure full (or nearly full) employment, a commitment set down in the 1944 White Paper on *Employment Policy* (Cmd 6527). It seemed a feasible commitment because Keynes's theory had provided a much clearer picture than before of how the economy worked, and because the basic statistics needed to fill in the picture and make it concrete had now been specified and supplied. The framework of the social accounts and the first estimate of U.K. national income had been drawn up in 1941 by two academic economists (J. E. Meade and J. R. N. Stone) in war-time government service.[3] As a secondary point, Keynesian economic management made the government budget, rather than traditional monetary policy, the main instrument by which the balance of the economy was to be maintained. Conversely, budgetary policy was henceforth to be governed by the overall requirements of the economy and not by government financing needs or shibboleths about 'balanced budgets' and 'genuine borrowing'.

By the time the Conservatives achieved power in 1951 there had been six years of peace, and the transition from war-time methods in the conduct of economic policy had been largely accomplished. Inevitably there had been some delay and confusion in rearranging the machinery of government, as well as errors and miscalculations in the measures taken (e.g. the 1947 convertibility experiment – which owed a lot to U.S. pressure). Moreover, the statistical picture of the economy and its operation was still inadequate in many details. Also, after the failure in 1947 of Hugh Dalton's experiment in ultra-cheap money, little thought had been given to the role that monetary policy might play in a world of full employment without war-time controls. But after 1947 the Labour Government displayed growing technical competence in the economic sphere, as shown by the impressive *Economic Surveys* for the years 1948 to 1951 and the performances of Sir Stafford Cripps and Hugh Gaitskell at the Exchequer. With the Conservatives' return to office this technical competence and sophistication disappeared. Economic policy was once again determined by Ministers and advisers who were barely familiar with the new thinking.

This does not mean that Keynes was totally ignored. One of the remarkable things about the Keynesian revolution, not only in the United Kingdom, is the way in which its basic notions were accepted in practice even by those who only half understood and perhaps in theory opposed them. But the erratic nature of Conservative economic management from 1951 to 1964 must be ascribed partly to the unfamiliarity of those responsible with modern economic thinking. Most of the Tory Chancellors were, in Samuel Brittan's words, not merely 'innocent of economic complexities, but ... did not even have the practical financial flair that one might reasonably expect from a party with business links'.[4] They relied for advice mainly on the traditional sections of the Treasury, where there was little economic expertise, and on the Bank of England, where there was even less. The Economic Section of the Treasury under Sir Robert Hall – and after 1961 Sir Alec Cairncross – was chiefly occupied with the technicalities of forecasting and had only a patchy influence on policy. There was, however, some improvement in the 1960s. The Economic Section was enlarged, as was the economic staff at the Bank of England; and Sir Frank Lee and Sir William Armstrong, successively Permanent Secretaries at the Treasury in the last four years of Tory rule, had more grasp of economic affairs than their predecessors.

The second point with major implications for policy was the new political power of the working classes. The inter-war period brought universal suffrage, a considerable strengthening of the trade union movement and the first two Labour Governments. Indeed the marked anti-trade union and anti-worker image of the Conservatives helped to give Labour its first really solid victory in 1945. Thereafter the Conservatives accepted the welfare state just as they accepted the Keynesian revolution in economic policy, and were anxious to acquire a more favourable image with the working-class voter. At the same time neither they nor their traditional middle-class supporters wanted more Socialism. Rather, they wished to reduce somewhat the size of the public sector and, if possible, the level of taxation, while completing the abolition of war-time controls and rationing. These various points did not add up to a coherent political programme or philosophy. They merely put the Conservatives under pressure to offer all things to all men, particularly as they won the 1951 election on a minority of the votes cast.

The emphasis in policy and propaganda shifted during the period. In the first half of the 1950s it was on liberation from Socialist controls and austerity – 'Conservative freedom works'. In the second half it was on stability and confidence, particularly of financial circles and foreign holders of sterling. This was largely a result of the external monetary difficulties experienced in 1955, 1956 and 1957. Finally, in the 1960s, faster economic growth became the watchword. Underlying these shifts of emphasis, however, was the constant theme of prosperity, affluence, 'Double our standard of living in twenty-five years' and 'You've never had it so good'. The Conservatives brought electoral politics firmly down to the bread-and-circuses level. This meant timing General Elections in relation to the business cycle, so that they coincided with the optimistic, upswing phase. In the post-Keynesian era, however, one can usually arrange the turning points of the cycle to suit the election timetable. The Conservatives' chief contribution to economic history was thus to invent, almost without realising it, the election budget.

The bread-and-circuses approach was further encouraged by the third background factor, the decline in Britain's world power, which made foreign affairs unpromising material electorally. This was most strikingly shown by the Suez episode in 1956. However, as that episode also showed, the decline of Empire was not accepted willingly. Attempts to ignore it, slow it down or halt it strained the country's resources and compounded the problems of economic management. The most important item here was the rearmament programme started by the Labour Government as a result of the Korean War. The share of defence spending in G.N.P. rose from 7 per cent in 1950 to $10\frac{1}{2}$ per cent in 1952. In a way the Conservatives were lucky to inherit this programme from Labour, since they were able to run it down gradually in the succeeding years, to their electoral advantage. But the run-down was too slow to prevent lasting damage to Britain's industrial competitiveness. Too much of the country's engineering industry was involved in defence work throughout the 1950s, when it should have been supplying machinery and other products for the investment boom on the Continent. In addition, defence expenditure overseas was a large and growing debit item in the balance of payments.

The decline and fall of British imperial attitudes can also be traced in U.K. policy towards Europe. At first it was very much *de haut en bas*. Britain held studiously aloof from anything that smacked of European federalism, declining to join either the European Coal and Steel Community (1951) or the Messina negotiations on the formation of a Common Market (1955). On the other hand, Sir Anthony Eden committed the country quite casually in 1954 to maintaining 55,000 troops (four divisions and a Tactical Air Force) on the Rhine. Concern about U.K. trading prospects was, however, aroused as plans to establish the E.E.C. went ahead, the Treaty of Rome being signed in March 1957. Britain backed a proposal put forward originally by the Six themselves for a large European free trade area in industrial goods only. The proposal was by no means unreasonable, but it took insufficient account of protectionist attitudes in France. The French wished not merely to protect their agriculture, as everybody else did, but to get the rest of Europe to protect it for them through a community-wide farm policy. This meant a direct clash with Britain, who insisted on continued access to her traditional and more efficient suppliers in the Commonwealth. Since, however, Britain had no intention of committing herself to the ideal of a federal Europe, she could not expect support from France's partners in the Six. The result was the breakdown of negotiations (1958) and the split between the E.E.C. and what subsequently (1959–60) became EFTA.[5]

Britain's first application for membership of E.E.C. followed in 1961. It clearly sprang from an increasing awareness of Britain's reduced position in the world. On the political side, the colonial liberation movement was in full swing, and Britain's influence in Asia and Africa was receding. So was its nuclear and other military capability in relation to that of the super-powers. On the economic side, the country was felt to be lagging in industrial growth, its output per head falling behind that of the continental countries and its share of world manufactured exports declining steeply (from 21·5 per cent in the early 1950s to 14·2 per cent in 1964). Also, its balance of payments was chronically weak. Retreat to a European base seemed a way of salvaging and consolidating what remained of British power; but such motivation was both negative and ill-founded. Positive political enthusiasm for membership of E.E.C. was confined to a tiny minority of U.K. opinion. And while business and financial support was more widespread, a solid economic case for joining was and remains conspicuous by its absence.

A hankering for past glories was even more painfully visible in the U.K.'s obsession with the international status of sterling. The chief pressure here came from the Bank of England, which cultivated the idea of sterling as 'a great international currency', in which nearly half or 40 per cent or one-third of the world's trade (the number declining as the years passed) was conducted. The Bank's practical objective from 1952 onwards, with intermittent Treasury support, was to restore external convertibility for sterling. Of course, the freer trade and payments arrangements which convertibility entailed were desired by everyone. But orderly progress was already being made in this direction, notably with the establishment of the European Payments Union in 1950 under the aegis of O.E.E.C. and the Marshall Plan. The trouble was that E.P.U. allowed sterling no special status, treating it as just another European currency, and this the Bank of England resented. What positive benefit it expected from a rush to convertibility is not clear. Presumably it hoped that foreigners would want to hold more sterling, that the City would expand its overseas business and that these two factors together would make a major contribution to improving the U.K. balance of payments. But all this has the air of rationalisation for a policy based chiefly on sentiment. As in the 1920s, the Bank got not only its priorities but its analysis of cause and effect upside-down. Even if the international status of sterling was capable of making an important contribution to the material well-being of the British people, demand for sterling could not be assured merely by convertibility together with judicious manipulation of interest rates, as had apparently happened before 1914. Rather, the first essential was to strengthen Britain's trading position and create confidence in her economic performance.

This was especially important because of the low level of Britain's reserves, which made sterling vulnerable to sudden outflows of funds. There are two aspects. First, the relaxation of exchange control, although primarily directed to the current account (i.e. trade and current invisible payments), affected short-term capital flows by facilitating changes in the timing of payments – the so-called leads and lags. These can be very large. In severe cases, if a currency devaluation or revaluation is expected, they may attain the value of several months' exports and imports combined – enough to overwhelm national exchange reserves far larger proportionately than Britain's. Moreover, in

Britain's case the dangers were increased because sterling was also used in the finance of trade to which Britain herself was not a party. The Bank of England tended to underrate these difficulties until a crisis occurred.

Secondly, there was the problem of the sterling balances and sterling's role as a reserve currency. This too was of nineteenth-century origin, but its size and structure after 1945 were basically due to the Second World War. The introduction of exchange control at the start of the war formalised the Sterling Area (or 'Scheduled Territories') as the group of countries whose transactions with Britain were not subject to exchange restrictions.[6] A large part of the United Kingdom's war-time overseas expenditure was financed by the accumulation of sterling liabilities to overseas Sterling Area (O.S.A.) countries. Altogether, Britain's net sterling liabilities totalled over £3,500 million at the end of 1945, compared with £500 million in 1939. This represented more than four months' output of the U.K. economy and was nearly six times as large as the U.K. gold reserve, which had risen only from £500 million to £600 million. About three-quarters of the balances were reserves held by official institutions, the bulk of them in the Sterling Area.

By 1951 U.K. reserves had risen to £800 million, but with the sterling liabilities still at £3,500 million, large net conversions of sterling balances into gold or dollars were clearly not feasible. If existing holders of sterling, official or private, were to be paid out, either new holders must be found or a steady surplus on the U.K. balance of payments must be achieved. The former was (in part) the aim and ill-founded hope of the Bank of England in promoting sterling convertibility. The latter was the real key to the problem. A surplus on the U.K. balance of payments would enable U.K. reserves to be built up and at the same time make sterling more attractive to hold. Its effect would thus be cumulative. Moreover, it would not merely strengthen sterling in the long run, but would ease the short-run problem of financing fluctuations in the sterling liabilities due to temporary deficits in the O.S.A. countries' balances of payments.

In the event the march to convertibility was actually accompanied by a weakening of the United Kingdom's basic balance of payments and by growing difficulties in the management of short-term capital movements, all of which laid the foundations of a fairly rapid decline in sterling's international status in the 1960s. At first, in the early 1950s, the aim was convertibility with a floating pound, because this seemed the only kind of convertibility that was feasible. In 1952 there was a danger that the gold reserves would run out, forcing the pound to float anyway. The original, secret plan for floating put forward at this time ('Operation Robot') was not only muddled but showed little regard to Britain's obligations to overseas holders of sterling and to her partner countries in E.P.U.[7]

There was further talk of floating in 1954–5 and again briefly in 1957, but generally the aim was now convertibility at the fixed parity of $2.80. This was achieved (together with other European currencies) only in December 1958, but a big step towards it was taken in February 1955, when the Bank of England was authorised to support the price of 'transferable sterling' on the free market in Zürich at a level close to the official parity. Short-term capital movements promptly proved troublesome in the payments crisis later that year, and were the dominant element in the crises of 1956 (Suez) and 1957. The 1957 episode appears in retrospect as a turning point for sterling's international position; its character and consequences may be briefly explained.

In the summer of 1957 the U.K. economy had been under the impact of mildly restrictive policies for over eighteen months. Output had scarcely risen, there was no excessive inflationary pressure on the economy, and the balance of payments was not in deficit. On the other hand money wages, costs and prices were still going up, to the alarm of financial circles which felt that the Government had lost its grip on the economy – especially as the memory of Suez was still fresh. In the first half of the year £70 million or more had moved into dollar securities through banks in Kuwait, where

125

there was a loophole in the Sterling Area exchange control. This 'Kuwait gap' was closed in July by amended U.K. regulations. In August, however, payment deficits in the overseas sterling countries and rumours of possible alterations in exchange rates (mainly an upvaluation of the Deutschmark) led to a flight from sterling. In mid-September the authorities took spectacular measures to restore confidence: Bank Rate was raised from 5 to 7 per cent, a ceiling was put on bank advances and public expenditure programmes were cut. These measures were mainly designed to have a direct and immediate impact on international capital movements, but also to check inflation and so prevent further deterioration in the United Kingdom's competitive position. They certainly helped to prolong the stagnation of output for another year and thus to give the basic balance of payments a false appearance of strength in 1958, when sterling was declared convertible. These events were a striking indication of the Government's short-sighted devotion to the world role of sterling.

As it turned out, however, the crisis helped to cause a major structural change in international finance which greatly reduced the status of sterling even though it consolidated that of the City. The new factor was the Euro-dollar market, whose rapid growth began when the U.K. authorities, during the 1957 crisis, imposed narrow limits on the use of sterling for financing trade outside the Sterling Area.[8] The indirect result was that even in the City of London sterling came to be increasingly overshadowed by the dollar as a trading currency. Sterling's role as a reserve currency also shrank in importance. Countries outside the United States built up their dollar holdings and by 1964 U.S. external liquid liabilities had reached $27,000 million. Nearly $16,000 million were official reserves; in addition, a further $1,000 million (estimated) of reserves was being held in the Euro-dollar market. Sterling balances, on the other hand, did not increase, for the U.K. economy was not strong enough to inspire confidence. Balance of payments surpluses could not be achieved without holding back the growth of out-

126

put and depressing the economy below full employment. This weakness became more pronounced as the years passed, and by the autumn of 1964, when the Conservatives left office, it was clear that the pound was in fundamental disequilibrium and would sooner or later have to be devalued.[9] The U.K. reserves and sterling balances then stood almost exactly where they had been when the Conservatives came in thirteen years earlier: £800 million of reserves against £3,500 million of net sterling liabilities.

During this period the Sterling Area concept survived by a mixture of luck, imperialist financial policies exercised from Whitehall[10] and awareness among the large holders of sterling of the crisis that would arise if they all tried to get out simultaneously. Up to 1954 sterling was accumulated by British colonies in Africa and the Far East who were benefiting from the boom in primary commodities. Thereafter balances were built up chiefly by Middle East oil states, chiefly Kuwait (and in the later 1960s Libya and the Gulf sheikhdoms), together with a hotchpotch of other Commonwealth countries including Hong Kong and some Caribbean territories.

The reluctance of many holders to retain their sterling reserves was shown by the tendency for them to 'diversify' into gold or dollars after the mid-1950s. Between end-1957 and end-1964 O.S.A. holdings of gold and dollars (excluding South Africa) rose roughly from £300 million to £600 million.[11] Diversification was tolerable so long as it did not involve net conversions of existing sterling balances, but occurred only when the O.S.A. countries' total reserves increased. It suggested, however, that the whole Sterling Area relationship would sooner or later be called in question.[12]

The liberalisation and rapid growth of international trade and payments, combined with the periodic shakiness of sterling, meant that U.K. reserves looked increasingly inadequate as the years went by, even though the sterling balances were themselves more widely distributed than before and smaller in relation to the British economy. The inadequacy of U.K. reserves was highlighted in March 1961 when the 5 per cent revaluation of the Deutschmark and the Dutch guilder triggered a record outflow of more than £300 million from London to continental centres in antici- pation of further exchange-rate changes. In contrast with 1957, the U.K. authorities now seemed powerless to contain the movement by themselves and a forced devaluation of sterling was on the cards. The situation was brought under control by a series of short-term loans from continental central banks to the Bank of England, arranged at the regular monthly meeting of the Bank for International Settlements, the central bankers' club in Basle. This episode marks the start of the active co-operation among central banks which has transformed the management of short-term capital movements in the 1960s. It also indicated that in exist- ing circumstances sterling as an international currency could no longer be managed by the U.K. authorities on their own.

But central-bank credit arrangements were only a technical defence. They could not produce the basic strengthening of the U.K. balance of payments which was required to rehabilitate sterling. Unfortunately, the international status of the pound, and especially its position as a reserve currency alongside the dollar, helped to prevent devaluation from being seriously contemplated. Of course the Conservatives were op- posed to devaluation anyway, both because they assumed it to be electorally unpopular and because of their City connections and 'sound money' leanings. The international position of sterling enabled them to argue more respectably that devaluation would (a) be tanta- mount to defaulting on U.K. debts and (b) threaten the stability of the world monetary system as a whole. These points drew attention to problems that had to be faced. But they could not be a decisive case against devaluation, because they ignored the effects that altern- atives to devaluation would have on the home economy. With wages and prices inflexible downwards, these alternatives would eventually involve a drastic fall in Britain's economic well-being, in the form either of severe unemployment or of a progressive withdrawal from international trade through import restrictions, etc., or both. Besides being wasteful and immoral, such a repetition of the inter-war years would be electorally suicidal.

A constructive approach to the problem would have involved at least considering how and to what extent overseas official holders of sterling should be compensated for the loss in dollar terms which would be imposed on them by a sterling devaluation. In fact, politicians, civil servants and central bankers regarded all this as unthinkable and did no more than reiterate the old clichés, which were wearing thinner every year, about the greatness of sterling. Indeed, in its evidence to the Halsbury Committee on Decimal Currency in 1962, the Bank of England cited the world role of sterling as the crucial reason why decimalisation should be based on the pound as the major unit, rather than on a 10 shilling or 100 penny unit. The Bank's view was decisive in causing the Halsbury Committee to recommend and the Government to accept the retention of the pound in a decimal system.

In the post-war world of full employment and Keynesian economic management, the importance of a large public sector has been twofold. First, it affects the ways in which aggregate demand can be controlled. Second, there arises the question of how to allocate resources efficiently within the public sector and between it and the private sector.[13]

A large public sector creates both opportunities and problems for the management of demand. The important question is how much weight should be put on variations in public expenditure, and especially public investment, compared with other means of stabilising the economy such as taxation and monetary policy. The received view from early post-Keynesian economics was that it should play a big role; but the practical problems involved, such as executive time-lags and the danger of disrupting capital programmes by precipitate cuts, had not been thought through. This was partly because the policy was originally conceived in terms of quick upward adjustments to prevent slumps rather than quick downward adjustments to contain excess demand. Also, under the Labour Governments of 1945–51 the question of controlling public investment as such did not really arise; *all* investment was subject to controls in one way or another, and budgetary policy had a partial rather than an overall role in managing aggregate demand.

At first the Conservatives were mainly anxious to reduce the role of the public sector all round, and believed monetary policy to be sufficient for stabilisation purposes. Public-sector purchases of goods and services as a share of G.D.P. declined from a peak of 30 per cent in 1952 to under 27 per cent in 1955; half the drop came from defence cuts and much of the rest from switching house building to the private sector. The later fifties saw a much more determined and not unsuccessful effort to use short-run changes in public investment as a means of controlling the economy. The volume of public investment was reduced in 1957–8, substantially increased in 1958–9 and again restrained in 1960. An attempt was also made in 1957–8 to hold back *current* outlays by delaying pay increases in the public sector. It was, however, difficult to act effectively in these ways without disrupting public industry. In the 1960s the emphasis swung back, towards a smoother increase in spending and more medium-term planning. The new approach was outlined in a White Paper on *Public Investment in Great Britain* (Cmnd 1203, 1960) and in the Plowden Report on *The Control of Public Expenditure* (Cmnd 1432, July 1961). With public outlays such a large part of the economy, this gave encouragement to the idea of medium-term targeting or 'planning' for the economy as a whole. The new approach was also associated with a more constructive attitude to public expenditure. 'The tide of Socialism' had clearly been stemmed over the previous decade, and opinion moved in favour of a bigger allocation of resources to such areas as roads, hospitals and universities. Between 1960 and 1964 an upswing in public investment pushed the public sector's share of G.D.P. from 26 to 28 per cent.

This brings us to the second aspect, that of efficiency

in public spending. Economic efficiency means the allocation of resources among properly costed alternatives in the light of social choices and priorities. The basic principle is that resources should be committed in a particular direction only if the outputs thus obtained are at least as valuable to society as the alternative outputs which could be obtained by using the resources differently. In the private sector this principle is fulfilled in a rough and ready way through the profit motive, together with appropriate taxation policies and government controls. Its fulfilment in the public sector requires proper criteria for (i) undertaking investment and (ii) setting prices. The prospective social return on new investment should be similar to that in the private sector after tax. Prices – where there is a marketable product, as in the nationalised industries – should be related to marginal cost, i.e. the cost of the resources that would be released for some alternative use if output was reduced or not increased by a small amount.

Application of these rules is often far from straightforward. For example, marginal cost on the railways may be the cost of providing extra or longer trains on certain services, or the cost of keeping a whole line open instead of closing it. What is marginal cost in the latter case is mostly overheads in the former. If the line is kept open, the aim must be to charge these overheads to those most willing to bear them, i.e. those whose custom would not be lost at a higher price. But this involves price discrimination, which may be technically difficult or politically unattractive. Problems of price discrimination also arise when there are peak demands at certain times of day, involving increased production costs (e.g. electricity, railways).

Still greater difficulties appear when the product is not marketable because it is a collective good (e.g. law and order) or an 'externality' (e.g. a quieter surrounding thanks to the construction of a by-pass); or when the Government decides that the product, though marketable, should be priced below cost for reasons of income distribution (e.g. health and education) or again of environment (e.g. rural transport services). In such cases it becomes difficult to measure efficiency, let alone improve it. Modern techniques such as cost–benefit analysis and programme budgeting are needed.[14]

In the 1950s the Conservatives failed to tackle these issues in any way. Policy concerned itself with organisational change in public industry – either outright denationalisation as with steel and road haulage, or restructuring inside the public sector. The restructuring was meant to encourage a more commercial approach and often involved a degree of decentralisation, particularly under the Transport Act (1953) and the Electricity Act (1957). In practice, the public corporations were neither given freedom to determine their prices and investments nor were the policies imposed on them by Ministers conducive to efficiency. Price increases were delayed or prevented in attempts to slow down inflation or avoid unpopularity at election times, while investment programmes were approved in a haphazard and uncritical way and their execution subordinated, as already explained, to the management of aggregate demand. This made it difficult for the corporations to fulfil their statutory duty of covering costs (including interest on capital) over a run of years, and generally undermined their sense of purpose.

At the end of the fifties a number of factors compelled the Government to take a fresh look. Economic changes were creating big problems for several of the industries. In the fuel sector the coal shortage of the first post-war decade became a growing surplus from 1957 onwards, as industry switched to oil. In transport the growth of private motoring, together with under-investment in roads and delayed modernisation on the railways, was causing road congestion and (after 1956) operating losses on the railways. Most important of all, the Select Committee on Nationalised Industries, created in 1956, produced increasingly outspoken criticisms of political interference and official incompetence in this field. Two major changes resulted. One was the shift towards medium-term planning of all public investment. This was of great importance from the efficiency point of view because, when properly established, it would require governments to take decisions

132

on the allocation of resources well in advance. Priorities and alternatives could then be discussed in a sensible way, something which was impossible when decisions were being taken haphazardly from year to year.

The other innovation was a policy statement, *The Financial and Economic Obligations of the Nationalised Industries* (Cmnd 1337, 1961), putting public corporations explicitly on a commercial footing by laying down that they should aim at a target rate of return on their capital employed comparable to that of private industry (the average rate being 8 per cent). This was a marked improvement on the previous state of affairs, but several important points were still being evaded or confused. The nationalised industries were stated to have 'social' obligations in addition to their commercial ones, but no clear line was drawn between them. Political control-without-responsibility over prices and allied matters was not renounced.[15] And the target rate of return, which ought to be used as a criterion for new investments, was in fact applied to all existing assets. This had the effect of turning it into a rather arbitrary *pricing* rule, with the purpose of securing a 'substantial degree' of self-finance for the industries' capital projects. Price increases were appropriate in most of the nationalised industries in the early sixties, because prices had previously been kept too low. In general, however, financing is quite a different question from resource allocation, and should not be confused with it.

These deficiencies meant that the 1961 White Paper was still way behind the best economic thinking and also way behind experience in other countries, notably France and the United States. However, together with the 1960 White Paper and the Plowden Report it helped to initiate a decade of progress in this area.[16]

Monetary policy is the traditional method of regulating a market economy, and it was natural for the Conservatives to restore it to an active role. However, the mechanism by which monetary policy influences private spending is imperfectly understood. To some extent it works by affecting business and consumer expectations, and its dependence on this psychological link must be all the greater when the economy is very liquid – as it still was at the start of the fifties owing chiefly to the war. The impact of monetary policy was therefore likely to be specially unreliable until more normal monetary relationships were restored. This turned out to be a long process, not fully accomplished until the end of our period.

The authorities seemed not unaware of these difficulties to begin with. On the one hand they sought, by various technical means, in 1951 to restore official control over the volume of bank deposits. On the other hand they made it clear (sensibly) that they would not rely on controlling deposits. Requests to banks to limit advances were an established procedure, and a passage in Sir Anthony Eden's memoirs indicates that the Conservatives saw it as a back-stairs substitute for direct controls on imports or investment. In addition, the new weapon of hire-purchase restrictions was introduced in February 1952. And Bank Rate was raised from $2\frac{1}{2}$ to 4 per cent in March.

Developments during 1952, however, were not a good test for monetary policy. The boom created by rearmament gave way to an export-led recession centred on the textile industry. At the same time raw-material prices fell and stockbuilding in the United Kingdom levelled off, so that the balance of payments deficit disappeared despite falling exports. The monetary measures can have had only a marginal effect in all this, but Mr R. A. Butler (Chancellor from 1951 to 1955) and his advisers seem to have attributed a great deal to them. They thus came to overrate the ability of monetary policy in any circumstances to curb a boom quickly and smoothly.[17] They also seem to have been in a muddle about the effect of monetary policy on the balance of payments. There can be a direct impact on the reserves through movements of monetary capital. But any impact on the current account must spring from a prior effect on expenditure. In conditions of full employment there is no magic way in which monetary restraint can improve the balance of trade without cutting home investment or consumption.

The events of 1955 and after forced a change of view. In order to curb the boom in progress at the start of the year, Bank Rate was raised to 4½ per cent in February and hire-purchase restrictions were reintroduced. At this time also the Bank of England began to support 'transferable sterling' in Zürich, which temporarily put an end to speculation and helped the U.K. reserves. Butler wrongly concluded that the boom was under control and felt free to cut taxes by £150 million in the election year (1955). Credit restraint had to be sharply tightened after the election, and in the autumn another run on sterling forced a supplementary budget which reversed half the previous tax cuts. Further restrictive measures, both monetary and fiscal, were taken by the new Chancellor, Harold Macmillan, in February and April 1956. Even then, although output stopped rising and pressure on the labour market eased, the level of that pressure remained high until the further round of deflationary measures of September 1957.

This protracted sequence showed the risks of heavy reliance on credit policy, and established the strategy of the 'package deal', comprising both fiscal and monetary measures, when a major shift of policy was required. It also prompted the authorities to seek a firmer intellectual basis for contemporary monetary policy. The Radcliffe Committee was appointed in April 1957 to investigate the working of the monetary system.

However, Macmillan's successor Peter Thorneycroft did not wait for the committee's views before expressing some unorthodox ones of his own. In announcing his September 1957 measures, he claimed that control of the money supply was necessary to check rising prices, and that such control required the money value of public-sector spending as well as bank advances to be held constant. Thorneycroft's ideas were not well received, and he resigned in January 1958. His Cabinet colleagues found them unacceptable because, with prices still rising, constant public spending in money terms would have meant a cut in real terms, and because it was political folly to seek completely stable prices at the cost of a big rise in unemployment. Bankers and economists also found much to criticise in Thorneycroft's analysis, but from a practical standpoint his main mistake was to be ten years and several Governments too early. It was left to a Labour Chancellor to apply his medicine in something like its full rigour.

The Radcliffe Committee, whose report was published in August 1959, denied the quantity of money any special significance. They emphasised the imperfection of the credit and capital markets and the importance of deliberately rationing money, in order to enforce a 'squeeze', but they argued that the authorities could achieve these effects by acting on interest rates. In this they have been refuted by subsequent events. In the following decade it became clear that even substantial and deliberate rises in interest rates (long rates reached 9 per cent by the end of the sixties) might be insufficient by themselves to curb spending. An effective monetary squeeze required (i) directives to banks and other institutions to curb their lending to the private sector, and (ii) a tight budgetary policy which, since taxes could not be raised without limit, implied some ceiling on public expenditure. This corresponded closely to Thorneycroft's recommendations. Had he expressed his views in a more guarded way, and taken greater care to formulate them in Keynesian terms, his critics would not have had such an easy job demolishing them.

II. *Economic Policy and Performance*

Since 1945 the objectives of economic policy in the advanced industrial countries have included:

(i)   full employment;
(ii) reasonably stable prices;
(iii) a healthy balance of payments;[18]
(iv) a satisfactory rate of growth;
(v)   reasonable steadiness of this growth from year to year.

To these we should add:
136

(vi) social and industrial objectives, influenced to some extent by party ideology.

This is a long and ambitious list of objectives, and to assess how far they have been achieved is difficult for two reasons. First, they are not very precisely defined. Full employment is a band rather than a single figure, and on such matters as price inflation, steadiness of growth and income distribution standards of 'reasonableness' and 'fairness' vary a good deal. Moreover, many of the aims sooner or later conflict. The most commonly discussed conflicts are between efficiency and fairness, between full employment and price stability and between full employment and a fixed exchange rate. Secondly, to assess what policy has achieved one must know what it is capable of achieving, and our knowledge here is very imperfect. There is no doubt about the extensive responsibility of policy-makers with regard to objectives (i) and (iii); with regard to the others it is less certain and we must be cautious in our judgments.

Britain's employment record, like that of other European countries, has been excellent in the post-war period. Registered unemployment averaged under 2 per cent of the labour force in all but four of the thirteen years of Tory rule and under 2·5 per cent in all but one, that one being 1963 when the figure of 2·6 per cent was due to exceptionally bad weather in the first three months of the year. These are very low totals.

Professor Matthews has recently pointed out that government policy cannot take all the credit for this, as there were also powerful autonomous factors boosting the demand for labour after 1945.[19] By comparison with pre-1914, the growth of the capital stock and the absorption of labour surpluses has helped to stabilise the demand for labour in the face of output fluctuations. And compared with the inter-war period, private investment has been exceptionally buoyant, partly by way of reaction from its depressed level in the previous forty years and partly because technological change has been faster since the war. Tax concessions on industrial investment, especially the investment allowances (see

137

below), may also have contributed. The fact remains that the public sector as a whole (including its capital spending) has had a sizeable financial deficit throughout the period. In any case, as Matthews also points out, a more deflationary policy on the Government's part could undoubtedly have spoiled the employment record – and the British balance of payments problem could well, in itself, have brought such a policy about. Some critics have in fact maintained that the measures taken in the 1957 payments crisis amounted to a (temporary) abandonment of the full-employment objective in favour of price stability. This, however, seems a hasty judgment. While there was concern about inflation, unemployment was still very low (1·5 per cent) and, above all, there was still a three-year horizon to the next General Election.

The only shadow on the employment scene has been the regional problem. Unemployment rates in Scotland (3–4 per cent), Wales (3 per cent), Northern Ireland (6–10 per cent) and some parts of northern England ($2\frac{1}{2}$– 3 per cent) have been considerably higher than in the Midlands and South (about 1 per cent). This is a problem of long standing and reflects the excessive dependence of these regions on a small number of heavy industries, often with declining employment opportunities, such as shipbuilding, coal and steel. Policies to overcome this by attracting new industry to the 'development areas' were begun in the 1930s. In the first ten years after the war the problem was veiled by the very high level of aggregate demand, but it became more conspicuous in the later 1950s when demand pressure was slacker. In 1958 the Conservatives began to make more positive use of control over industrial building (the system of Board of Trade Industrial Development Certificates dating from 1947) to steer industry to high-unemployment areas. Provisions for financial assistance were also widened. The localities eligible for assistance were redefined in the Local Employment Act (1960), but this was in some ways a retrograde measure. It gave even more emphasis than before to high unemployment as the criterion for assistance, instead of aiming to encourage self-sustained development in the areas. In

138

other words it focused too much on the symptom and not enough on the cause.[20] Improvements came in 1963, following the recession of the previous winter. White Papers on Central Scotland (Cmnd 2188) and North-east England (Cmnd 2206) shifted the basis of policy in these regions away from simple relief of unemployment towards planned diversification and development. Also, financial assistance to all the depressed zones was stepped up, notably through more generous building grants and freedom for business to amortise their plant and equipment purchases at whatever rate they chose ('free depreciation').[21]

These policies were developed further by the Labour Government after 1964. They did not eliminate regional employment in the 1960s and they neglected certain aspects of the problem, especially that of retraining labour.[22] Nevertheless, without them the problem might well have got worse; certainly the population drift to the South-east and the problems of congestion there would have been aggravated.

The record in controlling inflation is less satisfactory, but nearly everyone would regard the objective as much less important than full employment. Retail prices rose by about $3\frac{1}{4}$ per cent per annum from 1952 to 1964.[23] This cannot be blamed on the movement of import prices. Although they rose by 18 per cent between 1950 and 1952 on account of the Korean War, they then fell by 10 per cent between 1952 and 1954 and fluctuated with little net change for the rest of the period. Just about the entire price inflation of the period 1952 to 1964 was thus due to the 'normal' functioning of the U.K. economy, whereas previously special and external factors had played a big part.

The inflationary process basically took the form of a wage–wage and price–wage spiral. The main rise in incomes came at the peak of the boom (1955–6, 1960, 1964) and prices followed on with a slight time-lag. The increase in U.K. money income per head (6 per cent a year) was not exceptionally fast by international standards, but it meant a faster rise in U.K. costs and prices than elsewhere because output per head in the United

139

Kingdom was increasing less.

A debate developed in the course of the fifties as to whether the rise in U.K. prices was primarily due to independent increases in costs, first of imported materials and then of unionised labour demanding higher wages ('cost push'), or to excessive pressure of demand on resources ('demand pull'). While the debate itself was inconclusive, an important set of policy questions emerged from it. Those who believed that inflation was caused mainly by pressure on wages tended to favour direct government intervention in pay negotiations – in short, an incomes policy; while those who believed that excess demand was the trouble tended to favour a slight increase in unemployment. In the Treasury Sir Robert Hall was a strong advocate of incomes policy, and he had outside support from academics such as G. D. N. Worswick and Thomas Balogh. Other academics, notably Professors A. W. Phillips and F. W. Paish, were sceptical and believed that a quite moderate increase in unemployment, to 2 or $2\frac{1}{2}$ per cent, would substantially reduce the rate of inflation.

The Government found itself in a dilemma. Unemployment was not palatable, but neither was an incomes policy, since it entailed interference with 'free collective bargaining' and risked a clash with the unions – which the Conservatives had been careful to avoid. After ineffectual gestures in the direction of wage restraint (Eden in 1955) and a 'price plateau' (Macmillan in 1956), it was decided in July 1957 (Thorneycroft) to appoint a three-man Council on Prices, Productivity and Incomes with the job of keeping price and wage trends 'under review'. The Council issued four reports, in February 1958, August 1958, July 1959 and July 1961. There was never much prospect that its utterances would influence wage negotiations, but its practical demise came quicker than expected when, under the influence of its initial economist member, Sir Denis Robertson, it took a tough 'demand-pull' line in its first report and approved the restrictive financial measures taken in September 1957. The T.U.C. promptly boycotted the Council for good, even though its later reports showed more awareness of the complexities of wage bargaining and refrained from sweeping judgments.

A more serious attempt to set up an incomes policy was made by Selwyn Lloyd in July 1961. The payments crisis of that year, suggestions that sterling was overvalued (see note 9) and a major O.E.E.C. report on *The Problem of Rising Prices* which lent support to the cost-push view of inflation[24] all played a part in this. Lloyd secured a six-month 'pay pause' and attempted to follow this with a longer-term strategy involving a $2\frac{1}{2}$ per cent 'guiding light' for pay increases and a National Incomes Commission to vet individual claims. The N.I.C., however, was stillborn, as the T.U.C., annoyed by the wage pause, by the fact that it had not been consulted in advance and by surtax concessions in the April 1961 budget, refused to co-operate. After 1964 N.I.C. was transmuted by the Labour Government into the National Board for Prices and Incomes.

Selwyn Lloyd's pay pause, like Cripps's wage restraint in 1948–50 and Harold Wilson's in 1966, showed that the movement of money incomes can be held up for short periods. But over the longer term the evidence hitherto from Britain and from most other countries is that incomes policy makes little difference to the rate of inflation. If anything, it adds to the injustice and inefficiency caused by inflation, because those in underunionised occupations, who tend to lag behind in the incomes race, are also the most vulnerable to income restraints and 'guidelines.'[25] It is conceivable, though not proven, that incomes policy could accelerate productivity gains by encouraging 'productivity bargaining'; but this would increase inflation rather than reduce it, because the essence of productivity bargaining is that large pay rises are awarded in return for the abandonment of restrictive practices, and such pay rises cannot be stopped from spreading to other parts of the economy.

The alternative, Phillips–Paish suggestion is to run the economy at a slightly lower average pressure of demand. The trouble with this proposal, apart from political objections, is that it argues 'from the experi-

141

ence of short post-war recessions to a situation in which a given unemployment rate is maintained as a permanent policy. In the second situation unemployment would be steady rather than rising and – in contrast to recession situations – the background would be one of steadily rising output and profits.'[26] It is difficult to believe, therefore, that a small increase in the economy's average margin of spare capacity would have very striking effects on the trend of money wages and prices. All the more so, as a further decade of inflation has gone by since the proposal was first advanced. People have become more accustomed to inflation, expect it to continue and show some signs of adapting pay claims to their expectations. The spiral may thus tend to accelerate, and if it does the conflict between full employment and price stability will become more serious, because price stability will simultaneously assume greater importance as an objective and require higher unemployment if it is to be realised.

As yet, however, we remain some way short of this. In the fifties and sixties price inflation as such was a nuisance rather than a menace, and its main impact was on the balance of payments.

The Conservatives came to power in October 1951 to face a record balance of payments deficit for the year of nearly £700 million. They left office thirteen years later leaving another record deficit of £750 million. The difference between the two was that while the 1951 deficit owed a lot to extraneous and temporary circumstances, the 1964 deficit mainly reflected a basic weakness in the United Kingdom's competitive position which had developed over the years and could no longer be corrected without a devaluation.

The deterioration in the position seems from Table 4.1 to have occurred between the fifties and sixties. This, however, is rather misleading. It should first be noted that the deterioration was wholly on current account. In fact the capital account moved somewhat in Britain's favour, because foreign (chiefly U.S.) investment in the United Kingdom rose faster than U.K. investment and long-term lending overseas; U.K. capital exports were, of course, restricted by controls, especially exports of portfolio capital. The surplus on current account in the fifties, however, was unsoundly based. It rested on the improvement in the terms of trade and on the restraint of home demand from 1955 to 1958.

Table 4.1

United Kingdom Balance of Payments, 1952–64

	1952–9	1960–4
	(annual averages, in £ million)	
Trade deficit	−140	−252
Government services and transfers (net)	−145	−358
of which: Military	−70	−219
Private invisibles (net) plus net interest, profits and dividends	+435	+524
Current account	+150	− 86
Long-term capital (net)	−175	−147
Basic balance	− 25	−233
Balancing item	+ 55	+ 53
Overall balance (or balance of monetary movements)	+ 30	−180

Source: Bank for International Settlements, *38th Annual Report*; and *United Kingdom Balance of Payments, 1969* (Pink Book).

The United Kingdom's terms of trade (the ratio of merchandise export to import prices) showed a windfall improvement of 10 per cent from 1953 to 1958. This meant that by 1958 the 1953 volume of exports was buying £300 million more of imports than before. The current account surplus in that year was an exceptional £350 million. As regards the curbs on home demand in 1955–8, had the United Kingdom been in a sound competitive position, restraint at home would have been offset by faster growth of export volume and a rise in the ratio of exports to G.D.P. Output would have increased and the fall in the U.K. share of world manufacturing exports would have slowed down. In fact exports were sluggish and their ratio to G.D.P. static at around 14 per cent. U.K. industrial production showed almost no increase for three years and the export share declined at much the same pace as before.

There were many reasons for Britain's uncompetitiveness and their relative importance is not entirely clear. But a major role was played by two factors already mentioned – wage inflation and military expenditure. From 1954 to 1959 total labour costs per unit of output in U.K. manufacturing rose by 25 per cent, about twice as fast as in other industrial countries. The deterioration in Britain's cost competitiveness ceased in 1959–64, some gain vis-à-vis Europe balancing a decline vis-à-vis the United States, but by then the balance of payments was in fundamental disequilibrium. As to defence spending, having risen to $10\frac{1}{2}$ per cent of G.N.P. in 1952, it was still absorbing 9 per cent in 1955, including 24 per cent of shipbuilding and 14 per cent of engineering output.[27] In the early 1960s, as Table 4.1 shows, defence and other government spending overseas contributed directly to the deterioration on current account. The cost of keeping troops abroad, in particular, rose steeply with inflation and the ending of National Service at the end of the fifties. The figures exaggerate the importance of such spending, because a proportion was offset directly or indirectly by a gain on the visible trade balance (higher exports to areas where British troops were stationed, German offset purchases, reduced imports into the United Kingdom for the troops themselves, and so on). But the offset for military outlays (perhaps 25 or 30 per cent) was lower than for development aid (well over 50 and perhaps as high as 70 per cent) and the net balance of payments burden was undeniable.

In the same period competition from other countries became steadily more intense. Germany and Japan re-entered world markets in the early 1950s, and Germany's export total caught up with Britain's in 1958. Britain's import controls were gradually relaxed, and discrimination by the Sterling Area countries in favour of British goods declined as world trade and payments were liberalised and as colonial territories gained independence. It may be noted that the relatively slow growth of the O.S.A. economies was not an important cause of Britain's poor export performance; it was chiefly her *share* of their markets which declined. In any case the geographical spread of U.K. exports is not God-given, and industry could have switched its efforts more rapidly to the fast-growing markets of Europe.

In sum, Britain's trading position was not strong enough to ensure the maintenance of the $2.80 exchange rate. The authorities must have been half aware of this. At any rate, an official estimate in 1953 put the desirable U.K. surplus on current account (sufficient to provide for capital commitments and some increase in reserves) at £350 million, and this figure had risen to £450 million by the end of the decade.[28] But there was never any proper strategy for achieving the target.

Had the Government been serious about holding the exchange rate after the 1961 payments crisis, its only sound policy would have been to wait for the slack created by Selwyn Lloyd's deflationary 'package' to be taken up with rising exports. There was clearly no room for major growth 'experiments' resting on expansion of home demand. Yet this was just what Reginald Maudling, Chancellor after 1962, and his advisers embarked upon – full of half-digested ideas about 'virtuous circles' in which growth leads to more growth by accelerating productivity gains. Whether or not the notion of a 'virtuous circle' is useful, its proponents never claimed that reckless expansion at home was the way to strengthen a weak balance of payments.

In his 1963 Budget speech Maudling agreed that expansion might initially lead to an external deficit and suggested that 'In so far as there is a stocking-up movement related to expansion, it is perfectly reasonable and sensible to finance such a movement out of our reserves or out of our borrowing facilities in the I.M.F. and elsewhere.' But, as Milton Gilbert has trenchantly put it, it is not 'perfectly reasonable and sensible' at the start of an expansion to anticipate an external deficit and to count on financing it by borrowing reserves from abroad; the external position at the low point of the cycle should be a significant surplus which would cover the increased import demand that is to come with expansion of the economy. It not only suggests the intention to ignore balance of payments discipline, but also strongly implies that the currency is in fundamental disequilibrium. For a situation in which the economy cannot be expanded to the level of full use of productive resources without falling into external deficit is a fundamental disequilibrium, and the only remedy for it in the Bretton Woods system is to adjust the par value.[29]

Because the Labour Government after 1964, with U.S. support, took the mismanagement of Britain's balance of payments to unheard-of lengths, it was possible for the Conservatives to maintain (at least in public) that the mess was none of their making. The claim can hardly be taken seriously.

The growth of U.K. output per head since 1950 has been slow by comparison with continental Europe (let alone Japan). The figures to 1964 are shown in Table 4.2. It was estimated that all the other countries of north-western Europe had surpassed Britain in output per head by the time the Conservatives left office. It could be argued that one should not pay much attention to fine comparisons of this kind. Nobody did before Keynes, because there were no national income statistics. More important, measured output per head is a crude and even misleading indicator of economic welfare. It takes no account of income distribution, of the proportion of output devoted to such pursuits as putting men on the moon and killing Vietnamese peasants, or of the environmental damage caused by modern technology and overcrowding.[30] Of course growth, even in rich countries, also makes desirable things, such as better housing, modern hospitals, more leisure and even improved military striking power for

146

Table 4.2

Growth Rates of Real National Income (Total, per Person Employed, and per Capita), 1950–64 and 1955–64

Country*	National income		National income per person employed		National income per capita	
	1950–64	1955–64	1950–64	1955–64	1950–64	1955–64
			(percentages)			
Germany	7·1	5·6	5·3	4·3	5·9	4·3
Italy	5·6	5·4	5·2	5·4	4·9	4·7
France	4·9	5·0	4·7	4·7	3·8	3·7
Netherlands	4·9	4·3	3·7	3·1	3·5	2·9
Norway	3·8	3·9	3·6	3·7	2·9	3·0
Denmark	3·6	4·8	2·7	3·5	2·9	4·1
United States	3·5	3·1	2·2	2·0	1·8	1·4
Belgium	3·4	3·5	2·8	3·0	2·8	2·9
United	2·6	2·8	2·0	2·3	2·2	2·1

Source: Edward F. Denison, assisted by Jean-Pierre Poullier, *Why Growth Rates Differ: Postwar Experience in Nine Western Countries* (Brookings Institution, Washington, D.C., 1967).

* Countries are listed in the order of growth rates of total national income from 1950 to 1964.

national defence easier to obtain. But this way of putting it emphasises that growth is not an end in itself – it is not something whose maximisation should be the prime target for an already rich society. Unfortunately, economists do not understand the growth process at all well and are not in a position to say at what point the pursuit of faster growth becomes on balance inimical to economic well-being. Even if they knew more, value judgments would come in sooner or later and make a clear answer difficult. In Britain, for instance, faster growth may mean quicker slum clearance and more modern hospitals, but also greater destruction of the countryside and more deaths on the roads. Who is to say where the right choice lies?

Anyhow, rightly or wrongly, it is a political fact that the rate of growth of output, and particularly output per head, has become an object of public concern, in rich countries even more than in poor ones.

The Conservative Government did not begin to worry about Britain's slow growth until the end of the fifties. There were three reasons for this. First, the faster growth of the continental countries could be attributed in earlier years to the greater war-time destruction they had suffered or to the fact that their real income levels were still behind Britain's. By the late 1950s this was no longer plausible. Secondly, up to 1958 there was considerable compensation for the slow growth of output through the improved terms of trade and declining defence effort. Brittan points out that 'between 1952 and 1959 (when the Conservatives won the third successive election victory with an increased majority) net national output measured in constant prices rose by 20 per cent, yet personal consumption rose by 25 per cent and personal disposable incomes by 28 per cent in real terms'.[31] And, he might have added, gross fixed investment rose by nearly 40 per cent. Taking the election of October 1951 as the starting date, improved terms of trade were by 1958 providing over £1,000 million a year (at 1958 prices) in additional resources, while the decline in the share of G.N.P. going to defence (from 10·4 to 7·7 per cent) released some £550 million. These trends were much less prominent after 1958.[32] Thirdly, the restraints on demand in 1955–8 were deliberate, but disappointment followed when the economy again appeared to come up against its full-capacity ceiling in mid-1960, after a short sharp upswing of only eighteen months.

Since Britain's slow growth over the decade was not due to underutilisation of resources, policy-makers had no obvious way of speeding it up. However, both policy-makers and industrialists had various criticisms of each other. Officials felt that large parts of U.K. industry

148

were inefficient and unenterprising compared with their continental and American rivals. This was hard to verify, but it received support first from journalists and others who found evidence of technological lethargy, outdated industrial relations and casual attitudes to marketing, and later from more academic analysis which suggested that U.S. subsidiaries in Britain were more profitable than British firms in the same industry.[33] Anyhow, officials took the view that additional sticks and carrots should be found to urge industry to a better performance.

Industry for its part objected to the seemingly erratic and piecemeal nature of the Government's economic management. First, the growth of aggregate demand had been not only slow but unsteady. By 1960 there had been two stop–go cycles since 1951, and there was to be a third to 1964. These fluctuations were not much smaller than those of 1870–1914, and the feeling grew that such ups and downs had a discouraging effect on business investment. Secondly, policy measures had tended to bear heavily on narrow sectors of the economy. This was true not only of controls on the nationalised industries but also of hire-purchase restrictions, which hit the motor and consumer-durable industries. A wider spread of controls seemed desirable.

All these considerations, together with concern about inflation and awareness of Britain's declining world position, led in 1961 to a series of new initiatives in economic policy. First, Britain applied to join the E.E.C. One motive behind this was certainly the idea of sticks and carrots for U.K. industry – competition being the stick and 'wider markets' the carrot. But the rationale of this was weak.[34] Secondly, additional weapons of economic management were sought. Selwyn Lloyd's effort to set up an incomes policy has been mentioned. Another development was the introduction of the tax 'regulator', giving the Treasury power to vary indirect tax rates (excise duties and purchase tax) by up to one-tenth in between budgets. Authority to change taxes in months other than April was obviously desirable, but the regulator did not represent a significant step forward. There had been

149

'autumn budgets' before, even (as in 1955) involving tax increases. The important thing, as Ian Little has pointed out,[35] is to remove the aura of crisis and opprobrium from autumn budgets, and this the regulator does not do, at least not sufficiently. What is probably needed is two or three routine 'budget days' a year rather than just one, on which taxes can be changed as a matter of normality.

The third and most far-reaching group of measures was concerned with medium-term policy and planning, and came to centre on the idea of a five-year growth target for the economy. The obvious use of such a target is in smoothing out the stop–go cycle and, more particularly, in planning public expenditure. Dampening the cycle means correcting deviations in the rate of growth of output. Planning public expenditure means determining the approximate share of national output to be absorbed by individual public services and by the public sector as a whole. The target itself is obtained by projecting the economy's productive potential in the light of recent productivity trends and the expected growth of the labour force. The object of planning would thus simply be to produce steadier growth, perhaps in the hope that this will lead to faster growth, but not counting on it.

There is, in fact, little evidence that steady growth and fast growth go together or that continental Europe's growth was faster because it was steadier. Still, Britain might be a special case. It was widely suggested that stop–go had inhibited private industrial investment, causing the United Kingdom to lag behind in the expansion of its capital stock and the applications of new technology. The United Kingdom was certainly at the bottom of the European investment league as well as of the growth league, in spite of generous, if fluctuating, tax concessions on business investment.[36] But one could also argue, as Professor Kaldor has, that Britain's low investment ratio by comparison with other countries reflected the exhaustion of labour reserves in the primary sector and consequent low structural opportunities for growth.[37] The implication of this would be that, if the authorities did succeed in jacking

150

up the investment ratio either by eliminating stop–go or through bigger fiscal incentives, this would chiefly lower the social return to investment and have only a small effect on the rate of growth.

A different set of arguments, however, suggested that dampening the cycle and keeping the economy at something less than maximum pressure would improve the underlying opportunities for expansion. It would do this by opening the way to export-led growth. The reasoning was that the speed of the upswing in the U.K. cycle and/or the pressure of demand near the top of the cycle had impaired U.K. competitiveness, directly by causing supply bottlenecks and indirectly by causing inflation. Contain the upswing in U.K. demand and exports would forge ahead, pulling investment with them as they had in Germany and drawing more labour into manufacturing industry where necessary. Essentially this was the Paish thesis, or a variant of it. Paish himself placed the main emphasis on controlling inflation; others emphasised the force of demand as such. While mismanagement of the cycle doubtless contributed to the United Kingdom's inflation and hence to its balance of payments problem, it was no longer plausible by the early 1960s to suggest that better control of the cycle would suffice to eliminate the payments problem within a reasonable period of years.

None of these arguments was actually put to the test, for the Government never envisaged the growth target as a mere projection. Instead it tried to run before it could walk, by using an over-ambitious figure to raise business optimism and hustle the economy along. This risky form of pseudo-planning was the background to the Maudling experiment.

The idea of stepping up the growth rate simply by persuading industry that it was going to be stepped up sprang partly from fashionable talk about 'virtuous circles'; but it also reflected a sudden naïve enthusiasm for the French style of indicative planning. The French *Commissariat du Plan* had an impressive technical staff, carried weight in the French government machine and had close relations with industry through the *commissions de modernisation*. The French economy had certainly shown rapid growth since the war. But did this actually owe much to the plans? Why had Germany managed to grow even faster than France without indicative planning? And anyhow, could the apparatus of French planning be effectively transplanted into Britain's very different industrial and institutional set-up?[38] Such questions were hardly asked, let alone answered. Moreover, what if French planning brought us French rates of inflation? Did we stand ready to devalue the pound every few years? Rather than pursue high-flying ideas about planning, the authorities would have been better advised to study a much more down-to-earth episode in recent French policy, namely the stabilisation programme of 1958-9, with its two devaluations and tough financial restraint, which turned out a brilliant textbook success and ensured a sound balance of payments combined with fast growth for the best part of a decade.

The approach to indicative planning in the United Kingdom began slowly. Selwyn Lloyd, with support from only a limited circle in business, the Treasury and the Cabinet, set up the National Economic Development Council ('Neddy') in 1961–2, with the twin task of providing (a) a forum where both sides of industry and the Government could meet to discuss problems of growth and modernisation (including incomes policy); and (b) an 'office' outside the Treasury and on the fringe of the government machine (modelled on the French *Commissariat*) to work out medium-term projections and give advice on growth problems. At the same time, partly by coincidence, the internal organisation of the Treasury was reformed so as to give it a less predominantly financial slant and encourage more attention to questions of resource allocation. During 1962 the 'Neddy' Office drew up several reports focusing on the implications of a 4 per cent growth rate in Britain's G.D.P. between 1961 and 1966. Past trends did not suggest that a figure as high as this could be achieved, and the N.E.D.O. studies were ostensibly of a hypothetical nature. In practice, the 4 per cent took on the nature of a target and was formally approved as such by the N.E.D.C. in February 1963, almost half-way through the period to which it referred![39]

The Tories were voted out of office before the failure of their 'planning' episode had become fully apparent to the public, and their Labour successors, instead of learning the lesson, carried on with the same mistakes for another two years with the so-called National Plan. The lesson surely is that inflated 'targets' for national output and spurious inter-industry 'co-ordination' have no place in genuine growth policies. Such policies should concern themselves with the micro-foundations of growth at the level of the firm, the industry and the trade union, suggesting how modernisation can be promoted, flexibility of working methods improved and so on. They do not need an 'overall framework' beyond that provided by the Government's commitment to full employment and to free trading relations with other countries. Projections and forecasts should, of course, be made by individual firms and industries, and the Government should publish its own projections of national output and public expenditure as a background (as it began to do in the 1960s). But the Government's object should be to manage aggregate demand so as to *match* the economy's productive capacity, not 'stretch' it.

On this view the important part of the planning machinery so far as the private sector is concerned is not N.E.D.C. itself but the 'little Neddies', the Economic Development Committees for individual industries, analogous to the French *commissions*. These began to be set up in 1964 and by the end of that year there were nine of them, covering just over one-quarter of the working population. In the later 1960s several of them produced interesting reports on their industries and may well have had some effect on firms' policies.

Quite apart from the question of planning, the Government could have reduced the economy's fluctuations in the fifties and sixties by conducting its stabilisation policies more efficiently. Policy interventions should have been made sooner and this would probably have allowed them to be smaller as well. The reason why they were not made sooner lies in the events and economic indicators which determined official action.

These were (1) the current level of unemployment, (2) the current level and rate of change of the gold reserves and (3) the next General Election. The first two are known as 'lagging indicators'. Changes in employment typically lag behind changes in output by several months, in some cases as much as nine months.[40] By focusing on the politically sensitive unemployment figure, policy-makers were led to over-expand demand when a cyclical recovery had already started (1958–9, 1963). Similarly, the reserve position is an unreliable indicator of basic balance of payments trends or demand pressures in the economy. Large reserve losses often reflect breaks in confidence and outflows of short-term capital, which tend to occur when the boom is past its peak (1955, 1961, 1964), thus again delaying policy responses. In 1955 and 1961 major packages of restraint came a year later than they should have done. In addition, the reserves may drop for reasons quite unconnected with the U.K. cyclical situation (1956, 1957). As to (3), the tax cuts in April 1955 and the inaction of the summer of 1964, both obvious errors from the stabilisation point of view, were largely influenced by impending elections.

Poor short-term forecasting, it may be noted, was not an important reason for these deficiencies of policy. Of course forecasts were not always accurate, and might have been improved if relationships such as that between output and employment had been worked out earlier. But the main trouble was that policy-makers looked at the wrong variables and paid insufficient attention to underlying economic forces. As Dow expresses it, 'in most years the forecasts appear to have been good enough to make it seem in retrospect worth while for policy to have tried to deal with the situation they indicated'.[41]

The Conservatives came to power in 1951 on a wave of distaste for Crippsian austerity and general revulsion against 'planning', on which they capitalised with their slogan 'Set the People Free'. In practice their policies were less radical than their slogans; the limits of manœuvre were narrow if they were to retain full employment, the social services and the confidence of the trade unions. Despite the party rhetoric, policy remained broadly bipartisan. The Conservatives claimed credit for removing controls on private industry and consumer rationing, but in fact the process had already been started with Harold Wilson's bonfire of controls in 1949. By the end of 1954 most of the controls had disappeared.

There were at least three areas, however, where the Conservatives made larger concessions to market forces than Labour would probably have done. The first was in the field of housing policy. The aim of a property-owning democracy implied a shift to private building; and with the improvement in the housing situation towards the mid-fifties it became reasonable and indeed urgent to deal with private rents, which were still frozen at their 1939 level. This the Conservatives did with the Rent Act of 1957.

This Act freed from control all new unfurnished lettings (i.e. following vacant possession) and also existing lettings of property above a certain rateable value (about 8 per cent of all private rented dwellings). Other rents could be increased, but at most to a level which in terms of real purchasing power still left them 22 per cent lower than in 1939. Further decontrol by ministerial Order, subject to parliamentary approval, was authorised but not carried through because of the heated opposition aroused by the Act both in Parliament and outside. However, the fuss soon died down as the comparatively limited scope of the measure became apparent. Some cases of hardship and of hasty eviction by landlords were reported and amending legislation to deal with this was passed in 1958. But most rent increases were moderate and affected better-off tenants well able to pay them. From 1957 to 1964 another 2 million rented dwellings became decontrolled, mostly through the tenants moving out, 'which suggests that a very large proportion of controlled tenants were both willing and able to pay more for their housing'.[42]

Even so, the housing situation in the 1950s, although not marked by a serious overall shortage, remained unsatisfactory precisely in the sector covered by the 1957

Act. That Act may have done something to improve the supply and utilisation of private rented accommodation, but it did not remove the financial discrimination against this form of housing by comparison both with owner-occupation and with local authority housing. This meant hardship for people in the lower-income brackets who were neither fortunate enough to be council tenants, yet could not afford to buy their own homes.[43] In fact, Conservative policy on housing finance and rent was rather like their initial policy towards the nationalised industries, though in practice less open to criticism. This policy was one of legal or organisational change towards freer markets without, on the one hand, going to extremes or, on the other hand, engaging in any systematic analysis of the problem from an economic and social point of view.

The second area where Conservative attitudes to the market made themselves felt was capital exports. In Conservative and City circles overseas investment was regarded as not only profitable but virtuous. National self-interest, tradition and imperial solidarity all appeared to require it. Freedom of U.K. capital exports to the overseas Sterling Area was in any case a key feature of the sterling system and was retained without qualification while the Conservatives were in power. During the 1950s direct investments outside the Sterling Area were also freely authorised. The social advantages of this policy were, however, extremely dubious. The primary purpose of encouraging capital exports should be to maximise the social productivity of U.K. investment. To this end, investment overseas should be taken to the point and only to the point where its yield at the margin is the same as on home investment. The Reddaway Report of 1967 provided strong evidence that in manufacturing and mining the yield was in fact considerably less.[44] The return on overseas investments after payment of foreign taxes appeared to be no higher (at 8.5 per cent) than the after-tax return on investment in Britain; but taxes paid in Britain, in contrast to those paid abroad, are themselves part of the U.K. social (though not the private) yield of the investment. This constitutes the main reason for discouraging direct investment overseas, whether inside or outside the Sterling Area.[45]

Thirdly, cuts in personal taxation, especially direct taxation, were a definite objective of the Conservatives during the 1950s. It was the natural counterpart of their wish to check the growth of the public sector. They attached more weight to individual enterprise and initiative than did Labour, and less to equality; and they tended to complain that the weight of taxation was squashing these desirable qualities out of the British people – or, more strictly, out of the British middle classes. Major investigations of the tax system, its impact and fairness, were set on foot, but with few practical consequences.

The tax burden had indeed increased steeply since before the war, and the structure of incomes both before and after tax had become less unequal.[46] The reduced inequality of pre-tax incomes mainly reflected the rapid growth of employment income, both wages and salaries, relative to self-employment and investment income. This in turn was due on one side to the absorption of pre-war unemployment, and on the other to the run-down of industrial capital during the war, rent control, low interest rates, dividend restraint and differential taxation of profits. After the middle fifties these trends were reversed to some extent. From 1957 to 1963 salaries and professional incomes both rose faster than wages, while investment incomes rose faster still. These developments probably understated the change in trend away from greater equality, because there was also a big rise after the middle fifties in land values and equity prices, which must have mainly benefited higher-income recipients.

For post-tax incomes the reversal of the previous equalising trend was also clear. Between 1957 and 1963 the proportion of total income tax and surtax collected from the top 5 per cent of incomes fell from 54 to 47 per cent, though that from the 6 to 10 per cent band rose from 9 to 11 per cent.[47] The standard rate of income tax was reduced in three stages from 9s 6d in the pound (or 47·5 per cent) in 1951 to 7s 9d (38·75 per cent) in 1959; and in 1961 the starting level for surtax on earned

157

income was raised from £2,000 to £5,000, which particularly benefited higher-income earners. In addition, the rich tended very naturally to avail themselves of legal arrangements designed to remove parts of their income from the tax net, though the quantitative importance of this is uncertain.[48] The Conservatives also reduced indirect taxes, particularly purchase tax, but cut food subsidies, which is equivalent to increasing taxes;[49] the net effect here must have been regressive.

While all these changes in taxation were not negligible, they added up to a marginal rather than a major shift in the U.K. tax structure. Conservative complaints about taxation were not in fact justified if directed to the total burden on the British taxpayer as a proportion of G.N.P., for this has been no worse than average compared with other industrial countries. Nor has the U.K. system been particularly progressive, except at the very extremes of the income scale.[50] Taxation has been less important as a redistributive measure than public expenditure, particularly on the health service, education and social security payments.

It is surprising in retrospect that the Conservatives did not do more to lower the very high rates of tax on the top range of incomes and to reduce the heavy discrimination against unearned income. One may assume that they were inhibited by electoral considerations from going further.

The Conservatives' predilection for market freedom did not prevent them from stepping in to regulate markets where it seemed desirable to do so. Notably successful were the control of the denationalised steel industry after 1953 through the Iron and Steel Board, and the financial support given to the contraction of the Lancashire cotton industry by the Cotton Industry Act of 1959. Less justified was the merger programme forced on the aircraft industry by Duncan Sandys in 1959. But probably the most important aspect of industrial policy was the (bipartisan) attack on restrictive practices, designed not so much to interfere with market forces as to stop private industry from interfering with them. This

158

was begun by Labour with its Monopolies and Restrictive Practices Act (1948), which set up the Monopolies and Restrictive Practices Commission. The Commission's work led the Conservatives to pass the Restrictive Practices Act (1956), which required all restrictive trade practices to be registered, with a view to their subsequent elimination unless justified under specific exemption clauses before the Restrictive Practices Court. By 1964 nearly 2,500 agreements, mostly on prices, had been registered; two-thirds of them were voluntarily abandoned, chiefly as a result of test-case decisions by the Court. Other agreements were probably abandoned without being registered. The Resale Prices Act (1964) extended the Court's jurisdiction to resale price maintenance, which was declared illegal in principle, but open to justification in particular cases, much like the practices covered by the 1956 Act.

No doubt some restraints on competition were now being achieved in alternative ways not covered by the two Acts ('information agreements' and the like). However, the fact that the parties to some agreements attempted to defend them before the Court suggested that substitute arrangements were not always easy to devise. The abandonment of R.P.M. certainly led to short-run price cuts. It was left to the next Labour Government to strengthen anti-monopoly policies further with the Monopolies and Mergers Act of 1965.

The Conservatives chose a good moment to return to office. Historical circumstances and the world environment were both very favourable during this period. The world economy was showing steady and unprecedented expansion. The spectre of an American slump, which was so feared in the early post-war years, gradually receded from view, and the mild recessions which did occur had a negligible effect on economic growth in Europe. Britain's own imperial past was something of a burden both economically and psychologically, and contributed to blunders in policy; but it was not allowed to interfere with the general climate of prosperity.

Looking at the broad sweep of Conservative economic policy, one is struck by the extent to which it was, in effect, bipartisan. This applies not merely to the mechanics of budgetary policy in the post-Keynesian era, but to particular areas such as regional policy, restrictive practices and aid to industry, and also to broad swings in the climate of opinion, away from 'controls' in the early fifties and towards some form of 'planning' in the early sixties. The Conservatives showed themselves as generally undogmatic, willing to try out new policies if it seemed appropriate, and anxious to consolidate their grip on the economy.

On the other hand their very pragmatism made them weak on basic principles and inclined to take half-baked theories as a substitute for serious analysis in guiding economic strategy. Butler's reliance on monetary policy in 1952–5, Thorncycroft's attempt to control the money supply in 1957, and Maudling's growth experiment in 1962–5 all fall into this general pattern. Comparing the Conservative with the Labour administrations which preceded and followed them calls to mind the story about the Western economist who met a Russian colleague during the Soviet wheat crisis of 1964–5. 'What's your harvest going to be like this year?' he asked. 'Oh, average', replied Ivan. 'What do you mean – average?' 'Well, not as good as last year – but better than next year!' Average seems about the right verdict.

Notes

1. A full-length treatment which does go into the chronology in detail is Samuel Brittan, *Steering the Economy* (1969), an expanded successor to his earlier Penguin book, *The Treasury under the Tories* (1965). See also J. C. R. Dow, *The Management of the British Economy, 1945–60* (Cambridge, 1965); G. D. N. Worswick and P. H. Ady, *The British Economy in the 1950s* (Oxford, 1962); R. E. Caves and associates, *Britain's Economic Prospects* (Washington, D.C., 1968); and A. R. Prest (ed.), *The U.K. Economy: A Manual of Applied Economics* (Manchester, 1966).

2. This applies equally to the repercussions on economic theory, which are beyond the scope of this essay. One of the best simple accounts of the essentials of *The General Theory* is in M. Stewart, *Keynes and After* (1967).

3. For a description, see J. R. N. Stone's contribution to D. N. Chester (ed.), *Lessons of the British War Economy* (Cambridge, 1951). It may be noted that these landmarks were closely paralleled in the United States. The U.S. national accounts were compiled during the war in the Department of Commerce and in 1946 an Act of Congress formally committed U.S. Governments to a full-employment policy. However, the nature of the U.S. Constitution, combined with the pre-Keynesian attitudes of Congress and of a large section of relevant U.S. public opinion, prevented the development of Keynesian fiscal policy along U.K. lines. Things have improved a bit in the 1960s, but not much.

4. Brittan, *Steering the Economy*, p. 113. Brittan exempts Reginald Maudling from this general judgment, but with little justification. Like Peter Thorneycroft, Maudling was articulate on economic matters and had ideas of his own; but his ideas like those of Thorneycroft were half-baked and liable to create blunders in policy.

5. The essential difference between a customs union (like E.E.C.) and a free trade area (like EFTA) is that, while both aim to reduce tariffs on each other's goods to zero, a customs union also establishes a common tariff system vis-à-vis third countries, whereas a free trade area allows members to preserve their separate national tariff systems. Also EFTA did not share the E.E.C.'s pretensions to supranationality and did not aim at a fully unified market in agricultural products.

6. All these countries had strong economic and other ties with Britain and most were members of the Commonwealth. All of them except South Africa held the bulk of their reserves in sterling, and it was an unspoken bargain, after the war as well as during it, that this would continue in exchange for exemption from U.K. exchange controls, especially controls on the export of U.K. capital.

161

7. Sterling newly earned by non-residents was to be freely convertible, but the bulk of existing sterling balances was to be blocked! In Britain both exchange control and import quotas would remain. Overseas governments were to receive little or no advance warning of the change. See the Earl of Birkenhead's life of Lord Cherwell, *The Prof in Two Worlds* (1961) pp. 284–94, and Arthur Salter, *Slave of the Lamp* (1967) ch. 15, for accounts from first-hand sources. Cherwell and Salter played a major role in getting 'Robot' rejected by the Cabinet. For further discussion, see Dow, *The Management of the British Economy*, pp. 80–90, 97–8.

8. The new restrictions were seen by the U.K. authorities as a temporary curb on speculation and were in fact relaxed in 1959 and 1962. However, in 1957–8 some of the banks most affected, such as National and Grindlays and the Bank of London and South America, began to switch their business to dollars instead, bidding for dollar deposits in competition with the New York money market and offering dollar credits to their customers round the world. The growth of this business was greatly boosted by the return to convertibility of the major West European currencies in December 1958. Thus the Euro-dollar market was transformed in a short space of years from a small and purely local institution in the City into a massive world-wide credit system.

9. This conclusion had already been reached in 1961 by the National Institute of Economic and Social Research (in its quarterly *Economic Review*), as well as by international institutions such as the Bank of International Settlements (in its 31st *Annual Report*, March 1961, part 1).

10. On this see A. Shonfield, *British Economic Policy since the War* (1958) chaps. 5–6, and P. M. Oppenheimer, 'Monetary Movements and the International Position of Sterling', *Scottish Journal of Political Economy* (February 1966) pp. 114–5.

11. Gold holdings alone rose approximately from £180 million to £300 million.

12. Diversification accelerated after 1964, but a

serious crisis of the sterling system did not occur until the devaluation of November 1967.

13. Between 1951 and 1964 the share of gross domestic product absorbed by public-sector outlays on goods and services (including capital formation) fluctuated between 25 and 30 per cent. In addition, transfer payments (including subsidies and debt interest) stood at around $15\frac{1}{2}$ per cent. In 1938 the percentages had been: goods and services 20, transfers $12\frac{1}{2}$. Note, moreover, that the economy was not fully employed in 1938, so that the public and private sectors were not competing for scarce resources.

14. Cost–benefit analysis seeks *inter alia* to assign money values to intangibles such as human life saved, time spent, noise avoided and so on in assessing the return to an investment project. Programme budgets classify expenditure on collective or zero-price goods according to outputs rather than inputs, so that more informed decisions can be taken on where to increase or reduce outlays. The cost of the police, for example, is divided into crime detection, traffic control, ground cover, etc., rather than into wages, uniforms, buildings, etc.

15. In November 1961 Mr Selwyn Lloyd's 'pay pause' (see below) was broken by a pay award in the electricity industry. The Government was consulted by the Electricity Council during the negotiations, refused to intervene and then publicly rebuked the Council for the outcome! See Brittan, *Steering the Economy*, p. 164.

16. Progress was also helped by some good appointments to top positions in public industry, such as Lord Robens at the Coal Board, and by the recruitment and training of more economic specialists.

17. The ideological predisposition in favour of monetary policy must not, however, be forgotten. There was no similar enthusiasm for import controls, which the Conservatives reimposed on a big scale in 1951–2 to deal with the balance of payments deficit.

18. Strictly speaking this is a necessity rather than an objective, since it merely reflects the need to live within one's means. In the absence of international

trade or transfers there would be no balances of payments, but the need for each country to live within its resources would remain (indeed would become more compelling, since trade enables countries to specialise according to their comparative advantages in production).

19. R. C. O. Matthews, 'Why has Britain had Full Employment since the War?', *Economic Journal* (1968).

20. There were two particular deficiencies. First, the 'development districts' designated by the Board of Trade under the 1960 Act tended to be too small. Secondly, they were liable suddenly to lose their designation when their unemployment declined and reacquire it when unemployment rose again – which hardly helped firms to plan their investment. For full discussion see Gavin McCrone, *Regional Policy in Britain* (1969) chap. v.

21. Some of the other financial measures were of more doubtful merit, particularly the cheap Exchequer credits for shipbuilding (see Prest, *The U.K. Economy*, p. 187) and the loans to developing countries tied to orders for industry in U.K. depressed areas (see Brittan, *Steering the Economy*, p. 176).

22. For forceful criticism, see Clive Jenkins, 'We Haven't Got Enough' in R. Blackburn and A. Cockburn (eds), *The Incompatibles* (1967). What Mr Jenkins does not make clear is that one of the major reasons for the shortage of retraining facilities is the (literally) medieval attitude of many unions on questions of apprenticeship, skilled status, etc.

23. This was less than half the rate of 1946–52, and also a good deal slower than in 1964–9.

24. It is not generally known that the origins of this report owed a good deal to Sir Robert Hall's desire for influential support in his efforts to convert the U.K. Government to the idea of an incomes policy. However, he left the Treasury just as the report appeared. For some of the other personalities involved in the 1961 policy, see Brittan, *Steering the Economy*, pp. 163–4.

25. Comment tends to focus on injustice to nurses, teachers, etc., when their pay falls behind. But in the long run efficiency is the more valid argument. If some

girls are sufficiently dedicated to become badly paid nurses, that is their choice. But it is not the community's choice to force the closure of hospital wards for lack of such girls.

26. Brittan, *Steering the Economy*, p. 273.

27. Of course, this need not have affected the export propensity if the Government had been prepared to make room for it by cutting other domestic outlays; but continued austerity on the consumption side was electorally risky almost a decade after the war, and domestic investment was (reasonably enough) judged necessary to foster modernisation and growth.

28. *Economic Survey for 1953* (Cmd 8800); and *Radcliffe Report* (Cmd 827) paras 62, 734.

29. Milton Gilbert, 'The Discipline of the Balance of Payments and the Design of the International Monetary System', a Charles C. Moskowitz Lecture presented at New York University, November 1969.

30. See E. J. Mishan, *The Costs of Economic Growth* (1967). The polemical tone of this book should not blind the reader to the incisive and rigorous quality of its analysis.

31. Brittan, *Steering the Economy*, p. 245.

32. The terms of trade did improve by another 6 per cent from 1959 to 1962, but slipped back 3 per cent in 1962–4.

33. The major research here has been done by Professors J. H. Dunning and D. C. Rowan. See their articles in *Business Ratios* (Autumn 1966) and in *Banca Nazionale del Lavoro Quarterly Review* (1965 and 1968). For earlier, more journalistic discussion, see, for example, Rex Malik, *What's Wrong with British Industry?* (1964); Eric Wigham, *What's Wrong with the Unions?* (1961); and Michael Shanks, *The Stagnant Society* (1962).

34. For an excellent discussion of the main arguments, see P. P. Streeten, *Economic Integration: Aspects and Problems* (Leyden, 1963).

35. I. M. D. Little, *Fiscal Policy*, in Worswick and Ady, op. cit. p. 241.

36. Gross fixed non-residential investment as a proportion of G.N.P. from 1955 to 1964 was 14·5 per cent

in the U.K., 17·0 per cent in France, 18·0 per cent in Italy, 21·7 per cent in Germany and 21·8 per cent in the Netherlands. See O.E.C.D., *National Accounts Statistics, 1955–64* (Paris, 1966).

37. N. Kaldor, *Causes of the Slow Rate of Economic Growth of the United Kingdom* (Cambridge, 1966).

38. The industrial and institutional background is described interestingly, though in a very slanted way, by Andrew Shonfield in *Modern Capitalism* (1965).

39. The chief N.E.D.O. reports were *Growth of the U.K. Economy to 1966* and *Conditions Favourable to Faster Growth* (both published in 1965). Brittan points out *Steering the Economy* (p. 282) that the rapid growth of the labour force in the early 1960s made the 4 per cent target moderately rather than grossly over-ambitious. But that was just the trouble: the figure was high enough to cause trouble but low enough for the Government and nationalised industries (at any rate) to take as a basis for policy.

40. The first full piece of analysis on this is R. R. Neild, *Pricing and Employment in the Trade Cycle*, chap. 3, which was published in 1963; but the Treasury forecasters evidently had some suspicion of the relationship by the late 1950s, if not before.

41. Dow, *The Management of the British Economy* chap. v.

42. A. J. Merrett and A. Sykes, *Housing, Development and Finance* (1965) p. 22. The other method of decontrol was through purchase by the tenant making him the owner-occupier.

43. Labour policies in the later sixties did no more to solve this problem than the Tories had. The following structural data may be of interest: at the end of 1963 it was estimated that, out of a total housing stock in Great Britain of 17·1 million dwellings, 44 per cent were owner-occupied, 26 per cent let by local authorities (or government departments) and 30 per cent let by private landlords or housing associations: ibid., p. 27.

44. W. B. Reddaway (assisted by J. O. N. Perkins, S. J. Potter and C. T. Taylor), *Effects of U.K. Direct Investment Overseas, Interim Report* (Cambridge, 1967) and *Final Report* (Cambridge, 1969).

45. The Reddaway finding accords with *a priori* reasoning in that one would expect firms to equalise the marginal *private* returns on home and overseas investment, disregarding the destination of the taxes they have to pay. There are a number of other factors, besides taxes, which suggest that the private propensity to invest overseas may be higher than the social interest would warrant. Of these, the effects on real wages may be the most important.

46. See H. F. Lydall, 'The Long-Term Trend in the Size Distribution of Income', *Journal of the Royal Statistical Society*, series A (1959); and R. J. Nicholson, 'The Distribution of Personal Income', *Lloyds Bank Review* (1967) from which the data in this section are taken.

47. Ibid., p. 17.

48. See R. M. Titmuss, *Income Distribution and Social Change* (1962).

49. Cuts in food subsidies in 1952–3 and 1955 totalled 2 per cent of G.N.P. and offset two-thirds of the net reduction in other taxes (including National Insurance contributions, which were increased) in the years 1952–5. See Dow, *The Management of the British Economy*, Tables 7.6 and 7.7, pp. 200–2.

50. A tax or tax system is defined as progressive, proportional or regressive according as the proportion of income taken in tax rises, remains constant or falls with income. U.K. income tax on the great majority of incomes is only mildly progressive, while indirect taxation is on balance regressive (because of the high taxes on tobacco and alcohol). See A. J. Merrett and D. A. G. Monk, 'The Structure of U.K. Taxation', *Bulletin of the Oxford University Institute of Economics and Statistics* (1967).

5 Lessons of Suez*

Robert Skidelsky

Is there anything new to be said about Suez? Judging
from the mountain of books produced on the subject,
the answer would clearly seem to be no. We now know
almost all that there is to be known – at least from our
side of the story. Egyptian and Russian policy-making
still remain mysterious. Would the Russians have inter-
vened had Britain and France not agreed to a cease-
fire on 6 November? Was Nasser ever prepared seriously
to compromise or negotiate? And if so, what tactics
would have been most efficacious to secure that result?
We cannot be sure. However, there is no reason to
suppose that the present outlines of the story will be
substantially changed in the future.

Why then return to the subject? The answer is,
because the historical treatment has been curiously unsatisfactory. Serious historians have, on the whole, refused to pass judgment. They have fitted together all
the pieces, often with consummate skill.[1] But a certain
timidity, or perhaps ordinary prudence, has inhibited
them from taking up the broader issues. They have preferred to remain above, or perhaps below, the battle of
ideas. The partisan accounts tend to be faulty in
another way. They assume agreement with (largely) un-
stated premises or prejudices, Left-wing or Right-wing,
pro-Arab or pro-Israeli. They do not really pretend
to present a reasoned case one way or the other. An exception is Professor Herman Finer's *Dulles over Suez,*
a powerfully argued condemnation of American foreign
policy in the crisis. Anthony Nutting's recent pro-Arab
book on Suez is entitled *No End of a Lesson,* but I cannot
for the life of me discover what the lesson is meant to be.

To make up for their lack of a truly critical approach
to the arguments advanced in 1956, the historians have

* See chronology on p. 191.

168

resorted to some fashionable psychologising. The Anglo-French reaction to the nationalisation of the Suez Canal has been described as an 'imperial reflex' – a reaction based on prejudices and attitudes inherited from the nineteenth century but quite inappropriate to the modern world. But historians have been loath to define what these attitudes were and to explain exactly why they were inappropriate. Hugh Thomas suggests that the graceful surrender of Empire and influence had built up vast resentments in Britain which demanded for their release a 'spot of adventure', 'a daring stroke', one last final fling, before the nation was prepared to settle down to sedate and unexciting middle age.

Eden's actions have been subjected to similar psychological, even physiological, scrutiny. The Tory Press's demands for the 'smack of firm government' began to prey on his over-sensitive nature; he wanted to prove himself a Churchill; his political position needed restoring by a bold coup. Illness played its part: 'the poison from the damaged bile-duct', writes Anthony Nutting, 'was eating away at his whole system'. Thus he too was driven into deviation: for a mad, intoxicating moment, Talleyrand saw himself as Napoleon.

These explanations are not without value or interest, but they should not absolve the historian from the task of examining the actual reasons adduced and arguments deployed. Professor Popper has described as 'a widespread and dangerous fashion of our time ... the fashion of not taking arguments seriously, and at their face value ... but of seeing in them nothing but a way in which deeper irrational motives and tendencies express themselves'. The historians of Suez have by no means been immune from this fashion.

This historical approach is particularly disappointing because Suez brought into sharp focus certain fundamental questions about the nature of our response to the modern world: questions about the morality and practicability of the use of force in the nuclear age; questions about the consequences of the new nationalisms for peace and international order; questions about the role of Britain in the world and the purpose and scope of the United Nations. In other

169

words, the Suez episode has many lessons to offer which the historical literature has largely ignored, or dealt with only by implication.

It may be objected that history has no lessons to teach; that each historical situation, like every other kind of situation, is unique. Yet people's thoughts and actions are in fact modified by experience; and history is, after all, only a special kind of experience.

In fact the main participants in the Suez drama were very free in their appeals to history. Much anti-Suez opinion argued that the price of attempting to solve disputes by force had become unacceptably high. Others thought that what Eden was trying to do was, in a vague way, historically 'not on'. 'Suppose', E. H. Carr wrote in his book *What is History?*, 'that someone informed you that he proposed to devote himself to conducting a campaign for the reunion of [Britain and America] under the British crown; you would probably reply that he would be wasting his time. If you tried to explain why ... you might even commit the cardinal sin of speaking of history with a capital H and tell him that History was against him.' Pro-Suez opinion, as is well known, set great store by the 'lessons of Munich'. It viewed Nasser with eyes haunted by the vision of Hitler, and argued that experience showed that the appeasement of force merely whetted dangerous appetites. Even Eisenhower searched round, somewhat desperately, for historical arguments to convince Eden of the need for patience. In the first draft of a letter, he wrote: 'It took your nation some eighteen years to put the original Napoleon in his place.' The sentence was cut out when Dulles pointed out that Napoleon had been overthrown by force.

There is another motive for returning to the subject of Suez at this moment. Every account so far has preceded the Arab–Israel war of 1967. Certain complacent observations uttered before that event now appear, to say the least, somewhat dated; for example, the comment in the B.B.C. symposium *Suez Ten Years After*: 'The Canal today is, of course, in better condition than it was before the Suez crisis began'; or again Herbert Nicholas's remarks in the same book: 'What the world

actually got out of Suez was ... a peace-keeping force.'[2]
The conclusions which follow from these statements
need revision.

Historians apart, informed opinion was nevertheless
bound to draw certain conclusions from the Suez affair.
And the failure of the Right's policy has seemed in
retrospect to vindicate the view of the Left, viz., that
the attempt to discipline smaller nations by Great
Power force having failed, as it was bound to fail, the
only secure hope of international peace and order lay
in strengthening the United Nations. In my view the
attitude of the Left has turned out to be as illusory as
the policy of the Right was obsolete; and in the following pages I will try to indicate why.

If the initial British reaction to Nasser's nationalisation decree of 26 July, 1956 was an 'imperial reflex',
then it was certainly one very largely shared among all
sections of opinion. The Press and Parliament were
unanimous in condemning his action. But what is of
interest is the terms of the condemnation. Imperial and
Great Power affront were very much in the background;
what we heard was the authentic voice of liberal internationalism raised up in protest against the actions and
style of nationalistic dictatorship. This was as true of
Conservative reaction as of Labour. There is a tendency
to regard the authentic voice of Conservatism as the
voice of a primitive atavism; but as E. H. Carr has more
justly remarked, 'a typical English Conservative ...
when scratched turns out to be 75 per cent a liberal'.

Now how does this reaction square with that of imperial affront? Are we to reject the 'imperial reflex'
thesis? By no means; for the two terms, imperialism
and internationalism, are, in British experience, very
largely interchangeable.

By imperialism we mean that process whereby the
major white nations established a hegemony, physical,
economic and cultural, over the rest of the world. Now
it is perfectly true that Nasser's action threatened
British hegemony in the Middle East, latterly based on
the Baghdad Pact and the Hashemite dynasties in Iraq
and Jordan; although Eden undoubtedly overestimated

171

Nasser's power to enforce the rather romantic dreams of Arab power outlined in his book *Philosophy of Revolution*. His action also challenged Britain's economic interests: the uninterrupted flow of oil was vital to the British economy. As Eden put it, a man of Nasser's record could not be allowed to 'have his thumb on our windpipe'. Personal antipathies played their part: both Eden and Pineau, the French Foreign Minister, detested Nasser. 'I want him destroyed, can't you understand?', Eden bellowed over the telephone to Anthony Nutting. The French believed that Nasser's destruction was the key to victory in Algeria.

But that is by no means the whole story, or even perhaps the major part of it. For it does not exhaust the definition of imperialism to say that it is the domination of one power over others. It establishes common conceptions and systems of law and justice, rights and obligations; it promotes economic interdependence; it preserves peace, stability and order beyond the bounds of the nation-state; it encourages the intermingling of peoples and the interchange of ideas; all of which to the internationalist are undeniably good things, even if, in the case of empire, they stem from the original act of force or colonisation. The British were the true internationalists among the nineteenth-century empire-builders. Owing to its island position and its early reliance on trade, Britain had pioneered the idea of economic interdependence. The free movement of capital and goods, the prompt payment of debts, the sanctity of contract, freedom of navigation, international peace and stability – these were all national interests which evolved over time into an international code of mutual benefit. This code flourished in the confidence that every reasonable person would recognise it to be in his own best interest that it should; with the true cultural evangelism typical of the age, the nineteenth-century English liberal did not doubt that God had given to the British nation the duty of universalising the principles of true felicity, and looked forward to the time when such residual Great Power supports as economic sanctions and the British Navy would no longer be necessary.

To the critic – whether in nineteenth-century Berlin or in mid-twentieth-century Cairo – it seemed only too obvious that the true felicity these principles ministered to was that of the English middle classes, and that the facts which sustained them had less to do with universal human nature than with British economic and naval strength. With his eyes fixed on the vistas of universal free trade, universal democracy, universal disarmament and world government, the English liberal gave little thought to the energies, frustrations, resentments and passions bottled up by the Pax Britannica.

Balkanisation ought to have given him a clue as to the likely outcome of a withdrawal of imperial power; but at the time he believed that there was nothing in that situation that could not be put right by a railway from Berlin to Baghdad and the development of democratic institutions. The First World War was a more profound shock, but that could just about be explained away as the last agonised writhings of the beast in man. Since then the shocks have come fast, furious and frightening: the world economic collapse of the 1930s, Hitlerism, Stalinism, Auschwitz, Hiroshima, the nuclear threat, racial struggle, surging nationalisms, the ever-shrinking area of liberal democracy. It was certainly a period of transition, but it was less easy to feel optimistic about the outcome. The favourite international institutions beloved of the liberal mind seemed at best marginal: instead of the concert of powers envisaged by the United Nations, there was the balance of terror.

Yet the English liberals clung to their faith in world order and British responsibility for it, even though the voices of men like Eden and Gaitskell seemed particularly ill-attuned to the increasingly raucous noises of Black Power and White Power, of Red Guards and Young Turks. They spoke of 'theft' and 'law' when something more primitive stirred. They crossed Parliamentary swords with old-fashioned courtesy, while the sorcerer from Cairo 'conjured up from the bowels of the earth the legions of hate and fury'.

The deepest theme of Suez is, as Martin Wight well puts it, 'the quest for civilised behaviour in a world of dissolving standards'. Both Eden and Gaitskell, for all their inability to get on with each other – Eden wrote of Gaitskell: 'in all my years of political life I had not met anyone with his cast of mind and approach to problems'[3] – shared a civilised, middle-class disgust at the actions and style of an upstart and a *parvenu*. Both men had felt the same about Hitler, and would have felt the same about any Englishman who had challenged his opponents with the words 'May you choke to death on your fury'. As Morrison put it, 'it is not a civilised . . . way of conducting business'. Nuri es-Said, an ex-Ottoman aristocrat, would not have acted like that not just because he knew which side his bread was buttered on, but because it would have been beneath his dignity. In Nasser's place he might have accomplished most of what Nasser accomplished in real terms, without evoking anything like the same response. Hitler, too, could have got 80 per cent of what he wanted, without unduly alarming the Western powers, had he behaved more reasonably.

Both Eden and Gaitskell were, of course, conditioned by the experience of Hitler. Indeed Gaitskell was the first Parliamentary speaker to draw this analogy: 'it is all very familiar. It is exactly the same that we encountered from Mussolini and Hitler . . . before the war.' What impressed them was the similarity in style rather than the similarity in power; and if Britain's security was not directly at stake in the same way, Israel's certainly was. Like Hitler, Nasser was out for theatrical effects. 'He wanted,' said Gaitskell, 'to make a big impression. Quiet negotiation, discussion round a table . . . would not produce this effect.' And this was why both Tory and Labour leaders felt that he could not be trusted. He was not a gentleman – unlike General Neguib, for whom Eden cherished fond memories. He had 'torn up' agreements concluded with the Company only a few weeks before. He had acted, according to Gaitskell, 'suddenly, without negotiation, without discussion, by force'. 'One can have no confidence – no confidence', Eden repeated the word for emphasis, 'in the behaviour of a man who does that.'

The consequences for the international order of the new nationalisms exemplified by Nasser's Egypt were thus well to the forefront of the early Parliamentary debates on Suez. Two statements illustrate the point. First, Herbert Morrison (Labour):

> I say ... that we can have a situation in which the foe of genuine internationalism can be the modern nationalist, hysterical state, determined to act on its own irrespective of the interests of the rest of the world.[4]

Second, Sir Robert Boothby (Conservative):

> I believe that the rabid nationalism which is now developing is reactionary and atavistic – a revolt against the demands of the modern world and of life itself. ... [Nasser's language] is the language of Hitler and the rule of the jungle; and if we were to allow him to get away with it, it would be a most damaging blow to the whole conception of international law....[5]

Few Labour, and no Conservative, M.P.s dissented from these remarks. An exception was Anthony Wedgwood Benn who, pointing out that the Company concession would in any case revert to Egypt in 1968, asked: 'Can it possibly be an act of aggression to anticipate something that would be lawful in twelve years time?' – which showed at any rate that Wedgwood Benn had a strange idea of law. On the whole, though, Epstein is perfectly right in his summary that 'there was no substantial dissent from the Prime Minister's statement ... that Britain could not accept an arrangement leaving the canal in the unfettered control of a single power'.[6]

It could be argued that this arrangement had in fact been accepted by the British Government in 1954 when it agreed to withdraw its troops from the Canal base. At that time Antony Head, later the Minister in charge of the military preparations against Colonel Nasser, had said: 'I do not see the slightest reason why the Egyptian Government should close the Suez Canal, because it is as much of a life-line to them as to anyone else.'[7] Jo Grimond was more sceptical: 'Have the Government any proposals for putting the Canal under international control or putting in an international force to protect it, if we are not there ourselves?', he asked.[8] In Eden's defence it could be said that at that time Neguib, a moderate, was still in power; the regime, according to Eden, 'showed no signs as yet of those wider ambitions which Colonel Nasser was later to proclaim and pursue'.[9] Besides, the Company's presence seemed to offer practical guarantees of effective maintenance, service and development of the Canal; it was a buffer between Nasser and physical control of the Canal, which is why Eden was later to claim that it was an integral part of the 1888 system guaranteeing free navigation.

The common aim of the British Government and Opposition was thus to restore some kind of international control of the Canal; but differences soon emerged as to the means. It has sometimes been claimed that the Labour Party retreated from the strong stand taken in Gaitskell's speech of 2 August, 1956. Technically this is not so. Such inconsistencies as were to emerge in the Labour position were already present in that speech. What Gaitskell said may be paraphrased as follows: Nasser's action was abhorrent to civilised people; it reminded him of the style and methods of Hitler and Mussolini; it was not only a challenge to the West's position in the Middle East which had to be taken up, but also vitally threatened the future of Israel, and of civilised international behaviour. But the British Government in its reaction to that challenge must not go beyond the measures laid down in the United Nations Charter. These limited the use of force to self-defence or to collective military measures approved by the United Nations. It followed that Britain would be justified in using force if the United Nations sanctioned it; but 'we must not ... allow ourselves to get into a position where we might be denounced in the Security Council as aggressors, or where the majority of the Assembly were against us'. Earlier he had laid it down as a principle of British foreign policy to avoid 'any international action ... contrary to the public opinion of the world'.[10] Eden agreed with Gaitskell's assessment of Nasser's action, but he argued that it followed from that assessment that Britain should as a last resort be prepared to use force to impose international control even if United Nations authorisation was withheld.

These differences became clearer in the debate of 12–13 September. By this point the Government had committed a major tactical error. The sequence of events as originally envisaged by Eden seems quite clear and straightforward. First there was to be the 22-Power Conference; if that failed to find a satisfactory solution, there was to be an appeal to the Security Council; if that failed, the military expedition was to sail. The recall of Parliament in September was to coincide with the second stage of this strategy, the appeal to the United Nations. This was the 'clean line' that would have made it difficult for the Labour Party to divide the House.

This strategy was sabotaged by Dulles. He saw that the Anglo-French proposals would be vetoed by Russia in the Security Council, giving the British and French Governments an excuse to use force. He was determined to keep the parties talking, come what may, till after the United States presidential election. He therefore introduced the red herring of the Suez Canal Users' Association, 'the poisoned apple' as Finer puts it, or in Paul Johnson's words 'The Dulles Double-Cross'. Briefly this plan envisaged a consortium of users who would sail their ships in convoy through the Canal, using their own pilots and paying dues to a central office and not to Nasser. If Nasser tried to stop the users' ships, Dulles argued persuasively to Eden, then that would be a breach of the 1888 convention justifying stronger measures. Eden, in an effort to keep the Americans on his side, acquiesced reluctantly in this extraordinary proposal. But the Dulles plan made sense only if it was backed by sanctions. As Dulles gradually made clear, he intended none: he could not force American ships to pay dues to the Association rather than to Nasser; and if Nasser stopped the ships, well, then they would have to sail round the Cape. To the

177

British Labour Opposition the plan seemed both provocative and ineffective. They urged Eden to abandon it and go straight to the United Nations. When he refused, they voted against him.

Eden's capitulation to Dulles enabled the Opposition to claim that it was in favour of going to UNO while Eden was not. It obscured the real point at issue which was what would happen at and· after UNO? What should be done if the Russian veto were applied, or if, as was very likely, Britain and France failed to secure the support of the General Assembly, or even if, having secured a favourable resolution, Nasser ignored it? These questions the Opposition resolutely refused to face.

Since the appeal to UNO remained a purely hypothetical proposition on 12 September, 1956, the Labour Opposition was able to claim that Nasser was an honourable man; that he would, in the last resort, be prepared to respect the rule of law, provided only that sufficient 'moral' pressure was brought to bear on him. Indeed, they had to take this line, for they knew perfectly well that UNO would not sanction the use of force against him. Indeed the Labour Party was in a painful dilemma. For if Nasser were like Hitler, then only the threat of force would stop him; yet the Labour Party was renouncing the threat of force. This renunciation entailed a revision of Nasser's psychology. He was no longer a Hitler; his admitted refusal hitherto to negotiate had to be explained in other ways.

Thus the Opposition devoted the debate of 12–13 September to the task of rescuing Nasser from Gaitskell's unfortunate comparison of 2 August. His intransigence was now blamed on Allied provocation. Robens argued that he had refused to compromise because he felt 'insulted'; Eden's words were 'provocative'.[11] Kenneth Younger went further. 'The trouble was that [the 18-Power Plan's] chances of acceptance were largely ruined by its being put in the context of the Anglo-French threats.' He doubted whether even 'the Soviet Union would have opposed us if we had gone to the Security Council . . .'.[12] Crossman declared that if only 'the Government had started negotiating straight away,

178

a settlement could have been reached which would have been regarded as perfectly honourable and would not have looked like a triumph for Nasser'. Yet a moment later he declared that any settlement would have to end Egypt's right to blockade Israel. How easily, one wonders, would a settlement have been reached with that stipulation?[13]

Menzies formed a different estimate of Nasser's psychology, more in keeping with Gaitskell's original assessment. Eisenhower's renunciation of the use of force, Menzies wrote, fortified Nasser in his belief that all he had to do was to 'sit tight, reject the Dulles proposals, reject any watered-down proposals ... and continue the process until he had "written his own ticket". Meanwhile his practical grasp of the Canal would be consolidated, and the *fait* would be completely *accompli*.' Menzies' conclusion was: 'I cannot regard it as an element in statesmanship to relieve one's opponent of anxiety.'[14]

One or two Labour speakers did, it is true, deal with the possibility of frustration at UNO, but in an inconclusive way. Robens argued that 'a breach of a United Nations resolution would be a challenge to world authority, and no Government could successfully do that' – adding, it seems as an afterthought, perhaps remembering Israel, 'if the United Nations is to survive'.[15] Arthur Henderson, the son of Labour's 1929 Foreign Secretary, said that the correct procedure was to go to the Security Council, and if the Russians vetoed the Western proposals there, to activate the Uniting for Peace Resolution; this would give Britain the 'moral authority to enforce the recommendation'. Suppose UNO refused to recommend anything? 'That would be a clear indication,' Henderson went on, 'that we cannot look to the Charter as the instrument for safeguarding the security of the various nations of the world.'[16] In that case, would Britain be justified in using force on its own? Henderson did not say.

Instead the Labour Party as a whole contented itself with the restatement of the principle that no action must be taken contrary to the United Nations Charter. Force should only be used 'within the Charter'.[17] Given the composition of the United Nations, the Labour stand, in Epstein's words, amounted to 'the advocacy of inaction'.[18]

The United States position was equally ambivalent. In view of the fact that none of its own vital interests were involved, it could afford to take the high moral line; at the same time Dulles and Eisenhower did give Eden grounds for belief that in the event of an Anglo-French recourse to force, the United States would preserve a benevolent neutrality. In public, Eisenhower contented himself with statements whose moral flavour must have seemed as hypocritical as their meaning was obscure – for example, the following on 11 September:

> Now, if they are guaranteed the free use, then it – and it says – and then provides methods by which co-operation with Egypt may be achieved, I think that they are justified probably in taking steps and conferring with President Nasser looking forward to the free use of the Canal. But I don't – that doesn't mean that they are justified at that moment in using force. I don't think that – I think this: We established the United Nations to abolish aggression, and I am not going to be a party to aggression if it is humanly possible or likely to lead – to avoid or I can detect it before it occurs.[19]

The Anglo-French reaction to Nasser seemed to justify all Dulles's suspicions of colonialism and imperialism. Like all the actors in the Suez affair, he too was captive to a historical dream – that of America's mission to cleanse the world of the evils of colonialism, whether Soviet or British. In 1938 he had argued that the British and the French, with the typical arrogance of the 'haves', were trying to deprive such impoverished 'have-nots' as Germany and Italy of their rightful place in the sun. His arguments had not changed much since the 1930s.

Nor for that matter had the Labour Party's. They too were repeating in the new situation lines learned long ago. They wanted to stop Nasser, like Hitler, through collective security; they were even prepared to suggest force, so long as the actual question of using force never arose. And yet in the 1930s there was more excuse for trusting in collective security than in 1956. For then the League of Nations was dominated by big powers who at least had an interest in stopping Hitler; in 1956 it was dominated by the smaller powers willing to condone or support Nasser.

Of course, there was a new factor in the situation: the threat of a nuclear holocaust. 'The advent of the hydrogen bomb,' declared Aneurin Bevan, 'has stalemated power among the great Powers. The use of the threat of war ... is no longer available to statesmen ... without running the risk of universal destruction.'[20] This is a perfectly tenable view, but it was not the reason given by the Labour Party for its opposition to unilateral action. For in theory it was perfectly prepared to use force – if the United Nations agreed. And the threat of nuclear destruction might have applied equally to the collective as well as to the individual use of force. For example, would a United Nations intervention to stop Russia in Hungary or Czechoslovakia have been safe from nuclear retaliation?

Logically, Bevan's argument implied complete pacifism. It gave a *carte blanche* to the blackmailer anywhere in the world. He would have been on much firmer ground had he argued that in this case there was no British interest at stake sufficiently vital to run the risk of nuclear war. But, as I have indicated earlier, the argument was never primarily conducted in terms of interests. Had it been so, a more realistic debate could have developed round this very question, giving both sides an opportunity to consider in concrete terms what Nasser's action actually involved. What *actual* difference would it make to Britain's position? Would it deprive her of oil supplies? Could alternative supplies or routes be developed? These questions were hardly considered. In the evolution of British world attitudes they had become secondary to the moral aim of preserving civilised standards wherever Britain had once exercised responsibility – the mentality of a superannuated nanny.

The real dilemma of the Labour Party was different.

It had inherited the liberal ideal of orderly international behaviour, which it interpreted largely in terms of universalising British values. In other words, it willed the *end* of bringing back the Suez Canal to international control. But it could not bring itself to accept the means. It had a deeply ingrained hostility to the use of force, partly pacifist, partly 'progressive'. It had a deep mistrust of the motives of a Conservative Government. For, as in the 1930s when it was a question of supplying the National Government with the armaments to oppose Hitler, the Labour Party half suspected that the 'civilised' designs of the Conservative leaders were a cover for more sinister intentions. Only a Labour Government, in other words, could be entrusted with the use of force. For a Labour Opposition, therefore, the appeal to UNO, like the earlier reliance on the League, provided an ideal escape from the world of painful choices. It enabled a fine flourish of moral indignation at the expense of Eden and Nasser – and of reality.

If Labour's position was in the end impervious to facts, so, for different reasons, was Eden's. Let us concede that Eden had a reasonable grievance against Nasser. That alone would not be sufficient to justify the use of force. The aim of war is to secure a change for the better. If the result of war is going to mean a change for the worse, either because one will not be able to win it, or because the price may be too high, there can be no justification in starting it, however strong one's moral position. As John Vincent put it: 'Had the Final Solution been German policy in 1939, its wickedness would have afforded no reason for war, unless we had reason to suppose that war would enable us favourably to change matters.'[21] This kind of consideration is clearly a decisive constraint on the pursuit of a 'moral' foreign policy. Many people in 1956 were horrified at Russian action in Hungary. But they judged, rightly or wrongly, that the price of intervention was too high.

Eden can be criticised, then, for threatening and making war on two grounds: (1) that Britain lacked, even in conjunction with France, the military capability of mounting an action within the time-span necessary to secure immunity from wider adverse reactions; and (2) that even if the action had been militarily successful, there was no real possibility of gaining the political fruits of victory.

The military aspect of the Suez crisis has to be set in the context of the British decision of 1954 to withdraw from the Canal base; indeed Nasser nationalised the Canal about a month after the last British troops left. It is worth recalling the House of Commons debate in 1954. The chief strategic argument advanced by the Government was that the base had become untenable in the nuclear age; the chief political argument, that it was impossible to maintain a military base in a hostile environment. At that time everyone was obsessed by the Russian menace. This was the age of 'massive retaliation'. Dulles's strategy, to which the British Government subscribed, envisaged placing the whole of the non-Communist world under a gigantic nuclear umbrella. This had two basic weaknesses. It ignored the problem of what to do in circumstances when neither side would be prepared to risk nuclear war; and secondly, the Russian obsession blinded military planners to the possibility of disturbances which in themselves had little or nothing to do with the global Cold War situation. Perceptive critics of the Eden policy made this point in the 1954 debate; for example, Grimond said: 'surely what we are faced with very often is not a world war or a hydrogen bomb war, but local aggression ... such as we may see in the Middle East. It is against that sort of attack that we have to provide defences, just as much as for a full-scale world war with hydrogen bombs.'[22] At the time, these opinions were ignored.

The main Labour charge in 1954 was that the withdrawal had left a vacuum in the Middle East, potentially dangerous for Israel. The Government's reply took two forms. It pointed out that the base could be reactivated under certain conditions; and secondly, it claimed as a benefit of its policy a great gain in strategic mobility. Eden, replying to Attlee, said: 'There is no vacuum because as a result of these arrangements we shall be able to redeploy our forces and make them mobile to an extent which they have not been hitherto.' This policy implied building up a highly mobile strategic reserve, capable of being moved rapidly to centres of disturbance – a policy which would have permitted a rapid military reaction to Nasser's moves in 1956. But no such preparations were made before 1956.

To preserve some kind of effective presence in the Middle East, a number of Labour and Conservative speakers, including Crossman and Wigg, made a surprising suggestion: to set up a British base, with Israeli agreement, at Haifa.[23] This would serve the dual purpose of enabling British troops to get back rapidly into the Canal Zone should the need arise, and perhaps, more importantly, of deterring or dissuading Nasser from doing anything rash, such as moving against Israel or taking over the Canal. This suggestion was not followed up. The doctrine of 'massive retaliation' was designed to deter the Soviet Union; but there was nothing in existence that could possibly deter Nasser. The abandonment of the base in 1954 without thinking through clearly the political and military consequences was to cost the British Government dear in 1956.

Eden's inquiries at the end of July 1956 revealed that there was no chance of an immediate military riposte. There was no contingency plan for the reoccupation of the Canal Zone; parachutists had had no recent training; in any case there were no aircraft available to transport them. It was an axiom of British military planning that paratroops had to be supported within twenty-four hours. Yet the nearest feasible base, Cyprus, had no suitable harbours for naval ships; the naval expedition would have to sail from Malta, a thousand miles and six days' sailing time away. The shipping required had to be gathered together from all parts of the world; landing craft had to be got out of mothballs where they had lain since the Normandy landings of 1944. The French had similar difficulties. The fact was that the conventional military strategy of both powers was NATO-oriented; neither Britain nor France possessed an 'intervention' force, a commando group with its own aviation, shipping, amphibious vehicles, tanks

184

and artillery held in constant readiness for swift independent action. Moreover, even within NATO there was an absence of the integration that could have facilitated a joint operation. The British and French used a different type of rifle, different shell calibres, different bolt threads and engines for vehicles, different petrol, oils and lubricants, different signals and battle orders, and of course spoke different languages. 'The British soldiers,' the Brombergers observe, 'drink tea which makes the French soldiers throw up. French soldiers eat sardines in oil, which revolt the Tommies.'

Yet even when most of these difficulties had been overcome and the expedition stood ready to move by early September, the fundamental difficulty had not been resolved: namely, how to get the force into the Canal Zone quickly enough to forestall decisive political pressures at home and abroad. The military preparations, it seems, took no account of the international climate in which they would have to be conducted. The demands of each service escalated as each sought maximum security against real or imagined dangers. The expedition's scale, as one commentator remarks, 'was determined by prognosis of the very worst'. The result was that in the end a colossal armada was assembled: 80,000 troops, 150 warships, including 7 aircraft-carriers and 40 submarines; hundreds of landing craft, 80 merchant ships carrying stores; 20,000 vehicles. The French were more realistic. They wanted the emphasis placed on paratroop landings. The British remembered Arnhem and refused to contemplate using paratroops except as an advance guard of a much larger force. In vain, the French protested that it was the Suez Canal, not the Kiel Canal; that they were to fight Egyptians and not Germans. The British replied that as they had largely trained the Egyptian Army, it must be good.

In the event, the military and political difficulties were compounded by a double error. The first was the Anglo-French decision to use the Israeli attack as a pretext for their own intervention; the second was Eden's moral scruples about taking advantage of the foreknowledge he had of the Israeli attack to send the fleet from Malta in advance of the delivery of the ultimatum on 30 October. The less important consequence of the first mistake was to hold back the Anglo-French expedition for at least a fortnight while plans were co-ordinated with the Israelis. The more important consequence was to rob the Anglo-French intervention of any plausible connection with the initial action of Nasser to which it was intended as a riposte. Eden was forced to renounce the initial justification of force for the much weaker one of 'separating the combatants' – on terms manifestly to Egypt's disadvantage – a shift which largely destroyed Britain's moral position. The consequence of the second error was to delay the military operation for almost a week when every minute was vital to its success. As Elizabeth Monroe rightly observes, 'Deeds that stood a chance of taking the world's breath away if done quickly stood none by Day Six.' By the time the Anglo-French expedition was finally ready to go into action, Eden was in the process of being forced into a political capitulation.

Could he have resisted? Churchill is supposed to have said: 'I am not sure I should have dared to start, but I am sure I should not have dared to stop.' Dulles, after doing his best to sabotage the expedition, remarked to the British delegate at UNO: 'Why on earth didn't you go through with it?' Hugh Thomas has summed up as follows: 'Probably there would have been neither world war nor devaluation if we had continued for [twenty-four hours], and, having got so far, the morale of the Army and the Entente Cordiale, that incomparable friendship, would have been better served by going on at Suez. But the risk was imponderable....'[24] In the end it was the logic of the very internationalism for which Eden had gone to war that ruined him: he could not act in defiance of world opinion.

The cumbersome military preparations were not entirely the fault of the military planners. They were not given any clear indication of the political objective that force was meant to accomplish. The Government's instructions to them were of the vaguest kind: 'to mount joint operations against Egypt to restore the Suez Canal to international control'. What exactly did this involve? Would Egypt have to be reoccupied or not? Would a new Government be found for Cairo? These problems were never cleared up. The Army planners, having to divine government intentions, envisaged landings in Alexandria and Cairo leading to a temporary military occupation of Egypt; these were later altered to landings in the Canal Zone itself. The Government probably hoped it would not come to that; they seemed to assume that, with the appearance of Anglo-French forces in Egypt, Nasser would flee the country and the people would rally to the 'idol of the masses' General Neguib, or even more improbably to the discredited Nahas Pasha, the old Wafd leader. Some curiously inept leaflets were dropped over Egypt during the phase of 'psychological bombing' early in November to promote these ends. With the assumption of a friendly Government and a docile population, Eden did not have to think far beyond the military landings. But one of the chief reasons for the evacuation in 1954 was the belief that a base could not be maintained in a hostile country. And it seems clear that the British Government had given very little thought about what to do if the Egyptian people refused to accept their 'temporary occupation', but launched a guerrilla and sabotage campaign of the type common in other countries, and even then in progress in Cyprus. How, in particular, could the Canal be kept open in such circumstances? And how could there be any guarantee that oil from the other Arab countries would be kept flowing?

These were gigantic risks, and there is no evidence that they were weighed properly in considering the use of force. It may be that they would have turned out well. One cannot agree with Bevan's comment that 'the heroism of the civilian, as displayed in Hungary, makes nonsense of the power of tanks'.[25] In fact the power of tanks made nonsense of the heroism of the civilian. But Soviet Russia, in the maintenance of its interests in Hungary, was prepared to use force to a degree that would be considered entirely unacceptable for a democratic and liberal power like England. By using force at Suez without having a realistic and realisable

187

political objective, the Eden Government violated the fundamental maxim of war.

In the Suez débâcle, both Eden and Gaitskell were prisoners of an illusion – the illusion of Britain's special mission to preserve peace, law and stability in the world.

It arose in the imperial era, when, with superb effrontery, the British tried to remake millions of Asians and Africans – not to mention Europeans – in their own image; tried to enforce on them, or persuade them into, a code of behaviour which, while in keeping with Britain's own interests, could be generalised as a solvent for the world's problems. The Labour Party inherited the idea, divested it of its imperialist trimmings, infused it with a moral fervour, and tried to apply it through such post-imperialist institutions as the League of Nations, the United Nations and the Commonwealth of Nations. It was the white man's burden all over again.

The Suez crisis exposed its hollowness. Britain had neither the power nor the will to make it work. For the old international order depended on the existence of powerful policemen, confident in their right to impose the law in the areas under their control, and able to do so. Eden dubbed the Suez intervention a 'police operation'. Yet the post-imperial British policeman not only lacked credibility, in view of the existence of more powerful policemen round him, hostile to his pretensions, but perhaps, more importantly, lacked the old faith in his mission. He no longer believed that he had right overwhelmingly on his side. He had been educated for years into the belief that imperialism, the fact of power that made possible all his illusions, was dirty, exploitative and ignoble. He could no longer believe that he was acting from the loftiest, disinterested motives. Wasn't Suez really about preserving the oil companies, the Baghdad Pact, the client states, the whole system of influence, patronage and corruption which served Britain's Middle Eastern interests?

The British spokesmen appealed to world opinion and received the biggest shock of all. The United States refused to co-operate; the United Nations sided with the law-breaker, as did the Asian and African members of the Commonwealth; the white dominions extended only lukewarm support; most of Europe remained indifferent; while France came in from much less worthy motives, motives that had to be smothered by a pillow of cloudy international rhetoric. With dawning horror, the British realised that they were totally out of touch with the sentiment and feelings of the rest of the world.

If anything the Labour Party's illusion ran deeper. The Tories' concept of their post-imperial responsibilities rested upon the illusion of power. Once that illusion was shattered, little remained of that concept; the way was opened to joining Europe. But the Labour Party's illusion rested on something that no mere harsh facts could dispose of. The old imperial idea had been transposed into a dream of world brotherhood. It rested on the repudiation of power, the repudiation, in fact, of everything that goes up to make the real world. It was an imperialism with all the pain, the injustice, the cruelty and the oppression conjured out of existence by magic. It was the imperialism of the intelligentsia, both an atonement for past sins and a guarantee of status without tears.

Yet it must not be this illusion that goes down in history as the lesson of Suez. For the fact was that the United Nations failed to redress the wrong which most British people felt had been perpetrated by Colonel Nasser; what is more, it never stood a real chance of doing so. In the desperation of failure, the Eden Government claimed that at least it had given teeth to UNO. But in reality the United Nations proved quite incapable of preserving peace in the Middle East. For the resolution setting up the peace-keeping force accepted the original British contention that it was impossible to maintain a military position in a hostile country, and thus stipulated that it remain in Egypt only as long as Egypt wanted it to. In 1967 Egypt asked it to leave – and it did.

In the wake of Britain's final withdrawal from the role of a world power, and the increasing difficulties of the American position in Vietnam – difficulties which make it extremely unlikely that the United States will take on a similar commitment again – the collapse of a Western-sustained international order threatens to become complete. The world East of Suez at any rate is likely to undergo drastic and probably violent changes, over which the Western powers and UNO will have very little influence.

These changes will not be understood with a simple model of the replacement of Western-style internationalism by Communist-style internationalism; that would be replacing one kind of illusion by another. The Communist bloc, it seems, is subject to very much the same fissiparous and centrifugal tendencies as the non-Communist bloc. The convulsions in Eastern Europe, and the Sino-Soviet conflict, point to the break-up of the Communist monolith; 'working-class' imperialism has had an even shorter history than 'capitalist' imperialism.

With the decay of Utopian dreams of internationalism, whether of the Western or Marxist variety, a new politics is coming to the fore – a politics of race and regionalism. We may expect an increasing tendency to regional power blocs based on a common culture, or common economic interests, or a common enemy, or a combination of all three; each pledged to defend its integrity against outside interference. Any such concentrations of regional power will probably be accompanied by the creation of nuclear armaments, common market trading patterns, and common institutions. The old internationalists will not welcome any of these developments; but they offer perhaps the best hope of stability in a world in which empire is obsolete, nationalism destructive, and internationalism further away than ever.

Notes

1. e.g. Hugh Thomas, *The Suez Affair* (1967).
2. A. Moncrieff (ed.), *Suez Ten Years After* (1967) pp. 130, 139.

3. Earl of Avon, *The Eden Memoirs: Full Circle* (1960) p. 320.

4. *Hansard*, vol. 557, col. 1660.

5. Ibid., vol. 558, cols 143–4.

6. L. Epstein, *British Politics in the Suez Crisis* (1964), p. 64.

7. *Hansard*, vol. 531, col. 760.

8. Ibid., col. 785.

9. *Full Circle*, p. 260.

10. *Hansard*, vol. 557, cols. 1616–17.

11. Ibid., vol. 558, col. 176.

12. Ibid., cols. 334–5.

13. Ibid., cols. 91, 93–4.

14. R. G. Menzies, *Afternoon Light* (1967) pp. 165–6.

15. *Hansard*, vol. 558, col. 181.

16. Ibid., cols 40 f.

17. Ibid., col. 137.

18. Epstein, *British Politics in the Suez Crisis*, p. 67.

19. Department of State, *The Suez Canal Problem* (1957) 26 July–22 September 1956, p. 333.

20. *Hansard*, vol. 558, cols. 1708–9.

21. *Cambridge Review*, 1 May 1965.

22. *Hansard*, vol. 531, col. 785.

23. Ibid., cols. 760, 770, 791.

24. Thomas, *The Suez Affair*, p. 164.

25. Paul Johnson, *The Suez War* (1957) pp. xi–xii.

A chronology of leading dates

1956

26 July	Nasser nationalises the Suez Canal Company.
16–23 Aug.	The 22-Power Conference in London proposes an International Board to run the Canal.
9 Sep.	Nasser rejects the proposal.
12 Sep.	Eden announces in Parliament the plan for a Canal-Users' Association.
23 Sep.	Britain and France appeal to the Security Council.
16–28 Oct.	Anglo-French-Israeli talks.
30 Oct.	Anglo-French ultimatum following Israeli invasion.
5 Nov.	Anglo-French paratroops land at Port Said.
6 Nov.	Seaborne invasion followed by ceasefire at midnight.
7 Nov.	General Assembly agrees to set up U.N. Police Force.
22 Dec.	Last British forces leave Suez.

6 World Status without Tears

William Wallace

THE 1957 White Paper on Defence was published on 5 April, almost two months after the customary deadline for the annual defence review. One reason for the delay in its appearance was the change in Government which had come in mid-January; a new Prime Minister, Harold Macmillan, and a new Minister of Defence, Duncan Sandys, taking over tasks still heavily burdened by the aftermath of the Suez campaign, needed time to assess their new responsibilities. The new Government made it clear that more was involved in its review of defence than mere delay. In his first speech as Prime Minister, Macmillan promised that 'no vested interests, however strong, and no traditions, however good', would stand in the way of his Government's reassessment of the costs and commitments of defence. Sandys, the new Minister of Defence, declared that 'a turning-point' had been reached in British defence policy. In the weeks that followed, growing speculation in the Press helped to build up popular interest and expectancy. When it finally appeared, the White Paper presented itself as involving 'the biggest change in military policy ever made in normal times'.

The problem which the White Paper set out to tackle was one that had increasingly troubled the Government since 1945. The cost of defence had been rising, its claims on manpower and resources steadily increasing. Britain's Great Power commitments had also increased. Although the post-war withdrawal from India and the evacuation in 1954 of the Suez base had relieved her of some obligations, she was forced to commit four divisions and a sizeable air force to the defence of Europe. Yet Britain's economic ability to support these various commitments had considerably declined. The country seemed to face a clear choice between what Churchill

192

called 'the twin but divergent objectives of financial solvency and military security'.

To this dilemma the White Paper offered a third alternative. For developments in weaponry had, it was argued, altered the whole nature of warfare. Major conventional wars were now precluded by nuclear weapons sufficiently powerful to deter a potential aggressor. Under the umbrella of the nuclear deterrent, scattered local conflicts might still erupt, though limited in scale and in duration by the threat of nuclear intervention; but long-range air transport and mobile sea-borne forces gave the possibility of handling them primarily from a central reserve, with only a moderate supplement of fixed bases and garrisons to hold the line of communications. If Britain's defence strategy were recast to take into account these developments, the costs could be cut without a corresponding reduction in power. The same commitments, it was argued, could now be met with fewer resources and smaller forces.

The key to this transformation was the change of strategy; the primary aim of policy was to be, not defence, but deterrence. 'We believe,' Sandys argued, 'that the British people will agree that the available resources of the nation should be concentrated not upon preparations to wage war so much as upon trying to prevent that catastrophe from ever happening.' The primary emphasis must therefore be placed upon the nuclear deterrent. A smaller 'shield' of forces capable of resisting an attack for a more limited period was all that was needed on the conventional side. The impossibility of total defence against the airborne deterrent meant that resources could be concentrated on offensive capability; defence could be limited to that which would increase the credibility of the deterrent. For conventional forces, mobility and versatility could now substitute for bases and numbers. A small and highly equipped force would suffice to contain the short-term local conflicts and to police Britain's remaining colonial responsibilities. It would therefore be possible to end National Service and to rely on better-equipped all-regular forces.

The decision to end National Service and to concentrate on the deterrent created the most immediate impression on the Press and the public. But the strategic assumptions which underpinned this change were not so widely noticed. Foreshadowed in the reviews of the previous three years, but now for the first time spelled out, they represented the most ambitious attempt since the Second World War to reconsider the basis of defence policy and defence expenditure. The doctrine of deterrence offered Britain a way to world status without too many tears.

Until 1957 British military thinking had been imprisoned by traditional considerations deriving from the pre-war period. For until 1939 Britain's defence problem was relatively simple. Without any direct involvement in Europe, her position as a world power rested on the resources of her Empire and the control of her imperial communications. Security within the Empire could be maintained by a mixture of local forces and small garrisons; the Navy and the network of bases which supported it guarded the lines of communication and trade. Defence expenditure was not a pressing burden on the budget; moderate capital expenditure could maintain a large and efficient Navy, and supply the weapons needed for its scattered yet small Army. Between the wars defence expenditure averaged around 3 per cent of the Gross National Product; the total manpower in all three services was little above 300,000. The Air Force, still by far the smallest of the three services, was not a major consumer of resources. In contrast to most continental countries, Britain had no form of compulsory military service from 1919 to 1939. The cost of world-power status remained easy to bear.

The Second World War disrupted this happy situation. Its cost depleted the country's foreign investments, leaving its balance of payments heavily dependent on a sharp increase in exports and immediately vulnerable to the strains of expenditure abroad. The growth of nationalism increased the problem of imperial security, and decreased the availability of bases from which that security could be maintained. The failure to achieve a

194

European settlement necessitated the maintenance of occupation troops on the Continent and a supply of trained reserves. In general the pressures of the Cold War meant that the traditional 'breathing-space' of three or four years in which to rearm and to retrain her manpower was likely in future to be denied.

The problem of keeping pace with technical innovations also arose in an acute form. Development of new types of weapons and equipment was becoming more costly and time-consuming, and replacement more frequent; the cost of the weapons and equipment themselves was also rising sharply. The Air Force, which the war had established as a major element in warfare, made the heaviest demands on resources, with the increasing sophistication of aeronautics and electronics adding to the costs imposed by rapid obsolescence. In 1929 the R.A.F. had been allotted around a sixth of the services budget; in 1949 it was consuming almost a third, as well as the lion's share of the Ministry of Supply's budget. But the two older services were similarly affected by the revolution in technology, which had reduced the effective life-span of their equipment, raised its cost, increased it complexity and diversity, and required a huge 'tail' of non-combatant forces to look after its repair and maintenance. Further, the diversion of resources from heavy engineering, electronics, shipbuilding and vehicle production directly impaired the export drive. The costs of maintaining an adequate global defence was rising at the very moment when Britain had lost her old ability to meet her military commitments without strain.

The full implications of these changes were not fully appreciated. Post-war foreign policy, recognising the lost capacity for complete independence, was based upon the doctrine of the 'three circles' of British influence – the Atlantic, the Commonwealth and Europe. Of these, the most important was undoubtedly the Anglo-American relationship, through which Britain might hope to compensate for her loss of global independence by exerting influence on the more powerful partner. Only a little less important was the Commonwealth, which contributed directly to British power and which was the foundation of her world position. Europe, in which by necessity Britain was heavily involved, was seen as a sphere of influence complementary but subsidiary to these two. The status and influence gained from her relationships and commitments in each of these circles, mutually reinforcing each other, would provide the foundation for a continued global role.

Although in 1946, when the McMahon Act abruptly terminated war-time Anglo-American co-operation in weapon development, an independent nuclear programme had been instituted, the significance of atomic weapons was not fully appreciated. For the European theatre, where they would most probably be deployed, was seen as an area rather for intermittent intervention than for permanent commitment. The permanent commitments of British defence – communications with overseas territories and maintenance of imperial garrisons – did not appear to require a nuclear programme.

Further temporary factors kept postponing a defence review. The Government was preoccupied with Britain's immediate economic problems. The 'temporary' commitment of occupation troops to the Continent gradually became permanent. The disturbed situation in the Middle East, the outbreak of Communist insurgency in Malaya, and the insecure position of Hong Kong further extended British forces, and compelled an extension of National Service from twelve to eighteen months.

The outbreak of the Korean War therefore found British forces widely dispersed, heavily committed, inadequately equipped, and unprepared. When the United Nations called for troops, the Ministry of Defence had difficulty in assembling, from an Army of 400,000 men, one combat-ready brigade. The invasion of South Korea raised, in the eyes of all the Western nations, the ugly prospect of renewed global war. The countries of the Western Alliance therefore pledged themselves to hurried programmes of rearmament; Britain, as one of the Alliance's most important members, naturally pledging one of the most ambitious. The Labour Government put in motion a crash programme, phased over three years, to build up an Army of ten divisions, with large reserves, to strengthen both the Navy and the Air Force, and to speed up the re-equipment of all three services. National Service was extended to two years, and some reservists were recalled. Large numbers of aircraft were ordered; the naval building programme and production of armour and transport for the Army were considerably expanded. The effect on the country's convalescent economy was severe. Between 1950 and 1953 an extra 100,000 men were called into the services, at a time when there was a shortage of manpower. Expenditure on defence almost doubled, in 1952 accounting for 11 per cent of the Gross National Product. The balance of payments, which had run a healthy surplus after the devaluation of 1949, plunged back into deficit in 1951.

The first concern of the Conservative Government on their return to office in 1951 had therefore been the need to contain the economic burden imposed by re-armament. The progress of the programme which they took over had, in addition, run into trouble at several points. Shortages of materials and of skilled labour created bottlenecks in production; attempts to accelerate aircraft development came up against deficiencies in design and performance, unexpected delays and complications, and sharp escalations in cost. In the course of 1952 the new Government therefore decided to adjust the original plan, extending it to run over a fourth year and holding it to a lower target. To ease the pressure on materials and production resources, priority was given to fighter and strike aircraft, with such less urgent needs as re-equipment of the Army forced to take a secondary role. Privately, Churchill asked the service Ministries to consider plans for future economies – and to set in motion a major review of defence policy.

So from the late months of 1952 until the autumn of 1953 was conducted Britain's first post-war review of defence strategy. It was concerned with two main problems: the urgent need to reduce expenditure, and the need to reconsider strategy in the light of the development of new weapons and weapon-carriers. Britain had tested her first atom bomb during 1952, and the

Government was anxious to assess the impact of atomic weapons on warfare. An additional spur to economy was provided by the lessening of international tension during 1953, with Stalin's death and the conclusion of a Korean armistice.

The conclusions of the review were published in the 1954 Defence White Paper. This stressed the overriding importance of nuclear weapons in any future war, but did not see their effect on methods of warfare as wholly revolutionary. Since the first atomic strike might not be decisive, war might be expected to continue for some time in a 'broken-backed' form; large conventional forces and trained reserves would therefore still be needed, as well as an expanded system of civil defence and auxiliary forces at home to guard against invasion. Little consideration appears to have been given to the reduction of commitments, either in Europe or overseas, in spite of the continued deployment of almost the entire effective Army abroad – partly because these were accepted, in the White Paper's words, as the 'inescapable responsibilities of a Great Power intent on preserving peace', and partly because there was some hope that lessening tension would release Britain from several immediate obligations. The scope for economies was therefore very limited.

In line with the decision to place a greater emphasis on the striking power of nuclear weapons, the Army was downgraded in favour of the R.A.F., but the hoped-for savings on Army expenditure were offset by the rising cost of equipping the Air Force and of developing its future weapons. Accepting that the costs of development and re-equipment would continue to rise, the White Paper warned that in future 'we may not be able to afford both new weapons and conventional weapons of the same size'.

Britain was not the only country to have looked to the development of nuclear weapons to provide relief from the strain of rearmament. The United States had experienced similar problems of inflation, manpower shortages and a soaring budget, and a review of American defence policy had been put in train immediately the Eisenhower administration took office. In this it was strongly influenced by the prospect opened by the hydrogen bomb, the first test of which had demonstrated a destructive capacity far more catastrophic than the 'limited' destructiveness of the atomic bomb. The new defence programme, announced in December 1953, centred around a new strategy of deterrence, 'massive retaliation'. This strategic concept, by relying on the threat of nuclear force to prevent conventional war, made it possible to economise on conventional forces and so reduce total manpower and hold defence expenditure within a budgetary ceiling. For further economies it looked to the substitution of a central reserve with air mobility for troops permanently stationed abroad, and to progressive reductions in service strengths as the provision of improved equipment and weaponry enabled fewer men to meet equivalent commitments – a substitution of firepower for manpower similar, if smaller in scale, to that which the H-bomb itself promised.

The British review had only touched on the potential effect of 'new and unconventional weapons' upon future defence policy; for the Government, denied access by the McMahon Act to information on the effect of the H-bomb, was still unaware of its revolutionary consequences. But in this it was overtaken by the publication by the Chairman of the U.S. Atomic Energy Commission, in February 1954, of the results of the Eniwetok tests of eighteen months before. Churchill, who was particularly impressed with the catastrophic potential of this new weapon, set off for Washington to gather further information; the British programme to develop a similar weapon, which had begun in 1952, was given greater urgency.

The prospect which the hydrogen bomb offered to the British Government was appealing. It overwhelming power appeared to bring back equality of status for Britain with America and the Soviet Union, despite her much smaller resources; for, as Eden later wrote, 'if continents, and not merely small islands, were doomed to destruction, all are equal on the grim reckoning' – at least those who possessed the weapon. Even a small striking force might threaten an aggressor with an intolerable level of destruction. The 1954 Geneva Conference suggested to the Conservatives that it was also an invaluable aid to great power diplomacy. And, as Churchill argued strongly and repeatedly, possession of the nuclear deterrent made the outbreak of war less likely. Faced with the stark choice of nuclear war or peaceful negotiation, the powers would be forced to turn to diplomacy.

Its immediate impact on British defence policy, however, was limited. In the debate on the 1955 White Paper, Churchill declared that 'there is no absolute defence against the hydrogen bomb'; but he added that conventional forces would still be needed in adequate numbers to provide a defensive shield to 'identify aggression', to guard against the possibility of future Koreas, and to fulfil Britain's 'world-wide obligations', recently reinforced by Eden's pledge in September 1954 to maintain the existing strength of its forces on the Continent for an indefinite period.

In terms of strategy, then, the general decision had been taken to give first priority to the deterrent force; but the continuing requirements for forces for other roles remained. The commitments which the services were called on to fulfil remained global. Europe, the newest permanent commitment, was the largest single burden; but in the Middle East, for instance, the withdrawal from Egypt in 1954 had left troops in Jordan, Libya and Iraq, and in Africa and the Far East the traditional imperial obligations were aggravated by the Kenyan emergency and the continued fighting in Malaya.

Within Britain, questions of defence policy aroused little interest outside the Cabinet, the services, and the Ministries directly concerned. Few members of Parliament were experts. The Conservative Party's interest was largely limited to questions of prestige, and Labour's to questions of principle – German rearmament in the early fifties, and now nuclear weapons. There was no constitutional agency for the discussion and development of strategy on policy, and the coverage given to defence questions in the Press was generally low. The Minister of Defence had little power to coordinate the direction of policy, and little opportunity to consider the field as a whole; there had been four Ministers in the first four years of the Conservative Government, and there were to be three more within the next eighteen months. The direction of defence policy since the war had therefore been largely determined by negotiation between the three services, interrupted on occasion by overall directives from the Cabinet, without any real popular or Parliamentary interest.

Underlying this lack of interest was a general consensus about the position of Britain as a world power. The special relationship with America had been the cornerstone of the foreign policies of both the Labour and the Conservative Governments. The Commonwealth connection and its accompanying obligations was valued by the Conservatives for its contribution to Britain's world standing, and by the Labour Party for its commitment to multi-racialism, international co-operation and democracy. The Commonwealth, indeed, gave Britain's global policies real assistance, as well as the prestige of continuing greatness; consultations between Commonwealth defence staffs still took place regularly, and troops from the 'old' Commonwealth had fought with Britain in Korea and in Malaya. Though attitudes to Europe varied in their enthusiasm, few questioned that Britain's external obligations placed her to a degree apart from her continental neighbours. Further, there was general agreement that Britain had a special contribution to make to international diplomacy – for Conservatives, from her diplomatic expertise; for the Left wing, from her moral authority. With relatively few exceptions, the possession and retention of nuclear weapons was accepted as the badge of Britain's Great Power status, and as the necessary passport to a seat at the international conference table. (It occurred to no one to question the need for Britain to have a seat at 'the conference table'.) Rising individual prosperity concealed from the public the real decline in British power, and the weakness of her external economic position. Britain was still, in the eyes of the electorate and of their political leaders, one of 'the Big Three'; and the Government's diplomatic activities, in 1954 at the Geneva Conference and in 1955 at the Summit, helped to confirm this impression. In sum, there was little dissent on the fundamentals of British defence or foreign policy.

If Britain's role and status met with general acceptance, the size of the 'inescapable obligations' which this entailed aroused much wider criticism. Unfavourable comparisons were made with the lighter defence contributions of her continental neighbours, and the economic advantages which they were thus able to obtain. Resentment at the competition which reviving German industry offered in export markets was to be heightened at the beginning of 1956 by the German decision to limit their period of conscription to eighteen months. The necessity of peace-time conscription had never been fully accepted, and was coming under increasing attack. When the Labour Government had first introduced it, it had been attacked by the Liberals as an invasion of traditional civil liberties, and from 1953 the Labour Party itself began to agitate for its early reduction and eventual abolition. The trade unions were strongly opposed to it, and the employers resented its demands upon manpower. Further, it was unpopular in the Army, which retained its old preference for all-regular forces, arguing that the constant turnover of National Servicemen was bad for the forces' morale. It was, in addition, an inefficient means of supplying the needed manpower, now that the advent of the hydrogen bomb had destroyed the post-war need for the training of reserves. It is doubtful whether National Service was a very live issue among the bulk of the electorate; but it was sufficient that both political parties believed that there was advantage to be gained from advocating its abolition, and political danger in being seen as a party which favoured its indefinite retention.

The strongest pressure for change, however, came, as before, from the need for economy. In July 1955 a Treasury projection estimated that the cost of maintaining existing defence programmes over the next four years would rise by more than 25 per cent. Progressive reductions in American military aid, and the ending of Germany's responsibility for the occupation costs of

British forces, added to the cost of overseas commitments already in excess of £150 million, putting strain upon the economy and the balance of payments.

Some immediate cuts were made to alleviate the burden. Eden promised a reduced intake of National Servicemen for 1956. The Territorial Army was to be downgraded and reorganised for home defence, and the Home Guard disbanded. The size of the active fleet was to be reduced. The V-1000, which had been announced the previous year as the future mainstay of Britain's air transport system, was cancelled; small cuts were made in the proposed size of the V-bomber force, and larger cuts in Fighter and Coastal Commands. The number of projects were pruned through a closer co-operation on guided missiles with the Americans. Nevertheless, in the Budget of 1956 development costs continued to rise, while the impact of these piecemeal economies on the effectiveness of the active forces threatened to justify John Strachey's criticism that the Government by 'trying to get something of everything succeeded in getting enough of nothing'.

The wider implications of Government thinking – and the primarily political and economic motives behind it – were first made public in a speech by Macmillan, as Chancellor of the Exchequer, in mid-May. Speaking to the Foreign Press Association, he mused about the 'pipe dream' of a defence bill of half the present size, a saving of over £700 million, which would transform Britain's economic position, solve the problem of her balance of payments, and allow a considerable tax cut. Of course, he added, 'we know we can't have it, we are not going to behave in an irresponsible way'. But he went on to emphasise that Britain was carrying a far larger defence burden than her European allies, and that there must be some consideration of what would be her 'fair share'. 'By and large,' he concluded, 'Britain will have to go on carrying two rifles instead of the one carried by others'; but he made it clear that the Government was determined to economise, and was aiming to save over £100 million.

His speech, as was intended, sparked off controversy. There were rumours in the Press that the Government was aiming for a saving of £400 million; the Labour and Liberal parties, determined not to be outbid, demanded savings of £500 million. Behind the public debate, the Cabinet was reviewing all aspects of defence policy. It started from the assumption that a budgetary ceiling must be imposed on defence expenditure. Given that the size of the budget was thus fixed, the question of its distribution became vital. Of the four main areas of expenditure, the commitments in the Commonwealth and in the overseas territories were the most difficult to cut; responsibilities could only be reduced, if that was wanted, over a number of years. Expenditure on research and development could be pruned further only by taking considerable risks, or by abandoning major programmes. The major prospect of economy must therefore be found either in the deterrent programme or in the recent commitment to Europe.

In the context of the existing deterrent programme, a significant further economy would mean abandonment of a project on which successive Governments had spent much money. In the 1956 White Paper the Government had declared its firm intention to provide a contribution to the Western deterrent 'commensurate with our standing as a world power'; to go back on this now would be to admit that Britain could no longer aspire to such a standing. By contrast, the European commitment could be cut more easily. Now that the prospect of deterrent power made the outbreak of a major conventional war in Europe unlikely, this seemed the smallest military risk. From a domestic point of view, this was clearly the most attractive target. It was therefore decided to effect what was virtually a unilateral revolution in NATO strategy, increasing its reliance on the global deterrent and on the early use of tactical nuclear weapons, and reducing the role of its conventional forces to that of an immediate shield against a probing attack. By such a redirection of strategy the British ground and air forces in Germany could be cut by roughly one half.

Such a reduction opened the welcome political prospect of dispensing with National Service. The problem here was that the Army insisted that it needed at least

200,000 men, and it was considered extremely unlikely that any such number could be raised by voluntary recruitment alone. The services' answer was to move to a system of selective service; but the Government were well aware of the political difficulties of advocating a system which Labour was already attacking as 'unfair'.

Despite Macmillan's hints, the defence review itself aroused remarkably little informed discussion or criticism. The Opposition's spokesmen called for the early abolition of National Service and for major savings in expenditure, and at the same time for the maintenance of existing commitments and of the independent deterrent – a position which was more political than practical. Colonel Wigg dissented from his party in holding that National Service could not be abandoned within the framework of Britain's present commitments; Stephen Swingler demanded that those commitments be cut. *The Times*, alone among the serious newspapers, had questioned the necessity of the independent deterrent, a weapon which appeared to satisfy 'British prestige rather than military necessity'.

The review was intended to reach its conclusions in the autumn of 1956, allowing time for consultation with Britain's European and American allies and for the publication of the final decisions in next February's White Paper. But it was overtaken at the end of July by the seizure of the Suez Canal, and for the next six months politicians and servicemen alike were occupied with more immediate matters, as diplomatic reaction turned to military intervention, and intervention to a withdrawal before the military objectives had been gained, and in the face of a diplomatic defeat.

The events of the Suez campaign could not fail to leave a deep impression on Britain's defence and foreign policy, as on its domestic political situation. The course of the campaign itself, and the length of the preparations needed for it, re-emphasised the inadequacy of the armed forces. The economic weakness of the country brought home the limitations on Britain's freedom of action in foreign affairs. Worse, the two main pillars of Britain's world position refused to support her in the defence of what she considered her most vital interests.

Of the other members of the Commonwealth, only Australia and New Zealand supported her at the United Nations; while the United States, whose actions had done much to precipitate the crisis, was actively promoting a settlement which was against British interests. Veiled Soviet threats of nuclear retaliation were widely felt to have forced the British Government to halt its troops when only nineteen miles down the canal.

These events, however, were subject to more than one interpretation. In military terms, the slowness of the build-up and the lack of suitable equipment for such a limited operation suggested that what Britain needed was more mobile and more effective forces of intervention; as one officer had remarked when the Canal was nationalised, 'You couldn't keep it open with an H-bomb.' On the other hand, the lesson of Russian sabre-rattling was that no country could act independently in the future unless it could protect itself against 'nuclear blackmail'. The economic lessons, at least, were clearer. If Britain was going to retain any initiative in its foreign policy, then it must rebuild a position of economic strength.

Psychologically it was impossible for Britain to accept the implication that Suez spelled her demise as a world power. The mood of a wide section of public opinion, and in particular of the overwhelming majority of the Conservative Party, was one of wounded national pride, of deep resentment at the 'humiliating withdrawal' which had been forced by American 'betrayal' and Soviet interference. A motion deploring the American attitude to the British intervention secured the signatures of almost a third of the Conservative M.P.s. In one exchange in December, the Foreign Secretary denied that he included the United States or Canada among 'the enemies of this country'.

The man who inherited the responsibility for the decision, when in the New Year Sir Anthony Eden resigned, was Harold Macmillan. As Chancellor, he had, during the review of early 1956, been the strongest proponent of economy; in the last two months of that year he had been grappling with the economic strains which intervention had occasioned, and attempting to stem the flow from the reserves.

The position of the Conservative Party at this time was particularly serious; following the Suez withdrawal and Eden's resignation, its popularity had sunk disastrously. Britain's diplomatic position was also extremely difficult. Relations with the United States were so estranged that when in December the Foreign Secretary visited Washington he was unable to meet President Eisenhower; the Commonwealth was deeply divided, while the French were disgusted by what they regarded as Britain's betrayal.

In his first broadcast as Prime Minister, Macmillan set out the theme which his Government was to follow:

> Every now and again since the war I have heard people say: 'Isn't Britain only a second- or third-class power now? Isn't she on the way out?' What nonsense! This is a great country, and do not let us be ashamed to say so.... Twice in my lifetime I have heard the same old tale about our being a second-rate power, and I have lived to see the answer.

He admitted that in its economic resources Britain could not match the vast capabilities of the United States or the Soviet Union, though she was materially strengthened by 'close ties' with the Commonwealth and with her European allies. He emphasised that while Britain would maintain her defence obligations, it was wrong for her allies to expect her to carry 'more than our fair share'. On relations with the United States, he asserted that 'the life of the free world depends on the partnership between us'; but it must be a real partnership based on mutual confidence and respect, not an unequal relationship between master and servant. But his main concern was not with material resources or the details of international politics, but with the character and courage of the British people. Properly led, he was certain that British people still retained the capacity for greatness; and his Government would do its best to provide the leadership needed:

> So do not let us have any more defeatist talk of second-class powers and of dreadful things to come.

Britain has been great, is great, and will stay great, provided we close our ranks and get on with the job.

Such an appeal might do much to strengthen morale in the country, but it could do nothing to improve the economic situation. Although the reserves were now recovering, expected increases in the cost of the social services and the need for tight control over the size of the Budget dictated further economies in defence. In mid-February Peter Thorneycroft, the new Chancellor, announced that higher contributions would be necessary to meet rising social service costs. By the time the Budget was presented on 9 April, Mr Thorneycroft was able to state that defence expenditure for the coming financial year would be £79 million less than the original estimate, and to offer the country a cut in purchase tax as a stimulus to domestic expansion and a bonus for his party. The almost completed defence review was held back by the new Government for further consideration, with a determination to squeeze additional economies out of its planned future deployments.

Eden's Minister of Defence, Antony Head, refused to continue to serve on these terms. His successor, Duncan Sandys, had for three years been the Minister of Housing, but nevertheless had some previous experience of defence problems as Minister of Supply from 1951 to 1954, and earlier as a controversial officer in the Territorial Army and as a member of the war-time Government. He had the full confidence of the new Prime Minister, who now gave the Ministry of Defence increased powers over the three services Ministries. On 15 January the first economies had been announced: the R.A.A.F. and R.N.V.R. air units were to be disbanded, reserve training in the Army was to be reduced, and a £10 million cut was made in orders for fighter aircraft.

For wider cuts, the new Minister was forced back to reconsider the alternatives of the previous year. With abandonment of the deterrent now completely ruled out by the political emotions generated over Suez, the development programme and the conventional forces

208

offered the only possibilities for further reduction. The Government therefore decided to abolish National Service – a decision which avoided the unpopular alternative of some form of selective service at the cost of neglecting the forces' manpower needs. The Army was to revert to an all-regular basis, with a planned strength by 1962 of 165,000 men. This figure was not based on the Army's needs – estimated by the War Office at 200,000 – but on accepting as the future strength of the Army the figure which it was estimated could be recruited by voluntary methods.

Further alleviation of the burden of development clearly depended on the co-operation of her allies. For such co-operation the United States was by far the most valuable partner, the only friendly country which could offer Britain more than she had to give in return. Developments in this sphere therefore depended on the success of diplomatic efforts to repair the Anglo-American relationship. The path to a rapprochement was laid by the American change of heart on the Middle East, which came around the New Year, and by the departure of Eden. Both Eisenhower and Dulles sent warm messages to Macmillan on his appointment as Premier, and the American Secretary of Defence issued an immediate invitation to Mr Sandys to visit Washington. There were inspired rumours in the Press that the United States was prepared to assist Britain both in the development and the provision of guided weapons, although the continuing limitations of the McMahon Act prohibited giving her either full control over their use or the warheads to fit them. Within two weeks of his appointment Sandys set off for a five-day visit to Washington, accompanied by a party of experts in guided weapons and atomic research; he was greeted at the airport by Dulles, and his interview with President Eisenhower was the first granted to a British Cabinet Minister since Suez. For the Americans, now that their Middle East policy placed a priority on resisting Soviet expansion, the visit presented an opportunity to bolster an ally whose world position assisted the aims of their foreign policy. For the British, the resumption of close Anglo-American relations restored the most valued of their international links, and opened the prospect of welcome savings in research and development. Sandys returned with an agreement for closer collaboration in future development programmes and the offer of a number of intermediate-range missiles to supplement Britain's airborne deterrent until her own second-generation deterrent was ready for production.

Consultation with Britain's European allies, who were most affected by the proposed alteration in Britain's deployment of forces, took second place to the re-establishment of the Anglo-American partnership. While the American alliance brought a net gain to Britain in terms of diplomatic influence, weapons development and equipment, Europe was seen as a net drain on Britain's resources. The increasing cost of the British Army of the Rhine was made no easier to bear by the annual haggling over the German contribution which began again in December 1956 with a barrage of intransigent statements from both sides. The British felt justified in protesting at the unfairness of the burden they were carrying, when they alone of the European powers had a major portion of their forces permanently stationed outside the country, and when they compared the eight per cent of their Gross National Product spent on defence with the 6 per cent of the French and the 4 per cent of the economically booming Germans. At the NATO Council meeting in December, the British delegates had received only vague promises, which confirmed them in the intention of going ahead on their own. The future strategy of NATO and the shape of the British contribution, discussed during Sandys' visit to Washington, was not put before the French and German Governments until the Western European Union meeting at the end of that month. The continental countries were left with the impression of a rather perfunctory consultation by an ally whose mind was already made up.

With all these complications, the 1957 White Paper was delayed for nearly three months after Macmillan's Government had taken office. With one exception its fundamental decisions, as they finally emerged, did not differ significantly from those towards which the 1956 review had been moving. The major change was the reduction in the size of the Army, which would leave Britain even more desperately dependent on the deterrent in the event of war, and in the parallel announcement of the end of National Service. The research and development programme was squeezed still further; but in spite of the need for stringent economy, the Government had decided to protect the future independence of the deterrent force by developing an 'advanced type' of rocket, Blue Streak, using the promised American Thors as a stop-gap weapon.

But if the decisions themselves were not too different from what they would have been without the Suez campaign, the presentation of those decisions both in the White Paper and in the defence debate which followed had a different emphasis. This was mainly due to the altered atmosphere, which encouraged the Government to stress, even to exaggerate, the potential power and the independence of action which the new policy promised. To the Opposition's criticism, Macmillan was able to reply that the only alternative to his strategy was the continuation of National Service. Otherwise Britain's global role would be seriously diminished – which Labour wanted as little as the Conservatives.

The purpose of the deterrent was portrayed in a manner that differed subtly, but significantly, from that of the previous year. Where the 1956 White Paper had called the British force 'a contribution to the Allied deterrent', the 1957 White Paper noted that it would give Britain 'an appreciable element of nuclear power of her own' – a reference to the possibility, in the minds of politicians on both sides of the House, that her American ally might fail Britain again. The deterrent thus preserved Britain's diplomatic independence, and ensured that the Atlantic partnership would continue to be a partnership of equals. Further, it gave Britain the international standing and the diplomatic leverage necessary to play the role of peacemaker between the two super-powers – a role which both Conservative and Labour leaders considered Britain peculiarly qualified to fill, and one which Macmillan saw as a promising route to the recovery of his party's fortunes. 'Thus', he wrote in an open letter to his constituency chairman, 'we may secure our twin objectives, namely, peace based upon disarmament, and the preservation of the free world.'

The strongest reaction to the White Paper came from abroad. The European members of NATO were united in deploring the 'unilateral' nature of Britain's decisions, and the *fait accompli* which they presented to her partners in the Alliance. Germany in particular protested against the proposed withdrawal of troops and the lack of adequate consultation; Macmillan travelled to Bonn later in April to soothe their ruffled feelings. The continental countries might have been more sympathetic to Britain's case if they had felt that Britain's unwieldy defence burden was borne on their common behalf; but there was little European interest in the scale of Britain's commitments East of Suez, and little appreciation that the British deterrent force was a necessary or significant contribution to the strength of the Alliance. Rather, it seemed to them that Britain's defence plans represented the pursuit of an independent national policy of little relevance to the immediate concerns of the Continent, and one which demonstrated yet again the low priority which Britain placed on her European role. At home criticism was far more muted. Labour's front bench was visibly embarrassed by the disunity of its supporters, and limited its criticisms to points of detail. There were many within the Labour Party who doubted the adequacy of the conventional forces, but they were inhibited in their criticism by their commitment to abolish National Service, and were thus reduced to demanding a higher level of forces without explaining how the additional manpower was to be recruited.

The Government's new policy therefore passed through Parliament almost unscathed, though a scattering of Members protested at the damage its actions had caused to European relations, and one M.P. was daring enough to doubt whether the savings in expenditure would ever materialise. Outside Westminster criticism was similarly scattered and restrained.

There were rumblings in the Press on the wisdom of the Government's choice of alternatives, and on the accuracy of its financial and military calculations; the *Manchester Guardian* suggested that unless the objectives of the country's foreign policy were altered, expenditure could only rise. A few academic commentators questioned the validity of Sandys' strategic assumptions and argued that the existence of nuclear deterrents made limited conventional wars more, rather than less, likely. The Liberal Party declared itself against an independent British deterrent, urging that Britain accept the full implications of collective defence and make a more valuable conventional contribution to the Alliance. There were various protests against the deterrent, too, on moral grounds, though not yet organised into a coherent force. But by and large the White Paper met with general acceptance. The vast majority, politicians and public alike, shared the Government's belief in the necessity of continued global status, and its desire at the same time to reduce the level of expenditure and the drain on manpower without admitting to a decline in power. Both Sandys and Macmillan went out of their way to emphasise, in presenting the White Paper, that the economies proposed would not lead to a loss of striking power or to the abandonment of any of Britain's obligations. She would achieve the same influence for a smaller expenditure.

It was all something of an illusion; and Macmillan was the Great Illusionist. Better than any other member of the Cabinet, he knew the limitations of Britain's defence and foreign policies and the constraints imposed by her economic position; as Chancellor he had been particularly well placed to note his country's limited independence of action over Suez. Yet he chose to re-emphasise the theme of Britain's greatness, to deny that Suez had demonstrated the unreality of Britain's continued claim to world power. For the next five years he was to struggle, with a remarkable degree of success, to conceal from the electorate and from the more sceptical sections of his party the reality of Britain's decline, substituting the spectacle of global diplomacy for the lost substance of global power.

The Government deluded itself as well as others. The justification for the withdrawal of troops from Germany was that improved equipment and the extra firepower of new weapons would provide equivalent protection with fewer men. But in 1957 hardly any of the promised tactical nuclear weapons had arrived, and the programme of re-equipment had been delayed yet again to keep the defence budget within the financial ceiling imposed. That the withdrawal of troops nevertheless began immediately, indicated the priority of economic and political considerations over military and diplomatic. There was considerable doubt among informed opinion about the value or usability of tactical nuclear weapons in a limited European campaign, but the Government avoided facing the problem on the few occasions when its critics directly raised it. The transport aircraft to provide the air mobility essential to the reduction of overseas bases did not exist in 1957, and the scale of future orders made it clear that the forces would have to rely on the requisitioning of civil aircraft in any emergency. The Thor missile on which Britain was to rely for intermediate reinforcement of the pruned deterrent force was not available for use without American co-operation – another question which Government spokesmen side-stepped.

But the biggest question-marks were over the projected development programme. The unfortunate experiences of the early fifties had demonstrated the uncertainty involved in weapons development. Yet the future of the independent deterrent was to be dependent on the success of a single project still in the earliest stages of development, and the overall programme was organised on the expectation that costs would be held relatively stable. The Government had no choice but to plump for Blue Streak and resist the duplication of projects on which the Americans were engaged if it was to hold its military budget within the desired limits; but the risk it took was that it might put all its eggs in the wrong basket, and be left with a deterrent which was inadequate or even unworkable.

There were wide implications for the country's future defence and foreign policy which the Govern-

214

ment and most of its critics also preferred to ignore. Nothing much was done to implement the idea of collective defence stressed by Eisenhower and Macmillan at their meeting of October 1957. Only token efforts were made to extend the principle to European co-operation, and to allow the continental countries a greater say in Britain's military planning and a share in the benefits of her research. There was a refusal to accept the growing importance of the European relationship, and a failure to connect European diplomacy with Britain's defence objectives. The Free Trade Area negotiations were at a critical stage in the spring of 1957, though already bedevilled by continental suspicions of Britain's intentions; her unilateral alterations in the strategy of the Alliance, and the immediate cuts in her European forces, only increased their doubts. On purely military grounds, the Government was right to consider conventional war in Europe the least likely risk; but its disregard for the likely diplomatic consequences reflected its continued belief in the greater importance of the other two circles of British foreign policy – the Commonwealth and the American alliance. The illusion that the Commonwealth connection and the Anglo-American partnership gave Britain a status higher than that of her continental allies remained, to shape her defence policy and to plague her relations with Europe for years to come.

In terms of its effects on expenditure and manpower, the White Paper achieved its aims. Within the five-year period covered by its projections, the number of men in the forces was reduced from nearly 700,000 to under 400,000, and expenditure was held down to around 7 per cent of the Gross National Product. Forces in Germany were down to a figure of 55,000 by the end of 1958 (though strong American and German pressure prevented Britain attaining the original target of 45,000), and the strength of the air forces there was almost halved. The deterrent, too, was rapidly brought to effectiveness. The first British tests of hydrogen bombs, announced well before the publication of the White Paper, were completed in May 1957. Delivery of hydrogen weapons to the bomber force began in 1958, when the more advanced Victors and Vulcans were coming into service. With the Anglo-American relationship restored to its pre-Suez amity, Britain cut a splendid figure in the diplomatic councils of the world; the deterrent strategy appeared to have granted her a secure and impressive foreign policy at a cost which her economy could bear.

But beside these real achievements there remained considerable and continuing difficulties. Although the new stategy reduced the financial and exchange burden, Britain's defence expenditure remained the highest in Europe, and the strain it put on the economy was still difficult to bear. Only months after the White Paper was published, the new Chancellor was calling for further reductions in military expenditure. The level of such expenditure at home and abroad contributed to the immediate economic difficulties in 1957–8, and to the renewed pressures of 1960–2. The reduction in service manpower without a corresponding reduction in commitments produced severe strains on the capacity and the endurance of the forces. In 1958 there were over 100,000 men in the Middle and Far Eastern theatres, and the eruption of successive crises in these regions made it impossible to reduce the number committed in following years. The Jordan operation in 1958, when a brigade was despatched to offer protection against Egyptian threats, exposed continued deficiences in the strategic reserve and in the provision of air transport to make it effective. There was a chronic shortage of funds available for conventional re-equipment. In 1960 the British Army of the Rhine was still heavily dependent on war-time stocks, and their eventual replacement still left remarkable deficiencies in armour, transport and communications. Tactical nuclear weapons, around which its whole defence was planned, were still in short supply, and almost all were under American control.

Even more serious were the growing difficulties over the future of the deterrent, the basis of the new strategy. Information gained from the Americans in 1958 showed the Government how far behind it was in missile development, and cast considerable doubt upon the viability of Blue Streak. A sharp escalation in its cost reinforced those doubts. The 1959 White Paper contained the first hints of disillusionment, and Blue Streak was eventually cancelled just over a year later. Ironically, the linchpin of a strategy intended to reduce defence expenditure was cancelled partly on grounds of cost; its replacement, which turned yet again to the Americans for help, was a project of equally uncertain prospects at an equally early stage of development.

By 1959 the assumptions which underlay the strategy had also been badly shaken. The White Paper of that year contained no reference to strategic considerations, and Sandys did not answer the Opposition's charge that 'there is clearly no strategic doctrine now governing the Government's defence policy.' It had become apparent that the possession of a global deterrent did not prevent the outbreak of war; it placed strict limitations upon the area and level of conflict, but underneath the nuclear umbrella a whole range of limited wars was possible. And in such situations nuclear powers were as restricted as the non-nuclear in their choice of retaliatory weapons. If Britain could not have kept open the Suez Canal with an H-bomb, neither could she combat subversion and the threat of local attack with nuclear weapons; for effectiveness in limited war, conventional forces were vital. Faced with this realisation, opinion in the United States moved gradually away from the concept of 'massive retaliation' towards the idea of 'flexible response', which governed the expansion of conventional forces undertaken by President Kennedy.

This readjustment in strategy could only re-emphasise the gulf between the super-powers and their weaker allies, for such a wide range of options was totally beyond Britain's means. Her weakness in conventional forces was starkly exposed in 1961, when the coincidence of crises over Kuwait and Berlin found her forces over-committed and undermanned, compelling the Government to recall reserves and to take powers to retain remaining National Servicemen in order to bring its existing units up to fighting strength. The decline in domestic unemployment from 1960 on had led to a drop in recruiting, and there was considerable scepticism as to whether the target for the Army of 165,000 men would be met. But any renewed expansion of Britain's conventional forces could only be achieved either through abandonment of the nuclear deterrent or a major escalation in defence expenditure; and either alternative would involve the reintroduction of some form of compulsory military service. All of these courses were precluded by the decisions of 1957, and the continued political commitment of the Conservative Government to them, as also was the more radical departure of a reduction in Britain's military obligations. The Government therefore continued to rely heavily on the deterrent power of a weapon the effectiveness of which for defence purposes was less and less apparent, and for whose means of delivery it was more and more dependent on the Americans. The five-year defence plan initiated by the 1957 White Paper ended, appropriately, with the Nassau Agreement, confirming Britain's complete dependence on the United States.

And yet it is difficult to argue that at the time and in the circumstances of 1956–7 the Government had any practical political alternative. Britain was far from alone in refusing to face the problems or meet the demands of nuclear and European defence. The United States had opted for the comfortable certainty and the hoped-for cheapness of massive retaliation well before the British; indeed the Eisenhower administration maintained its budgetary ceiling and continued to reduce its conventional forces until the close of the fifties, in spite of growing criticism from military and civilian sources. France was no stricter with her NATO commitments than was Britain. German rearmament was remarkably unhurried, the Germans preferring undisturbed economic growth to greater security. While her allies were so careful of their own interests and so careless of the common defence, it was hard for Britain not to place her own interests first; while her major partner refused to face the conflict between security needs and economic objectives, it was only natural for Britain to adopt the same attitude.

If the attitudes of her allies were a limiting factor, the prevailing atmosphere at home was a much more powerful limitation. Almost no one in Britain of 1957 appreciated, amidst the signs of growing affluence and lessening taxation, the real decline in Britain's position, the loss of her traditional global status; even the most progressive accepted the desirability of Britain's world leadership, insisting on its moral quality rather than on its dependence upon power. In the aftermath of the humiliation of Suez, when Britain's traditional influence – or her moral principles – seemed temporarily to have deserted her, no politician could have admitted the reality of Britain's decline and hoped to retain his hold on the electorate. Within the narrow limits of economic necessity and political desirability the strategy of deterrence, already half-way to adoption as the future basis of defence policy, seemed almost the only way out.

It was easy, in retrospect, to see where the Government had gone wrong, where choices had been avoided and decisions badly taken. By 1961 it was possible for a Conservative critic to describe the Sandys White Paper, a little wistfully, as 'the last attempt by this country to maintain an independent status'. A sterner colleague in the same debate censured his party for attempting 'to live in luxury behind a wall of horror'. But neither of them had spoken up in 1957 against the assumptions on which that policy was based. Coming down in the world is a painful business, and one peculiarly difficult to accept; few in the mid-fifties were prepared to recognise that Britain must adjust herself to her reduced circumstances. Rather, in the wake of the Suez campaign and in the long-awaited flush of post-war prosperity, they demanded a reassertion of Britain's traditional position, even if they demanded too a lessening of its cost. Randolph Churchill summed up the feelings of most Englishmen on the proper role of British defence when in 1958 he proclaimed the achievement of the primary objective of the White Paper:

Britain can knock down twelve cities in the region of Stalingrad and Moscow from bases in Britain and another dozen in the Crimea from bases in Cyprus.

We did not have that power at the time of Suez. We are a major power again.

7 The Campaign for Nuclear Disarmament

Robert Taylor

Blessed are the peacemakers: for they shall be called the children of God.

MATTHEW V. 9

Let not England forget her precedence of teaching nations how to live. JOHN MILTON, *The Doctrine and Discipline of Divorce,* quoted by Commander Stephen King-Hall at the inaugural public meeting of C.N.D.

IN an age of so-called consensus politics, the Campaign for Nuclear Disarmament provided a dramatic and colourful diversion. For a brief period of about four years – from the spring of 1958 until the winter of 1962 – it became the focal point for many of the frustrations and fears of a vocal section of the British people over the problem of defence in a nuclear age, and the apparent inability of the political system to reflect those feelings. From its beginning, C.N.D. gave rise to intense, and often bitter, controversy. The movement's opponents in the national Press and among party politicians were numerous and vociferous. Hugh Dalton, one of the few Labour figures consistently opposed to Fascism and in favour of rearmament in the 1930s, denounced it as 'national egoism gone mad',[1] whilst Constantine FitzGibbon, the author of a lurid novel on the probable results of C.N.D. gaining political power in Britain entitled *When the Kissing Had to Stop,* felt it was symptomatic of a 'mood ominously reminiscent of the atmosphere prevalent in pre-Hitler Germany'.[2] Of course, its supporters saw the movement somewhat differently. J. B. Priestley wrote in 1961: 'We live now in a thoroughly corrupt society. We British no longer have any bright image of ourselves –

and perhaps, among other things, we went campaigning for that image.'[3] Even the New Left, although making characteristic ideological reservations when faced with a radical mass movement, concluded that C.N.D.

> had what many took to be the missing element in the politics of the time – the swell from below, the ring of anti-Establishmentarians, the self-activity and self-reliance, the converting zeal (unhinging fixed prejudices and opening minds), the participation and comradeship.[4]

Attempts have often been made to deny that C.N.D. had any importance at all. A recent study of British defence policy in the 1950s questioned whether the movement made any significant impact either on public opinion or on the Government's defence policies.[5] However, the fact remains that C.N.D. was able to attract a crowd of over 75,000 in 1960 and 100,000 in 1961 to the London finale of the Aldermaston March. Even the critical *Daily Telegraph* was forced to admit that the 1960 demonstration was the largest to be held in Trafalgar Square since V.E. night. No other mass movement in recent British history was ever able to equal such numbers.

Although disquiet over nuclear weapons had been evident in Britain since the dropping of the A-bomb on Hiroshima and Nagasaki in 1945, concern appeared to be intermittent and confined to a very small politically conscious section of the community. Neither the Hydrogen Bomb National Campaign in 1954 nor the National Committee for the Abolition of Nuclear Weapon Tests (N.C.A.N.W.T.), founded in February 1957, made much impression. The Emergency Committee for Direct Action, founded in 1954, hit the headlines occasionally with sit-downs at nuclear air-bases, but did not act as a catalyst to generate a mass movement against nuclear weapons.

However, in the winter of 1957 a number of coincidental, though largely unconnected, factors served to prepare the climate for the formation of a campaign for nuclear disarmament which would gain wider support than its predecessors,. The political atmosphere in Britain after the Suez operation was no longer one of amiable bipartisanship. For the first time since the 1930s a political issue had divided the nation, and many young people, previously without any interest in politics, were attracted to the Left. Moreover, the implications of the Government's reappraisal of Britain's defence policy – begun in 1956 – were brought home in a characteristically brutal fashion by Duncan Sandys in his 1957 Defence White Paper. The Conservative administration had decided to adopt the strategy of 'massive nuclear retaliation', even in the event of a conventional attack by the Soviet Union on the West. The White Paper also admitted that Britain was incapable of defending itself against nuclear attack. Paragraph 12 began bluntly: 'It must be frankly recognised that there is at present no means of providing adequate protection for the people of this country against the consequences of an attack with nuclear weapons.'[6] Plans for the construction of Thor missile bases in East Anglia, and the reported flights over Britain of the bomber patrols of the R.A.F. and U.S. Air Force, dramatised the country's vulnerability in the event of a global nuclear conflict. Anxiety was also building up over the effects of radiation from nuclear testing in the atmosphere. Ever since the *Lucky Dragon* incident in the Pacific in 1954, a series of medical reports on the effects of radiation had attracted public attention to the dangers of strontium-90. Above all, there was the apparent complacency of the British Government – unable to reach agreement with the Soviet Union over even partial nuclear disarmament and unwilling to inform the public of the horrors which a nuclear war would involve.

The 'real catalyst' for setting up a campaign against nuclear arms came from an article in the *New Statesman* by the popular novelist J. B. Priestley, entitled 'Britain and the Nuclear Bombs'. His simple and persuasive argument was that Britain should give a moral lead to the world and contract out of the nuclear arms race. By doing so, he argued, this country would increase its influence in the world and help to end the nuclear arms deadlock. Priestley sought to evoke the spirit of 1940 and Dunkirk – a time when he was as successful on the radio as Winston Churchill in capturing the public mood. As he wrote in his article, 'Alone we defied Hitler – alone we can defy this nuclear madness into which the spirit of Hitler seems to have passed, to poison the world.' He ended with an eloquent plea:

> The British of these times, so frequently hiding their decent, kind faces behind masks of sullen apathy or sour, cheap cynicism, often seem to be waiting for something better than party squabbles and appeals to their narrowest self-interest, something great and noble in its intention that would make them feel good again. And this might well be a declaration to the world that after a certain date one power able to engage in nuclear warfare will reject the evil thing for ever.[7]

The unexpectedly large and favourable response of *New Statesman* readers of the article led to a decision by the Editor, Kingsley Martin, to call together a meeting of prominent Left-wing figures to discuss the possibility of forming an organisation to try and propagate Priestley's argument.

In early January 1958, at a meeting at 2 Amen Court in the City, C.N.D. was born. The Chairman of the Campaign was to be Canon John Collins of St Paul's Cathedral. A one-time R.A.F. chaplain during the war and later a founding member of Christian Action, he had been devoting most of his energy before 1958 to the struggle against *apartheid*, and came into national prominence by his work for the South African Treason Trial Fund. Bertrand Russell, philosopher and mathematician, agreed to become honorary President. He had been active in peace movements since 1914. The full-time organising secretary of the movement was Mrs Peggy Duff, who had been working on N.C.A.N.W.T. With her organisational experience in Victor Gollancz's 'Save Europe' Campaign in 1945 and work in the mid-1950s for the National Campaign for the Abolition of

Capital Punishment, she gave a welcome touch of professionalism to the movement in its early days.

Canon Collins, at a Press conference held at the end of January 1958, declared that the aim of the Campaign was 'to channel the existing emotion in the country and create a climate of opinion which would make it essential for the political parties to follow'. Priestley claimed that he did not like campaigns and Press conferences and preferred 'his typewriter and plenty of tobacco', but that the pressure for such a campaign was overwhelming. 5,000 people attended the first public meeting of C.N.D. at the Central Hall, Westminster, in February 1958. Despite the lack of publicity, C.N.D. had been launched on its dramatic course. At the beginning, the movement tended to concentrate its energies on converting public opinion. It sought to bring home to people the urgency of the issue of the Bomb and heighten a feeling of moral concern and commitment. Robert Bolt, the playwright, wrote: 'Unilateralism has become merely a millennial gesture of faith in human nature. We have to live like Christians now or not at all. The brotherhood of man is no longer a notion. It is here.'[8] This spirit of revivalism and dedication was very apparent on the first Aldermaston March at Easter 1958, organised by the Direct Action Committee Against Nuclear Weapons. Although not a marcher himself, Canon Collins wrote of the spirit displayed there: 'It was one of expectancy, of dedication and of hope, more religious and more reverent than many church services that I have attended.'[9] Over 8,000 people gathered in Trafalgar Square on Good Friday prepared to walk the fifty miles to the atomic research establishment in Berkshire. It was a serious and highly respectable gathering. Political banners and slogans were deliberately discouraged by the organisers. The issue was to be portrayed as one of morality. As Canon Collins told the vast crowd, 'the H-bomb is the supreme moral issue of the day. The symbol of the cross must replace the symbol of the sword.' Many Christians, particularly Quakers, were attracted to the new movement. Notable churchmen like Father Trevor Huddleston and the Rev. Donald Soper gave their active support to the cause.

The C.N.D. leaders were no doubt surprised at the initial success of the movement's moral appeal. By March 1959 over 270 local groups and 12 regional committees had been formed in all parts of the country, but particularly in the London area, the North-west of England and Scotland. The readiest response to its appeal came from the younger generation – and especially among students from middle-class backgrounds. Although at no time during its history did the movement capture the support of a majority in the universities, for its first four years a large section of the politically conscious student population was attracted to it. A combined universities' Campaign for Nuclear Disarmament was founded in 1958. It became an important branch of the movement, for intellectual support and policy-making.

A. J. P. Taylor was complaining after only six months of the Campaign's existence that it appeared to be a 'movement of eggheads for eggheads'.[10] Certainly its list of original sponsors in 1958 read like a Left-wing intellectual *Who's Who*: John Berger, Philip Toynbee, Alex Comfort, Peggy Ashcroft, Doris Lessing, Herbert Read. Many of the new dramatists of the Royal Court Theatre like John Osborne, Robert Bolt and Arnold Wesker joined C.N.D. Its refreshing and simple moral appeal also attracted many artists, musicians and composers. They were to add colour and gaiety to the Aldermaston marchers. Lindsay Anderson made a moving film, *March to Aldermaston*, of the 1958 march. Pop posters, protest songs and banners proliferated. A distinctive badge was designed, which had an immediate appeal.

C.N.D. was essentially middle-class in its composition and character. Unlike nineteenth-century moral crusades, it lacked a vociferous working-class following. Affluent North London suburbs like Hampstead, Finchley and Golders Green were more responsive to C.N.D. than Limehouse, Stepney and Whitechapel. Its supporters placed moral issues above 'bread and butter' problems. Despite constant attempts to encourage supporters to work for the cause through their local councils and voluntary bodies, they were more interested in the politics of affirmation. Dr Parkin's survey of 800 activists shows that in order of priorities only 1 per cent put local politics first, as compared to the 56 per cent for whom international affairs were of supreme importance.[11]

The anti-political attitude of the rank and file was apparent from the beginning of the movement. The greatest enthusiasm, at the first Central Hall meeting, was reserved for those speakers who castigated politicians as wrong-headed or more often as evil. J. B. Priestley in his *New Statesman* article had spoken of British politicians 'surrounded by an atmosphere of power politics, intrigue, secrecy and insane invention', and concluded that they were 'more than half barmy'. Lord Russell was always ready to rake up such an anti-political stance, although by 1962 he was finding virtues in Mao Tse-tung and Nikita Khrushchev. When Emanuel Shinwell, the veteran Labour politician and ex-Minister of Defence, denounced Russell as a 'superannuated philosopher' and J. B. Priestley as 'about as woolly as any person I have known since the days of Ramsay MacDonald',[12] Russell wrote an angry letter in *The Times* saying that 'the problems raised by nuclear energy are not such as a politician's training enables him to understand'. In April 1961 he was to reach the heights of vituperation at the iniquities of power politicians in the West, when he suggested that President Kennedy and Harold Macmillan were more wicked than Hitler: 'They are the wickedest people who have ever lived in the history of man.' How such inherently evil men were ever to succumb to popular pressures was difficult to understand.

However, despite its moral appeal and castigation of power politics, C.N.D. was soon forced to make a decision as to whether ultimate success for its cause lay through trying to capture one of the political parties. A broad appeal to public opinion, with the assumption that once its simple message had received enough publicity all men of reason and common sense would join the cause, was soon judged by the leadership as an unsatisfactory strategy. It was clear, at least to the realists in C.N.D., that if they hoped to make an effective impact upon British defence and foreign policy, they would have to work through a political party. Attempts to attract all-party support in 1958 were not successful. The Conservative Party showed no interest. As many of C.N.D.'s leaders were members of the Labour Party, it was felt that the road to success lay through the Labour movement. Kingsley Martin wrote in 1960:

> I know of no way of obtaining a non-nuclear Britain except by converting the Labour Party. Unless they work through the Labour movement nuclear marchers are simply marching about to satisfy their own consciences and expressing their sense of sin and horror of nuclear war.[13]

Even A. J. P. Taylor conceded that the movement's attentions should be devoted to working through the Labour Party. As he wrote in the *New Statesman*, 'We have to convert the Labour Party, just as the Anti-Corn Law League converted Sir Robert Peel.'

At first sight it might have appeared that C.N.D. would make little impression upon the Labour movement. After all, it had been a Labour Prime Minister, Clement Attlee, who sanctioned the development of the British A-bomb, and a Labour Foreign Secretary, Ernest Bevin, who helped form the post-war European alliance system to contain the threat of possible Soviet expansion. In the early 1950s Labour in Opposition pursued a bipartisan defence and foreign policy. Whilst differences were expressed with the Government, they tended to be over matters of detail and emphasis. The fundamental aims of Britain's defence arrangements were not questioned by the Labour leadership, even though the issues of German rearmament and the development of the British H-bomb caused deep division in the party. At party conferences Clement Attlee – and later Hugh Gaitskell – cloaked their policies in the rhetoric of internationalism and spoke of the United Nations as the keystone of a future Labour foreign policy, whilst at the same time they gave support to the continuance of the alliance system of NATO, CENTO and SEATO and the independent deterrent. The leadership was firmly embedded in the thinking of the Cold War. The party's moral fervour was more usefully employed in denouncing South African *apartheid*, the Central African Federation and British policy in Cyprus.

Hugh Gaitskell, leader of the party after December 1955, was unwilling to bow to pressure from the Left on the defence issue. In the 1930s he had been forthright in his opposition to appeasement. Michael Postan believes that over the Munich settlement 'his attitude was probably more uncompromising than that of any other of the Labour men I knew, except perhaps Hugh Dalton'.[14] His distaste for Sir Stafford Cripps and the Socialist League was to reappear in his often contemptuous attitude to C.N.D. In 1958 Gaitskell was not prepared to go further than calling for a suspension of British nuclear tests and the removal of Thor missile bases from Britain, on strategic rather than moral grounds. On the issues of the independent nuclear deterrent and Britain's continued membership at NATO, he refused to concede an inch.

Moreover, in 1958 the leadership's position on defence appeared to have been strengthened by the conversion of Aneurin Bevan to the virtues of the party's official defence policy. At the 1957 Brighton conference, in a passionate speech, Bevan had poured scorn on his former Left-wing colleagues who supported unilateral nuclear disarmament by Britain. He accused them of suffering from an 'emotional spasm' and stated that he would 'not go naked into the conference chamber' or see Britain in 'diplomatic purdah'.[15] Although quibbling with Gaitskell over whether the party should favour stopping or merely suspending British nuclear tests, Bevan gave his powerful support to the Labour leadership on the defence issue. At a meeting of the Parliamentary Party in March 1959, he even went so far as to suggest that the acceptance of unilateralism by Labour would ensure it an electoral defeat of 1931 proportions.

However, despite the appearance of solidarity in the Labour Party leadership, within two years C.N.D. was in a position to capture the party conference. Its remarkable success was partly due to its ability to draw upon that traditional idealistic and moralistic element within the Labour movement which had been submerged under the rhetoric and propaganda of the Cold War. In a perceptive contribution to the *New Fabian Essays* published in 1952, Denis Healey wrote that 'the essence of British Socialism lies not in its contingent analysis or techniques, but in its determination to apply moral principles to social life'.[16] The Labour Party was particularly susceptible to this sentiment in its attitude to foreign policy. The combined influences of liberal Nonconformity and continental Marxism provided the party with its policy for international relations before the 1940s. As A. J. P. Taylor wrote of the Labour Party between the wars, 'It still held the outlook of Keir Hardie and E. D. Morel, of Brailsford and J. A. Hobson ... that imperialist capitalism was the cause of war – [that] Socialists should oppose both war and capitalism.'[17] British politicians of all parties, but notably Socialists like Ramsay MacDonald and Arthur Henderson, echoed the sentiments of internationalism and the brotherhood of man. Many looked to the League of Nations and the concept of collective security to secure world peace. At no other time were liberal principles so dominant in the conduct of British foreign policy. In the 1930s the Left believed in disarmament and were opposed to Fascism. They refused to believe that re-armament and war were the only way in which to defeat Fascism. Until 22 August 1939 they suffered from another illusion – that the Soviet Union was a peace-loving Socialist state. The Nazi–Soviet Pact shattered that belief, if only temporarily.

After 1945 there was a similar determination to build a new international order around the victorious allies, and a belief in the professed virtues of Stalinist Russia. Many were soon chastened by the onset of the Cold War in 1948, with the Communist seizure of power in Czechoslovakia, the Berlin air lift, and in 1950 the outbreak of the Korean War. On the Left of the Labour Party, however, there was much disquiet at the foreign policy of Ernest Bevin, which appeared to run counter to the idealistic traditions of the party. The Keep Left Group led by Barbara Castle, Ian Mikardo and Richard Crossman sought a Third Force – a balance of Western Europe between the United States and the Soviet Union – and questioned Britain's subservient support for the Atlantic Alliance. The Left also became intensely anti-American – a sentiment which was reinforced by the appearance of John Foster Dulles at the State Department in 1952 intent on launching a crusade against Communism, and by the McCarthy witch-hunts in 1953 and 1954.

C.N.D. was able to appeal to the traditional sentiments within the Labour movement, as well as to the feelings of frustration of many in the party at the dominant consensus within the political world on the fundamental principles of Britain's defence and foreign policy. J. B. Priestley was aware of the links which C.N.D. had with the Labour past when he wrote:

I grew up with the Labour movement and was writing little pieces for it nearly half a century ago. Conditions are very different now of course, but the fundamental character of a broad political movement, its inner nature, should not change if it is to keep its vitality.[18]

To Priestley, Labour's acceptance of the Bomb meant that it was 'cutting optimism and decency'.

Along with the nascent liberal idealism in the Labour movement, there were other factors which made the party particularly vulnerable to C.N.D. arguments. The Soviet invasion of Hungary in 1956 led to a mass exodus from the British Communist Party. Many moved into the Labour Party and strengthened its Left wing. They brought with them their old views – that the Cold War was a thing of the past and that Russia's intentions were essentially peaceful. After the events in Hungary this might have appeared a rather strange attitude to adopt. Yet the belief that there was both no moral difference between the two Great Powers and that the Cold War was irrelevant to Britain's national interest was powerful in the Labour Left.

At the same time there was a significant change in the balance of power within the Labour movement. Ever since the 1930s the leadership had rested its position on the loyalty of the big unions with their block votes at party conferences. In 1955 Frank Cousins became General Secretary of Bevin's old union, the Transport and General Workers. Although not consistently left-wing, his accession to power in the largest of the general unions added an element of instability to the position of the party leadership. The block vote of the big unions wielded in the early 1950s was no longer an automatic weapon in the hands of the party Establishment.[19] The combination of a resurgent moral idealism and changing power relations in the Labour movement made Gaitskell's position vulnerable. A. J. P. Taylor summed up C.N.D. strategy in the summer of 1958: 'We are not seeking to disrupt the Labour Party nor to challenge its leadership. We are seeking to win it over. We offer it the moral leadership of the world.'

This intoxicating appeal was to find many converts in the party's ranks in the next few years, particularly, according to Taylor, among those stalwarts who were active in Left-wing causes in the 1930s and remembered 'the Peace Ballot, sanctions and the Abyssinian War'. Whilst few workers were seen on the Aldermaston Marches, and attempts to interest workers in forming C.N.D. work cells in the factories came to nothing, there was a vocal and active group in the constituency parties and trade union branches sympathetic to the C.N.D. cause. If the movement's support had only encompassed middle-class intelligentsia who read the *New Statesman* and students who read the *New Left Review*, it would have been unable to expand in size beyond other Left-wing humanitarian pressure groups such as the National Campaign for the Abolition of Capital Punishment. A Labour Advisory Committee in C.N.D. under John Horner of the Fire Brigade Union and the Co-operative M.P. Frank Beswick linked the party activists with the movement. The Committee's success probably lay more in channelling existing feelings in local trade union branches through to the union nationally, than in the actual process of conversion.

232

For the period 1958 to 1961 the party Establishment found itself under an increasing threat from the traditional Left strengthened by the moral certitude of C.N.D. By the time of the 1959 march from Aldermaston to Trafalgar Square, Labour support was more apparent than in 1958. Robert Willis, Chairman of the T.U.C. for that year and General Secretary of the London Typographical Society, stood with C.N.D. leaders on the plinth of Nelson's Column, and Frank Cousins was seen among the vast crowd, although he refused to speak from the platform. About sixty Labour M.P.s were now sympathetic to the aims of C.N.D., including the Victory for Socialism Group led by Frank Allaun and Sydney Silverman. Michael Foot and *Tribune* led the struggle for unilateralism in the party outside Parliament.

The first sign of success for C.N.D. in the Labour movement came in early June 1959. The General and Municipal Union voted by 150 to 126 with 75 abstentions for unilateral action by Britain in ceasing to manufacture nuclear weapons and in prohibiting the use of all such weapons from British territory. Although it was suggested that the abstainers were busy having tea when the vote was taken, it was undoubtedly a setback to the Labour Party leadership. Gaitskell was no doubt shocked by this decision from the most loyal of the big unions and the one of which he was a member. As a *Manchester Guardian* report commented, 'Their decision was almost like a demand by the Congress of the Soviet Communist Party for the denationalisation of the basic industries.' There was a real possibility that other unions, such as the National Union of Mineworkers and the Amalgamated Engineering Union, would follow suit, even if there was every likelihood of a General Election in the autumn. A reappraisal of party defence policy became necessary.

However, Hugh Gaitskell was reluctant to accommodate C.N.D. A Labour Party campaign in the spring of 1958 to urge the Government to stop H-bomb tests had not gone far enough to satisfy C.N.D. supporters in the party. It was conceded that there was a political need to control this mass upsurge on the Left, but

Gaitskell was only too painfully aware of the implications of the C.N.D. appeal, which its leaders had not clearly thought out. After the inaugural Central Hall meeting, the C.N.D. Executive had re-written their statement of aims to the effect that they sought British repudiation not only of her own nuclear deterrent but also of any defence system which involved the threat of the use of nuclear weapons. This implied withdrawal from the NATO alliance and the adoption of a neutralist policy, but such an implication was left vague. In the early years many supporters believed that their concern was merely with the repudiation of the British bomb, and did not involve themselves in the question of whether they would have to go beyond this and demand that Britain leave NATO. As it was the visible manifestation of the alliance, with the missile bases under American control, which gave much emotional momentum to C.N.D., it is surprising that the neutrality issue was not faced and decided upon at an earlier date. From 1958 Gaitskell attacked his opponents in the party on this question of whether their policy involved leaving the alliances, and no effective reply was ever given to the charge.

But Gaitskell also went on to support the British independent deterrent – a policy which was not endorsed by everybody in the Labour Party outside the unilateralist Left. Ever since 1954 Richard Crossman and George Wigg had opposed the British bomb, whilst continuing to support Britain's membership of NATO. As Crossman argued in the 1958 defence debate, 'The trouble about the nuclear deterrent is that if we have one big enough to be militarily significant, we ruin the country, and if we have one within the economic resources of the country, then it is so trivial that it impresses no Great Power.' Gaitskell did not accept this view. He believed that possession of the Bomb enabled Britain to pursue an independent foreign policy, and used a similar kind of argument to his C.N.D. opponents later – that Britain had 'an opportunity of interposing between America and Russia' and being a 'modifying, moderating, mitigating influence'.[20] He also believed that the Liberal Party policy of a repudiation of the British deterrent whilst remaining in the NATO alliance would make Britain even more dependent on the United States, and concluded that it might even involve the country in another MacArthur-type adventure in South-east Asia.

With his fears about the implications of C.N.D. and belief in the independent deterrent, Gaitskell's room for manœuvre in the aftermath of the N.U.G.M.W. decision was limited. A joint committee of the T.U.C. and the National Executive drew up the 'non-nuclear club' idea to placate Left-wing opinion. It had been hinted at by Gaitskell in 1958 and recommended by Anthony Greenwood in March of 1959. The *Manchester Guardian* had been advocating it for some time. Although it did not satisfy Frank Cousins, it did prevent a split in the party. To most contemporary observers, however, it looked like a new policy dictated by internal party pressures and not a serious reappraisal of the defence question. It was notably equivocal on the actual stages for the club's development, particularly on whether it would mean a unilateral repudiation of the independent deterrent as a first step. While the club idea may have enabled the Labour Party to enter the 1959 General Election united on defence, in its bitter aftermath unilateralism was once more to become an explosive issue.

Throughout the next two years C.N.D.'s campaign was conducted almost entirely with the aim of capturing the Labour Party. Moreover, it was undoubtedly helped by the growing revolt against Gaitskell's desire to revise Clause 4 of the party constitution. The leaders of the old Bevanite Left like Barbara Castle and Anthony Greenwood began to identify themselves with C.N.D. for the first time in the spring of 1960. In March, Richard Crossman resigned from the Opposition front bench in protest at the 'futile and costly pretence' of trying to keep Britain an independent nuclear power. Whilst he did not join C.N.D., his action indicated that the party's official policy was becoming increasingly untenable. Over forty Labour M.P.s abstained from voting in the defence debate. In the early summer a number of the larger unions slid casually into the unilateralist camp, in varying degrees. With the defection of the Union of Shop, Distributive and Allied Workers, the Amalgamated Engineering Union, the National Union of Railwaymen and the Transport and General Workers' Union, who between them controlled over 2 million votes at the party conference, the solid trade union support had drifted away from Gaitskell. By June even his faithful supporters George Brown and Denis Healey felt that a reappraisal of the party's policy was needed, particularly when the Government announced that the Blue Streak missile designed to carry the deterrent was to be abandoned and that it was going to purchase Skybolt from the Americans. On his return from Israel in the middle of July, Gaitskell accepted that the party would have to abandon its support for the British deterrent. A new policy statement on defence was issued by the end of the month, which declared that the break-up of the Paris Summit Conference in May and Blue Streak's cancellation was responsible for the decision. Whilst reaffirming the party's traditional adherence to the United Nations and defence of West Berlin, the statement declared that 'Britain's future contribution to the Western armoury' would be in the development of conventional forces. The deterrent was to become a monopoly of the Americans. The fact that ultimate control over its use would rest with Washington was glossed over by vague talk of 'strengthening the NATO Council of Foreign Ministers and Defence Ministers.'[21] A demand that the United States should pledge itself not to use their deterrent without NATO's prior agreement was a totally impracticable suggestion, as the Cuba missile crisis of 1962 was to illustrate.

The new policy arrived too late to lead to a swing back by the big unions, and at the 1960 Scarborough conference Gaitskell decided to meet the unilateralist challenge by a policy of no more compromise. He was helped in this decision by the unsatisfactory case put up in the defence debate by C.N.D. supporters. Neither the A.E.U. nor the T.G.W.U. resolution went far enough, for neither explicitly called upon Britain to leave NATO. Frank Cousins made a confusing and emotional speech, which ended:

When I am asked if it means getting out of NATO, if the question is posed to me as simply saying, am I prepared to go on remaining in an organisation over which I have no control, but which can destroy us instantly, my answer is yes, if the choice is that. But it is not that.[22]

It was easy, therefore, for Gaitskell to expose the weaknesses of the opposition case. He was able to attack the implications of the two resolutions over neutrality. As he argued, 'If you are a unilateralist on principle, you are driven to becoming a neutralist – you are driven to becoming one of those who wish us to withdraw from NATO.'

Unlike Harold Wilson, Gaitskell did not see the issue as one capable of compromise or equivocation. Often accused by his opponents of intellectual arrogance and intolerance, he recognised the defence issue as a test of loyalty to his own leadership of the party. As the *New Statesman* admitted in an editorial entitled 'Wanted – a Leader', 'the successful vote for unilateralism was largely due to distrust of Mr Gaitskell'. Despite the repudiation of the independent deterrent by the new official defence policy, Gaitskell did not emphasise this fact in his speech to the conference. He preferred to concentrate his attack on the neutralist aspect of the question, and appeal directly to the principles of the majority of the Parliamentary Party, where his ultimate source of support lay and where C.N.D. could rely on no more than about eighty M.P.s to support their viewpoint. As he argued:

It is not in dispute that the vast majority of Labour Members of Parliament are utterly opposed to unilateralism and neutralism. So what do you expect them to do? Change their minds overnight? To go back on the pledges they gave to the people who elected them from their constituencies? ... People of the so-called Right and so-called Centre have every justification for having a conscience, as well as people of the so-called Left.'[23]

After Gaitskell's impassioned speech, the vote on the

official defence policy was surprisingly close. It was defeated by only 297,000 votes out of over 6 million cast. Ironically, C.N.D. triumphed by the use of the much criticised union block vote. The majority of the constituency parties followed the leadership. This was regarded as an unusual reversal of the traditional alignment in the Labour movement from the Bevanite days.

At the Scarborough conference the defence issue had been a catalyst for the dramatic and passionate collision between Left and Right. There was some fear, however, expressed by members of C.N.D. – notably George Clark – that their moral crusade was merely being used as a useful instrument with which to bring down Gaitskell, and that the Labour Left would not consolidate the victory which had been narrowly won. As early as the end of October 1960 Anthony Greenwood was telling a meeting at the Central Hall, Westminster, that it would be absurd for anyone to split the Labour Party 'on an issue which changes from day to day', and that 'neither side should be too dogmatic or too demanding'. When the unilateralist M.P.s supported Harold Wilson in his contest against Gaitskell for the leadership of the Parliamentary Party in the following month, it was clear that the leadership question was taking precedence over that of defence, for Wilson had been one of the main architects of the rejected official defence policy. He believed that party unity could not be achieved under Gaitskell's leadership and that the necessary personal trust which bound together the wings of the movement required a more suitable leader. Gaitskell won the election by 166 votes to 81. Although some non-unilateralist Left-wing M.P.s like Richard Crossman voted for Wilson, the bulk were C.N.D. supporters. Apparently there were few in the Parliamentary Party who accepted the argument that the issue was one of personality, not of principle. By their readiness to compromise, the Left in Parliament tarnished their moral image. At the 1961 C.N.D. conference there was much outspoken criticism by delegates of their behaviour. Attempts by Michael Foot, now M.P. for Ebbw Vale, to interest delegates in the Crossman–Padley compromise were unsuccessful. This was not very sur-

238

prising. Its only difference from the official policy lay in its view that NATO strategy should not be based on the threat of a first nuclear strike. The hostility in C.N.D. to the activities of the Labour Left brought criticism from the *New Statesman*. John Freeman, Martin's successor to the Editorship, complained of the movement's 'negative campaigning' and argued that anyway 'most unilateralists are frustrated multilateralists'.

C.N.D. had lacked any strategy of what to do once they had 'captured' the party conference. David Marquand, perhaps unfairly, concluded that their position was 'now as though the Salvation Army had suddenly inherited a majority shareholding in a Soho strip club'.[24] With Gaitskell's determination to reverse the conference decision and rest his leadership on the support of the Parliamentary Party, C.N.D. was divided about how to consolidate their victory. A pro Gaitskell body was set up under the general direction of W. T. Rodgers to reverse the Scarborough decision and mobilise Right-wing opinion – the Campaign for Democratic Socialism. Although it is difficult to assess its importance in the reversal of the Scarborough decision, C.D.S. helped to encourage the loyalists and prevent a further erosion of support for the official defence policy in the Labour movement.[25] C.N.D. was further frustrated by Gaitskell's own determination to carry on the struggle through the winter of 1960–1. Despite continued criticism and personal abuse, he toured the country, arguing passionately against unilateralism. Unlike his successor, Gaitskell took conference decisions seriously. By a combination of consistent argument and an appeal to traditional loyalty for the leadership, he was able to ensure that the Scarborough decision would be reversed. It now appeared that the Labour leadership was sincere in its opposition to the independent deterrent – a view which was to be strengthened by its hostile attitude to the Nassau Agreement. Even Denis Healey was ready to condemn the deterrent as 'a sort of virility symbol to compensate for the exposure of British military impotence'. No doubt these factors help explain the Blackpool conference decision to reject unilateralism. Yet the very close reversals at the U.S.D.A.W. and N.U.R. spring conferences of 1961 indicate that C.N.D.'s defeat was by no means certain.

Gaitskell's 'victory' at Blackpool was only partial. Resolutions against the Polaris base at Holy Loch and the training of West German soldiers in South Wales were both passed against the advice of the platform, although the official defence policy was supported by 4,526,000 to 1,756,000 and a neutralist motion defeated by a crushing vote of 5,476,000 to 846,000.

As over the Clause 4 dispute, Gaitskell was forced to concede to some demands of the Left. No doubt his repudiation of the independent deterrent owed much to his personal conviction of its impracticability after Blue Streak's cancellation, but by the summer of 1960 no other policy would have kept the Labour Party together. As the *New Statesman* pointed out, 'the Labour executive policy that was defeated at Scarborough last year was in many respects more radical than the early programme of C.N.D.'[26]

It was clear that the gulf between the Labour Left and the party leadership was not unbridgeable on paper, even if it was in spirit, as the attitude of the C.N.D. Labour supporters to Harold Wilson illustrates. David Marquand concluded that the result of both the Clause 4 row and the defence issue was to place 'Labourism' – 'that illogical and intellectually vacuous compromise between Socialist rhetoric and Reformist practice' – back 'in the saddle'.[27]

And yet perhaps this was not the most significant result of the impact of C.N.D. on the Labour movement. No doubt it helped, at least in theory, to prevent the Labour leadership following its European Social Democratic partners too far along the revisionist path. Richard Crossman was closer to the heart of the Labour movement than Anthony Crosland. But C.N.D.'s most important function was to have enhanced Gaitskell's reputation as a politician and made him the most dynamic and unquestioned leader of the Labour Party since the days of Ramsay MacDonald's ascendancy in the 1920s.

C.N.D.'s failure after Scarborough to consolidate its

victory was partly due to the exertions of the movement's opponents in the Labour Party. The desire for unity, particularly at the time when the Macmillan Government was becoming increasingly unpopular in 1961, also weakened C.N.D.'s influence in the party. But the divisions over strategy and personality which afflicted C.N.D. in the autumn of 1960 did much to dissipate its hard-earned triumph. Civil disobedience, which was always a source of anxiety to C.N.D.'s leaders from the beginning, was now to cause deep division. Since 1954 the Direct Action Committee under Michael Randle and Pat Arrowsmith had been in existence, pledged to militant methods of exerting pressure on the Government to change its defence policy. It continued after the formation of C.N.D., and although the new movement did not condone illegal activities, it did not disavow the Committee's aims either. Even Canon Collins, who continually doubted the expediency of militant action, admits in his autobiography that 'without them C.N.D. would have lost something vital to it, something of its soul'.[28]

The 'invasion' of the R.A.F. rocket base at Swaffham and a sit-down at the Atomic Weapons Research Establishment on Foulness were only two of many incidents during the period before the autumn of 1960. On the eve of the Scarborough conference, however, a disclosure was made in the *Evening Standard* that a new movement of non-violent resistance and civil disobedience was to be formed under the benevolent auspices of Bertrand Russell. A committee of 100 was to organise mass sit-downs of over 2,000 people in certain strategic places in protest at government policy. Whereas the old Direct Action Committee sought to persuade individuals to civil disobedience on grounds of conscience, the new Committee sought to disrupt the state by mass coercive means. The C.N.D. leadership opposed its creation. Canon Collins felt 'it was the greatest possible mistake', and Commander Stephen King-Hall, one of the founding members of C.N.D., declared that Russell's proposals were 'both improper and futile' – adding that it was 'through Parliament and only through Parliament that the basis of our defence strategy should be changed'. At the moment of its illusory triumph in the Labour Party, the C.N.D. leadership was bitterly divided by personality as well as by differences over strategy following the creation of the Committee of 100. After a series of bitter, and often comical, personal exchanges with Collins, Russell resigned the Presidency of C.N.D., and along with the Rev. Michael Scott and Michael Randle of the old Direct Action Committee, devoted himself with characteristic zeal and determination to the new campaign.

Although the Committee of 100 did not attract as many 'leading ballerinas' to the cause as C.N.D. originally did in 1958, they did recruit the Left-wing playwrights of the Royal Court like John Osborne and Arnold Wesker. Vanessa Redgrave, Herbert Read and John Braine were also members. After intense discussion, the Committee decided to stage a massive sitdown outside the Ministry of Defence in Whitehall on 18 February to coincide with the arrival in Scotland of the first Polaris submarine at Holy Loch, a stagingpost for the American nuclear fleet. The strain of militancy, endemic in C.N.D. since 1958, now came to the forefront with ever greater force. The Committee of 100 was closer to the heart of C.N.D. than the old leadership. While they had placed their faith in working through the Labour Party, the rank and file often gave the impression that they were not interested in the give and take involved in the usual methods of political persuasion. As it became clearer that the Labour leadership would not succumb easily to a full-blooded neutralist policy, many were to turn out of frustration to the instant delights of direct action. The worsening international situation over Berlin in 1961 added an urgency to the new movement. Pat Arrowsmith voiced their concern when she wrote: 'If we are not to become mere puppets we must be prepared to take radical direct action for what we believe to be right ... The spirit of democracy is sometimes better preserved when the law is broken – even though it may have been passed by a parliamentary majority.'

The first sit-down went ahead as planned on 18 February 1961, when about 4,000 people sat down for two and a half hours outside the Ministry of Defence. The authorities did not appear very dismayed. When Earl Russell sought to nail a petition to the door of the Ministry, one official came out and offered Sellotape as a substitute, which was accepted. Much to Russell's dismay, the police took no action against the demonstrators. As he complained to a Press conference on the following day, 'We do not want for ever to be tolerated by the police. Our movement depends for its success on an immense public opinion and we cannot create that unless we raise the authorities to more action than they took yesterday.' His recently appointed private secretary, Ralph Schoenman, the *eminence grise* behind the Committee of 100, summed up their aims: 'We want to put the Government in the position of either gaoling thousands of people or abdicating.'

In later sit-downs the Committee was to have more success in goading the police into action. At the end of April 1961 over 800 people were arrested and fined £1 each for sitting down, and breaking Section 52 of the Metropolitan Police Act of 1839. The Berlin crisis and the resumption of Russian and American nuclear tests in the atmosphere in the autumn of 1961 brought the Committee of 100 renewed support. Lord Russell was sentenced to a week's imprisonment, under an Act of 1361, for refusing to promise to keep the peace for a year. Feelings in C.N.D. rose sharply, and on Battle of Britain Sunday the Committee of 100 reached the culmination of its brief but dramatic expansion. Even a reluctant Canon Collins was drawn into the demonstration. 12,000 turned up at Trafalgar Square and thousands sat. 1,314 people were arrested, and the police acted with some violence. Even the unsympathetic Herb Greer admitted that 'after midnight when television cameras and reporters went home, they launched a deliberate and vicious attack against the scattered remnants of the crowd'.[29] One member of C.N.D. later believed that there was a revolutionary spirit in Central London on that day – but it was to be only momentary.

There was a growing tendency in the nuclear disarmament movement to search around for new sensations and means of gaining publicity. The constant desire of C.N.D. to appear law-abiding and respectable was being undermined. Some blame for these developments must rest with the Committee of 100, who legitimised civil disobedience and encouraged direct action. Most of the responsibility must, however, lie with the failure of the C.N.D. leadership to think out their strategy clearly. By 1961 there was a noticeable gulf appearing between the leaders and the led. As David Marquand put it:

> C.N.D. has always contained two quite different groups – the politicians, of varying hues, who hoped to use it as a weapon in some wider battle – and the rank and file who joined it out of a contemptuous indifference to all politicians of varying hues whatsoever. If the rank and file ever comes to believe that it is being used by the politicians in the movement, C.N.D. will collapse or disintegrate.[30]

This is precisely what was to occur. A concentration on trying to influence the Labour Party meant that failure to achieve complete success through a traditional political channel would be so much the more apparent and disillusioning. As a member of the Committee of 100, Nicolas Walter, wrote in the *Guardian*, 'the great majority of us are Socialists with libertarian and syndicalist tendencies who have been driven into the Committee of 100 by growing impatience with conventional political methods'.

Hatred of the Labour Party and its leaders now came to a head. Both Hugh Gaitskell and George Brown were the objects of attack at the 1962 May Day rallies of the Labour Party in Glasgow and Hyde Park. It was becoming increasingly clear that C.N.D. was no longer regarded as a pressure group seeking to influence the political system in the rejection of nuclear weapons, but as a vehicle through which to express resentment at the system itself. The Committee of 100, although by early 1962 almost bank-rupt of finance or support, began to talk of extending, as Tony Chandler put it, 'the philosophy of non-violence into all branches of life'. They contemplated trying to arouse the unemployed or the London homeless to stage sit-downs in L.C.C. hostels.

C.N.D. leaders resisted rank-and-file attempts to try and extend their interest into the fields of race relations and economic policy. A motion at the 1962 conference arguing that the Common Market was 'an economic arrangement for the perpetuation of the Bomb' was defeated. Demands for a campaign to ensure token and direct industrial action, including the blacking of work on armament projects, were ignored by the leadership.

While C.N.D. after 1961 became more fissiparous, at the same time it became more organised. Part of its success in the early years had been due to its spontaneity and flexibility in organisation, although the Executive Committee might have appeared to some to be a self-perpetuating clique of celebrities unrepresentative of the rank and file. However, as is inevitable in such a movement, pressure began to build up from below to democratise C.N.D. The London region led the movement for representation of provincial opinions. Attempts to satisfy this feeling by co-opting one representative from each of the twelve regions formed were not enough to satisfy rank-and-file opinion, and in 1961 a constitution was drawn up. With the creation of a mass membership, a delegate system to Annual Conference which enabled rotten-borough branches to sprout up in the country, and a growth in the number of full-time organisers, C.N.D. became ossified. Moreover, by giving the rank and file a louder voice in the affairs of the movement, it increased C.N.D.'s anti-political attitude. The Crewe resolution, which would have bound the leadership to call for either Soviet or American disarmament, was embarrassing to the leaders. As factions grew stronger in C.N.D., they were able to exploit the complexities and loopholes in the constitution to frustrate and disrupt the leadership's policy. As a prominent C.N.D.

leader argued, the situation in the movement by the end of 1961 was similar to that in the Labour Party at Scarborough.

The Aldermaston March also began to lose the moral impact of the early years. Many people began to see it as yet another institutionalised ritual of Easter like the Roses cricket match and Hampstead Fair. No doubt the carnival atmosphere had a liberating effect on the younger generation, although it appeared increasingly that this effect was to be seen more as an emancipation from the constraints of 'bourgeois' morality than as concern for the horrors of possible nuclear war. Although the national Press, radio and television tended to ignore C.N.D. at the beginning, for the period 1959 to 1961 they gave a reasonably sympathetic coverage to the movement's activities. By the time of the 1962 march there was growing hostility towards the marchers. The *Guardian* reporter on the 1962 march estimated that not more than one in twenty of the marchers were over twenty-one, and a high proportion under eighteen. With the weird array of dress, the long hair and beards, jeans and duffle coats, they became a hostile target for the Press. Indeed, one enterprising Sunday newspaper employed a reporter to write an article on the morals of the marchers.

The 1963 march caused a sensation with the circulation of a pamphlet in contravention of the Official Secrets Act, exposing in detail the whereabouts of the Regional Seats of Government to be used in case of nuclear attack. C.N.D. leaders were unable to prevent many marchers from invading one such establishment near Reading. After the Hyde Park Rally, when 30,000 people listened to the speakers at the end of the march, a number of C.N.D. followers ran amuck through the West End. As Peter Cadogan, leader of the 'March Must Decide' Committee, argued: 'We have changed the whole character of the March by these demonstrations. We have put it back on the front pages instead of the back.' In July there were renewed disturbances during the visit of Queen Frederika of Greece to London in protest at the mur-

246

der of a prominent Greek nuclear disarmer, Lambrakis. Canon Collins was to confess that there was a 'real ferment in the movement' which 'seemed to have left the purely nuclear issue behind'.

The militant activities of the Committee of 100 were symptomatic of a growing movement, not merely towards civil disobedience, but towards violence – a trend which became even more apparent in the later 1960s. The disturbances of 1963 were to herald a new phase in the revolt of the younger generation against Western society. The quietist and almost reverent atmosphere of C.N.D. in the early years had gone.

As the extremist groups increased their strength within C.N.D., the Labour Left began to leave. It is ironical that the militants should have captured the movement at the very moment when the strategic and economic implications of unilateral disarmament were being worked out. Mervyn Jones, in a pamphlet entitled *Freed From Fear*, sought to interest C.N.D. in the complexities of a defence policy, but such attempts were unsuccessful.

As it became apparent that C.N.D. was losing ground in the Labour Party, the old dilemma reappeared for those supporters who repudiated direct action but now realised that their success in the Labour Party was to be only a temporary one. In June 1962 INDEC was formed to run candidates in elections purely on the nuclear issue. As in the spring of 1959 when the Direct Action Committee sought to encourage a Voter's Veto Campaign at the South-East Norfolk by-election, the Labour Left found their loyalties divided. Although C.N.D. leaders repudiated INDEC, the inability of the Labour wing to revivify the movement's success in the Labour Party made it increasingly difficult to keep the loyalties of the rank and file in working through traditional channels.

The ultimate failure of C.N.D., however, does not lie in the growing evidence of its own contradictions and fragmentations. External events, which led to C.N.D.'s first successes, now worked against it. The Cuba missile crisis in the autumn of 1962 led to a

247

momentary increase in support for C.N.D. The alarm felt in Britain went far beyond the nuclear disarmers. But in the aftermath of the crisis several illusions nurtured by C.N.D. were destroyed. The deterrent theory was seen to work, and President Kennedy's self-restraint underlined the fact that the United States was not bent on world-wide aggression. In July 1963 the partial test-ban treaty, although a very limited step forward in a gradual *détente* between the United States and the Soviet Union, also weakened the C.N.D. case. It underlined the fact that the hostility of so many in the movement to the diplomatists and traditional methods of solving international problems was ill founded. Moreover, the ending of testing in the atmosphere by the United States, the Soviet Union and Britain meant that the visible signs and effects of the atomic bomb were no longer apparent. The most powerful emotional arguments could no longer be effectively deployed by C.N.D.

Harold Wilson's accession to the leadership of the Labour Party in February 1963 also helped to weaken C.N.D. By the autumn of that year, Michael Foot and Anthony Greenwood had decided to withdraw from the C.N.D. Executive. As the Labour Party closed its ranks for the coming General Election, the leaders decided to stop any further discussions about defence within its ranks. At the 1963 conference it was not even debated. By the time of the October 1964 election, indeed, it was Sir Alec Douglas-Home who was campaigning on the defence issue.[31] Fortunately for the Labour Party the electorate were more concerned with the cost of living, housing and pensions. Only 7 per cent of the Gallup sample saw defence as the single most important issue of the campaign. Harold Wilson devoted only one speech to the nuclear deterrent, although making speeches at Portsmouth and Chatham urging the further improvement of the Navy. 37 per cent of a Gallup sample, indeed, preferred the Conservative policy on defence, while only 21 per cent preferred the policy of the Labour Party.

Although C.N.D. might have influenced Harold
248

Macmillan in his attitude to the need for a test-ban treaty, its impact on public opinion, outside specific crises like Berlin or Cuba, was limited. After the 1964 election it appeared that C.N.D. had not only lost its support, but even its campaign against the independent deterrent. The Labour Government showed little inclination to abandon it or to renegotiate the Nassau Agreement. Denis Healey, the Minister of Defence, presided over the launching of a third Polaris submarine.

Moreover, international events seemed to make C.N.D.'s attitude even more untenable. Although the monolithic unity of NATO was shaken temporarily by the withdrawal of France in 1965, C.N.D. could take little comfort from the precedent. President de Gaulle believed that for a country to have any effective independence in the world it needed to possess nuclear weapons. Nor did this prevent him from being respected in the countries of Africa and Asia. Algeria even allowed France to test her atomic bomb in the Sahara.

The virtues of positive neutrality also began to appear less apparent. Fenner Brockway had spoken of 'a new force rising in the world, challenging the old powers – creative for Socialism and peace'.[32] Some leaders in C.N.D. had even believed that Britain could lead these uncommitted nations. J. B. Priestley wrote that if the movement's aim had been accepted by the Labour Party, Britain would have become 'the rallying point of sane world opinion'. He reflected that 'Asia and Africa would be accepting our leadership now'.[33] The spirit of the conferences at Bandung in 1955 and Belgrade in 1961 was regarded as 'a reaffirmation of traditional Socialist and humanitarian internationalism in an era when the world has become a single social system'.[34] It was to evaporate by the mid-1960s.

While C.N.D., as a whole, repudiated violence as a means of conducting a political argument, it did so at a time when it was becoming an accepted method of achieving one's ends. The threat of world nuclear destruction receded into the background, perhaps temporarily, to be replaced by the more immediate and realisable horrors of racial conflict. The Vietnam war was only the most brutal manifestation of such a development. The glorification of nuclear weapons now came from China, not the United States or the Soviet Union.

C.N.D. never evolved from being a movement of emotional and moral protest. The leadership were deeply conscious of their links with the radical movements of the past. The Levellers, the Chartist Movement and the Suffragettes were often evoked on C.N.D. platforms as worthy predecessors to remember and emulate. C.N.D.'s desire to put morality back into the centre of British politics recalled the political arguments used by nineteenth-century dissenting pressure groups like the Anti-Slave Trade Movement and the United Kingdom Alliance. Just as the removal of a specific moral evil, like slavery or drink, would lead to the New Jerusalem, so by Britain's repudiation of the nuclear bomb all the tensions and hostilities in the world would disappear. Unilateralism would, like free trade in Victorian England, ensure stability and peace.

C.N.D. was perhaps the last of the old radical movements. The dissenting tradition in British foreign policy has a long and respectable history, from the impassioned eloquence of Edmund Burke over the American War of Independence and the courageous stand of Charles James Fox over the war against revolutionary France. A. J. P. Taylor, one of C.N.D.'s most popular speakers in the early years, delivered his Ford Lectures at Oxford University on just such a theme in 1956. He often seemed to see himself as the John Bright of the movement. Just as Bright denounced the Crimean War and sought an acceptance of the principle of non-intervention by Britain in foreign wars, so Taylor sought to revive the moral sentiment of nineteenth-century liberalism to combat the nuclear menace. C.N.D. although often despairing of progress, was peculiarly optimistic in its belief that its cause would triumph, because its wisdom was so self-evident. Yet as statesmen in nineteenth-century England were only too painfully aware, moral indignation is only effective when coupled with military and diplomatic power. Britain in the late 1950s and early 1960s, despite the constant utterances of its politicians of all parties, was no longer militarily or diplomatically strong. The solid base for the pursuit of a moralistic foreign policy was lacking.

Although its success was partial and its momentum lost after 1961, C.N.D. brought some fresh air into the stuffy atmosphere of British politics. It ensured that generals and politicians could no longer deceive the public with soothing words of complacency on the consequences of nuclear weapons, or rattle their sabres with irresponsible abandon. But its importance lies in the fact that it became a liberation movement for the younger generation. In Eric Hobsbawm's words, C.N.D. was 'the political expression of "youth" as a recognisable group and not merely as a period of transition, to be got through as quickly as possible, between childhood and adult life'.[35] When all the antics of the Committee of 100 and the intrigues within the Labour party have been forgotten, people will remember this unique response of the young to C.N.D. The badges, the protest songs and pop culture underlined the spontaneity and commitment of the younger generation to the cause of nuclear disarmament. As the years went by, the movement degenerated into a collection of squabbling factions. It lost the innocence and purity of its formative period, but it always retained its youthful appearance.

A *Guardian* reporter in 1961 wrote of the Aldermaston marchers:

They are not marching to overthrow capitalism or even the Conservative party, to 'defend the Scarborough decisions', to back Cousins or 'knife' Gaitskell. Most of them are not even members of the Labour Party – many have no interest in its internal struggles. To them Aldermaston has become a symbol of the general demand for disarmament and a way of applying pressure towards it.'

Perhaps C.N.D. did make a contribution to that long and never-ending quest for world peace, but its younger generation has already passed away, and the new one

251

appears less concerned with that search, and more interested in violence and world revolution.[36]

Notes

1. Quoted by David Marquand in his article 'Bombs and Scapegoats', *Encounter* (January 1961) p. 45.

2. 'Politics and the Novel', *Encounter* (June 1961) p. 72.

3. *New Statesman*, 19 May 1961, p. 784.

4. 'Scarborough and Beyond: Consequences of a Conference', *New Left Review*, no. 6 (November–December 1960) p. 5.

5. William P. Snyder, *Politics of British Defence Policy, 1945–1962* (1964) esp. pp. 59–61.

6. The 1957 White Paper on Defence is discussed by C. M. Woodhouse, in *British Foreign Policy since the Second World War* (1961) pp. 87–8.

7. *New Statesman*, 2 November 1957, pp. 554–6.

8. Ibid., 24 December 1960, p. 1000.

9. L. J. Collins, *Faith Under Fire* (1966) p. 298.

10. *New Statesman*, 21 June 1958, p. 799.

11. F. Parkin, *Middle Class Radicalism* (1968) p. 37.

12. *Hansard*, vol. 583, 27 February 1958, col. 576.

13. Quoted by Canon Collins in *Faith Under Fire*, p. 329.

14. M. Postan, 'His Political and Intellectual Progress', in Rodgers (ed.), *Hugh Gaitskell*, p. 63.

15. For Bevan's speech in full, see *Labour Party Conference Report, 1957*, pp. 179–83.

16. Denis Healey, 'Power Politics and the Labour Party', in *New Fabian Essays*, p. 165.

17. A. J. P. Taylor, *The Trouble Makers: Dissent over Foreign Policy, 1792–1939* (1957) p. 199.

18. *New Statesman*, 19 May 1961, p. 784.

19. For a discussion of this, see Martin Harrison, *Trade Unions and the Labour Party since 1945* (1960) esp. pp. 224–46.

20. See Gaitskell's speech to the 1958 Labour Party Conference.

21. *Foreign Policy and Defence Statement*, July 1960.

22. *Labour Party Conference Report, 1960*, p. 180. Mr L. Misseldine, moving the A.E.U. resolution, remarked: 'The question of whether we stay in or get out of NATO does not fall within the moving of my resolution' (p. 177).

23. Ibid., p. 201.

24. 'Bombs and Scapegoats', *Encounter* (January 1961) p. 43.

25. There is an excellent account of this semi-clandestine pressure group in Lord Windlesham, *Communication and Political Power* (1966) pp. 81–150.

26. *New Statesman*, 31 March 1961, p. 501.

27. 'Passion and Politics', *Encounter* (December 1961) p. 4.

28. Collins, *Faith Under Fire*, p. 329.

29. H. Greer, *Mud Pie: The C.N.D. Story* (1965) p. 59.

30. *Encounter* (January 1961) pp. 43–6.

31. Leon D. Epstein, 'The Nuclear Deterrent and the British Election of 1964', *Journal of British Studies*, v 2 (May 1966) pp. 139–64.

32. Fenner Brockway, *Outside the Right* (1963) p. 181.

33. *New Statesman*, 19 May 1961, p. 786.

34. Peter Worsley, 'Revolution of the Third World', *New Left Review* (November–December 1961) p. 19.

35. E. Hobsbawm, *Industry and Empire* (1968) p. 250.

36. Three books have so far been written on the Campaign for Nuclear Disarmament. Christopher Driver, in *The Disarmers* (1964), describes its progress in a chronological account. Dr Parkin, in his *Middle Class Radicalism*, examines the social bases of C.N.D. Herb Greer, in *Mud Pie*, indulges in an exercise in polemics.

8   Looking Back On Anger

D. E. Cooper

LIKE most literary 'movements', that of the 'Angry Young Men' has a definite starting point – the publication of John Wain's *Hurry on Down* in 1953. Like most it has its apex – the twin furore over John Osborne and Colin Wilson in 1956 and 1957. And, as with most movements, it is more difficult to date its end. Certainly it is dead in 1970. The concept of Britain as the fertile breeding-place and deserving object of attacks by passionate young men has given way to the concept of Britain as the dynamic leader of popular culture. The images could not be more different. One difference is that the former image was generated on the stage of the Royal Court Theatre, or in the offices of Victor Gollancz Ltd, by native Britons. The contemporary image was born in the magazines of New York and Paris.[1]

If we are to understand the anger of the 1950s, it is useless to begin with a few *a priori* definitions – 'the basis of anger was . . ., etc.' The wiser, and less common, course is to look closely at the writings of the men who made up the movement. We may find that the real Lucky Jim, or the original Outsider, bear little resemblance to their counterparts so avidly discussed at Mayfair cocktail parties or in Hampstead coffee-bars.

But which writers? Fine novelists, like Iris Murdoch or Thomas Hinde, must be ignored; not because they were wanting in anger or talent, but because they do not figure in the *obvious* cadre of 'Angries'. This essay is not, primarily, one of literary criticism. Its purpose is to understand why a certain group of writers attracted a concentrated attention virtually unprecedented in recent cultural history, and why that attention should so quickly have waned. Such attention was only given to a very small number of men, and it is with these that we shall be concerned. The 'Angry Young Men' formed a small circle, then. However, each member – particularly Osborne and Wain – denied membership of this circle, together with the label 'Angry Young Man'. This is partly justified, for less scrupulous critics and journalists employed the label in such a way that the considerable differences that existed between members of the circle were hidden. But this disclaimer is not completely justified. I shall try to show, rather than assume, that these writers had a great deal in common. Several of them, moreover, were happy to subscribe to manifestos which were patent credos of anger, so bringing upon themselves a group-image. And, whatever the differences between them, they were all angry (I shall argue that this is the right word), they were all young, and they were all men.

On the one hand we have the writers of fiction and drama – John Wain, Kingsley Amis, John Braine and, of course, John Osborne. On the other we have the 'philosophers' – Colin Wilson and Stuart Holroyd. Even if the 'philosophers' wrote fiction as well, it is for their theoretical works that they are known. This division corresponds exactly to another important one – the division between those who have, and those who have not, attempted to supply answers, or remedies, to the problems they have discovered in post-war Britain. In general, the writers of fiction have denied that they were proffering any solutions to the troubles that angered them; some, like Amis, are quite adamant on this point. The 'Philosophers', particularly Wilson, have been equally adamant in their claim that their proposals would be the remedy to the contemporary 'sickness'. When discussing the first group, then, we shall be concerned solely with the 'Angries' criticism of society. When we turn to the second group, we shall be more concerned with the proposed improvements on that society. Perhaps this division is more apparent than real; perhaps the remedies of the 'Philosophers' add nothing to the movement. This is something we shall only discover by looking closely at the two groups. Only by doing this, also, shall we see the factors that goaded these young men into activity, and made for their raucous reception. And only by doing this shall we realise the extreme limitations of the movement.

Novels and Drama

What, then, angered Wain's Charles Lumley, Amis's Jim Dixon, Osborne's Jimmy Porter, and even Braine's Joe Lampton with his 'if you can't beat 'em, join 'em' philosophy? Of course they condemned what has always been condemned: selfishness, brutality, injustice. John Osborne, in his *Declaration* essay,[2] even says that his job is no more than demonstrating traditional values of justice in the strongest possible way. I think there is more to it than that. If there were not, the only problem would be to see why such a traditional outburst rose to shrieking pitch in 1955. Besides this, we want to look at the writings themselves, for there is surely something essentially modern about these writers' criticism of society, something beyond the eternal cries of the oppressed. Let us search for it by an apparently devious route.

In *Room at the Top*, Joe Lampton uses women for his purposes, and he thinks women deserve this. Even Alice Aisgill, the mature woman whom he loves, becomes an 'obstacle to be cleared from his path', As for Susan Brown, the virginal, simpering daughter of the town's wealthiest citizen, she is never more than a tool; seducing her is 'simply continuing the operation [of reaching the top] according to plan'. Joe mathematically grades women according to looks, style and class, and he knows bitterly that those in the highest grades will belong only to the richest men, whatever their feelings for these men. Women scheme, they deploy their bodies – but Joe can do the same, and he makes it his vocation to possess an Aston-Martin and a girl with a Riviera suntan. He does, too; but, as he realises, his goal is reached only at the expense of his being a 'real person'.

Joe, and the other heroes, are bitter not merely at

256

women for being as they are, but at themselves and all men for desiring such women, for allowing them to dictate so much of life. 'Women like this [the gorgeous Christine] are never on view except as the property of men like Bertrand' (the vile but wealthy 'painter', and son of Jim Dixon's professor). Yet Lucky Jim pursues the same Christine later in the book. Charles Lumley, in *Hurry on Down*, observed that a woman went to 'any crawling vermin who happened to have his pockets well-lined'. Charles, however, is humiliated by such a girl, who poses as the niece of the rich man who is her lover. Yet, on the last page of the book, Charles is willing to overlook even this.

These frontal attacks on women, and their powers, are mild by the side of Osborne's. Here is Jimmy Porter's description of his wife in *Look Back in Anger* : 'Sweet and sticky on the outside, and sink your teeth in it, inside all white, messy, and disgusting'. His greatest complaint is that women *devour* men, drain them of spirit and guts; Jimmy thinks of himself as the bulge around his wife's navel, a wife who appears to him like a gorging python. 'She'll go on sleeping and devouring until there's nothing left of me.' Later he asks, 'Why, why do we let these women bleed us to death?', and answers without hope, 'No, there's nothing left for it, me boy, but to let yourself be butchered by the women.' For Osborne, women symbolise everything which saps the life from men, and from the world. In an article, Osborne expressed his low opinion of women by saying that 'the female must come toppling down to where she should be – on her back', a view that was later tempered when he wrote on women for a leading fashion magazine.

In fact, what these writers really attack is not so much women, but a much wider target, *effeminacy*. One may of course respect women and condemn effeminacy, just as one may respect religious people and condemn puritanism or dogmatism. Effeminacy is simply the sum of those qualities which are supposed traditionally, with more or less justice, to exude from the worst in women : pettiness, snobbery, flippancy, voluptuousness, superficiality, materialism.

The effeminate society is one that displays all these. And it is against these, more than anything, that the attack of the 'Angries' is directed. This explains the sometimes violent tirade against women; for, while they are not of course fully responsible for the effeminate society, there is always Tolstoy's question: 'From where do we learn voluptuousness, effeminacy in everything ... if not from women?' It also helps explain the modernity of the 'Angries' criticism, the 'tart and tangy taste' of the literature, in Sartre's words. For just as 'straight-laced' or 'narrow' may have been the best word to summarise what was worst in, and peculiar to, nineteenth-century Britain, so 'effeminate' is the best word to characterise much of what is worst in, and especially belonging to, the Britain of the 1950s. Of course, to say that effeminacy is the main ill is not to carry explanation very far. 'Why the effeminate society?,' we want to ask. Here, there will be a myriad of factors to consider – including, naturally the growing influence of women. For the moment, though, effeminacy is a useful concept; for if we look at the various aspects of it listed above, we shall be able to account for a good slice of the 'Angries' attack.

Consider snobbery. It is a special type of snobbery that most angered these writers – not so much the serious snobbery that supplies jobs to Etonians but not to boys from grammar schools, but silly, petty, essentially effeminate snobbery. We find two ingredients in all the Angry novels: a snobbish character who arouses the wrath of the hero, and a sophisticated party, oozing snobbery, at which the brutish hero may fire. In *Lucky Jim* the villain of the piece is Bertrand Welch, a bad painter who believes that 'sensitive' artists like himself are a race quite apart from ordinary mortals. He is everything that Jim, in his prankish way, fights against. When Bertrand tells him that he is not good enough for Christine, that she requires someone more sensitive, Dixon turns on him and says: 'You think you're sensitive, but you're not; your sensitivity only works for things that people do for you. Touchy and vain, yes, but not sensitive.' Bertrand's snobbery is of the worst type. It is cultural, but it takes on a social form. 'The point is,' says Bertrand, 'that the rich play an essential role in modern society ... and shall I tell you what else I like? Rich people. I take pride in the contemporary unpopularity of that statement. ... I like them because they're charming, because they're generous, because they've learnt to appreciate ... beautiful things.' At the inevitable party scene, the drunken Jim tells him just what he thinks of this nonsense. The party itself is enough to anger Jim. It is a grotesque, cultural evening – complete with madrigal singing – arranged by a Professor of History who does not believe a man can be worth much who cannot tell a flute from a recorder. Amis includes a similar scene and criticism in his second novel, *That Uncertain Feeling*, where the mediocre John Lewis lashes out at a pretentious Welsh 'bard' during a cocktail party.

In *Room at the Top* the villain is Jack Wales, a tall mustachioed R.A.F. type, and the suitor of Joe Lampton's quarry, Susan Brown. The interesting thing about Wales is that he is not an unpleasant person at all. There is no conscious viciousness in his snobbery. Yet his habit of asking 'Do you know the so-and-so's?' (and the so-and-so's always have double-barrelled names), the assured look of confidence in his eyes, and the cut of his clothes, are enough to make him hated by Joe. Charles Lumley comes across as a similar sort of person; someone, again, who is not consciously unpleasant but whose very upbringing produces set views of people's places in society. After insisting that 'it takes a good bloke to play a decent game of rugger', the beefy Burge takes offence to Charles's having taken a job as a hospital porter. 'You ought to have taken on some decent job, the sort of thing you were brought up and educated to do, and leave this bloody slop-emptying to people who were brought up and educated for slop-emptying. ... [it's] letting the side down.' Lumley replies with predictable anger that he has 'no illusions about the division of human beings into cricket teams called classes', and is turned out of the party for his lack of illusions.

Despite this mention of class, the attack on snobbery is directed more towards petty, cultural snobbery, to class distinctions in the mind rather than in actual economic or social conditions. Of course, Socialism, the welfare state, competitive examinations, and so on, have removed much of the substance of class division and privilege. Amis, Braine and Wain seem to realise this – half realise it at least. What they demand is that the stupid residues of a divided society be dropped too. Drop the idea that the aesthetic sensibility of the rich is somehow naturally superior. Be rid of the illusion that manual work is in any way degrading. Let the manners and attitudes of people catch up with reality. Kenneth Allsop[3] is right to note that twenty years ago the reality of gross injustices would have produced cadres of steel-jawed Communists; the shadows of such times, in the brains of Bertrand Welches or Jack Waleses, produce instead the cynical but sensitive Lucky Jims.

Now consider superficiality. Our best starting point is John Osborne's notorious attack upon royalty, on what he calls the only English act that could top the bill, the 'amazing Windsors'. His objection to the institution is that it is not a 'truthful and worth-while symbol'; it symbolises nothing. Even the Pope symbolises a moral order, however perverse, while 'the crown simply represents a substitute for values'. His point, I think, is clear. While people can see the gloved hand waving from the golden coach, they feel assured that all is well with the nation, whatever its true state. Royalty, Osborne claims, is 'the gold filling in a mouthful of decay'. This is only one instance of Osborne's general attack upon symbols and surface appearances that serve to hide the truth from men. The Church is another obvious example. When Jimmy's wife in *Look Back in Anger* is persuaded by a friend to go to church, he launches a violent diatribe. The teachings of the Church create a false, gilt-edged optimism; they represent the 'selling-out of Reason and Progress'. And in *The Entertainer* Osborne insists, through the mouth of Jean Rice, that infatuation with the symbols of the Church only diminishes individual responsibility. How can you help people, asks Jean; 'Can you go up to a penniless mother and say "Madam, d'you know that Jesus died on the cross for you?" No, for there is no

God; we've only got ourselves. Somehow we've just got to make a go at it. We've only ourselves.'

The attack on superficiality is a broad one, by no means confined to the traditional enemies of Church and crown. Jimmy Porter sees a whole era, the Edwardian (and presumably our own), as built on symbols. The era subsisted on the image of croquet lawns, hot scones by the fire, and so on; but these merely create a false sense of stability and peace. 'It must have rained sometimes,' observes Jimmy. Joe Lampton is another who is intensely aware of symbols and surface values. He knows how much they mean to people. He is able to assess a person by the car he drives, the distance up the hill of his house, the perfume he buys his mistress, and the tan she wears. Joe is obsessed by such symbols, which give him 'the taste of prosperity as smooth and as nourishing as egg-nog'; obsessed, as we know, at the expense of his being a 'real person'. We see the theme continued if we turn to Kingsley Amis. 'The possession of the signs of sexual privilege is the most important thing, not the quality or enjoyment of them,' decides Jim as he looks at the world about him. Jim realises that this is not the only sphere where the surface has become more important than the core. It extends to the academic life in which he reluctantly moves. Instead of studying genuine history, he must waste his time writing an incredibly tedious paper on medieval ship-building. Indeed superficiality extends everywhere; everywhere there is produced the glittering, flashy stuff that would not hold up under a few seconds' examination. 'We must speak up against sham architecture ... the best seller, the theatre organ,' proclaims Jim. Charles Lumley is no less perceptive; he detests a world in which 'it was everyone's first duty to wear a uniform that announced his status, his calling, his ambitions'. For perhaps, if the symbolic uniforms were stripped off, callings, ambitions and status might change too.

Again, this line of criticism has a new ring. For while superficiality is itself scarcely a new phenomenon, it has never been so well and so professionally organised. Canned Scotch mist, and pop idols' gold lamé suits, are only the funniest of a widespread concentration on the tinsel exterior of life, the mammoth ability to take seriously the thinnest veneer. The writers we are considering have fixed on this point with savage accuracy. The isolated examples I have given cannot do justice to their terrier-like pursuit of all that has a false ring, of all that seems more than it actually is. In fact, the pursuit may be too hot. They seem to demand a degree of openness and, if need be, brutal honesty that would become quite unbearable after a few hours.

Now consider pettiness. This is not, like superficiality, taking surface appearances for the real thing, but concentration on the trivial, blindness to the important, the inability to feel strongly about what matters. It covers, then, John Osborne's prime stalking-horse: the lack of feeling in modern society, any sort of feeling. This, more than anything, is what makes Jimmy Porter the savage he is. His wife's placidity, his friends' silent perusal of the *News of the World*, and most of all their complete calm when he, Jimmy, lashes out at them with his remarkable battery of words. It is this mildness that drives him to such outbursts as the following: 'No one can raise themselves out of their delicious sloth. . . . Oh, Heavens, how I long for a little ordinary human enthusiasm. . . . I've an idea. Why don't we have a little game? Let's pretend that we're human beings, and that we're actually alive. Just for a while.' For Jimmy the most vicious word in the dictionary is 'pusillanimous', which he applies to his wife and her brother. This word, for Jimmy, sums up everything that is trivial, petty, low-geared, banal and lacking. The theme is repeated in *The Entertainer*. Archie Rice, the seedy, public-school comedian, whose life is really a conspiracy against ever showing his genuine feelings, eventually has a moment of self-analysis. His one wish is that he, and others, could only *feel* like an old Negress he once heard singing the blues in a dingy jazz-cellar. In his *Declaration* article, Osborne describes the purpose of his plays: 'I want to make people feel, to give them lessons in feeling. They can only think afterwards.' What Osborne demands, like Christopher Isherwood in *Lions and Shadows*, is that we should understand one another 'not coldly from the outside, but intuitively,

262

sympathetically from within'. The cold understanding can come from the statisticians – people are earning less than £y a year, there are x houses in Paradise Street without sanitation – and some solid thinking by social scientists and politicians may provide a type of answer. But before the thinking, before the figures, we must try to feel what it is like to live on only £8 a week, or without a bathroom. Undoubtedly there is something over-romantic in this concept of deep sympathy, identification with the oppressed. It rings a little of the ludicrous Tolstoyan communities set up at the turn of the century, whose hopeless failure was a striking comment on the dreamt of precedence of feeling over thought, of 'sympathy' over academic understanding. Equally, though, we can follow Osborne in his objection to a state of affairs in which, like the idealist Jean in *The Entertainer*, a person must apologise for 'getting steamed up' over a major issue.

In quieter mood, the same ideas are found in Amis and Wain. At times, however, Amis appears to be cynical towards strong feelings about major ideological issues. He speaks of 'the irrational capacity to become inflamed by interests and causes that are not one's own'. There appears to be some equivocation here, as Kenneth Allsop notes. Amis's heroes certainly have a good, robust sense of outrage against political dishonesty, or injustice generally. John Lewis refuses to accept a job from the hands of his mistress since, as he explains, 'one thing I feel rather strongly about is fiddles'. And as we have seen, Jim Dixon is quite able to become inflamed by the comfortable views of Bertrand Welch. Amis, it seems to me, does not wish to laugh at raw feeling over moral issues. What he does object to is the vague and abstract theorising produced by many on the Left. As Amis remarks in a letter in which he stated his refusal to subscribe to *Declaration*, 'I hate all this pharisaical twittering about the "state of our civilisation".'

John Wain is particularly opposed to the educational system, which not merely makes people unfeeling, but makes them unable to express what feelings may remain to them. Lumley reflects that 'the university had,

263

by its three years' random and shapeless cramming, unfitted his mind for serious thinking'. His respect for the working man as against the bourgeois stems mainly from the ability of the former to feel, and show what they feel. He rejoices when he finds that he has 'broken the sacred law of self-efficacy, mute compliance' that ruled his class. As against the dulled bourgeois, he admires 'raw, angular personalities who had been encouraged by life to develop their sharp edges'. His own sharp edges, he knew, 'had been systematically blunted by his upbringing and education'. Wain describes his purpose in writing as being 'to humanise society'; which means, in an age gripped by the machine and all that works on cogs and valves, to make people feel more, increase their understanding of one another, dig deeper into one another, and get excited about what really affects other people.

Susan Brown and her make-up, the bourgeois family and their television in Osborne's *Epitaph for George Dillon*, Lumley's academic acquaintance and his obsession for the minutest of problems, Archie Rice and his retreat into draught Bass, Burge and his divine rugby – all this is pettiness. Little things, however harmless and wholesome, are given giant stature, at the expense of 'the good, brave causes' which Jimmy Porter finds gone. Again, though, too much is being demanded – by Osborne at least. In *Epitaph for George Dillon* Ruth accuses George of wanting everyone to behave like characters from *Crime and Punishment*. George denies this; I am not sure that Osborne himself could deny such a charge.

It may seem that I have left out some of the main aspects of the 'Angries' attack. Of course, I could have mentioned that all these writers are Socialists.[4] We have the fiery Socialist, Osborne, one of whose characters can declare that 'Tory' 'is the most deadly four-letter word in the English – or any other – language'. We have the milder one like Amis, who says that he has always voted Labour and 'presumably' always will. Lucky Jim's Socialism consists in his simple belief that if you have to take a bun away from one of two men, you take it from the man with lots of buns. The writers are moreover

Socialists with a considerable contempt for politics and politicians as a whole. Both parties are a 'grubby lot of rogues' for Jean Rice, who thinks the difference between them is no greater than that between a male and female from the back. John Braine wants a 'world in which government is thought of only as a convenience'.

I could have stressed the anti-materialism of the writers to a greater degree. *Room at the Top* seems to me to be an anti-materialist Odyssey, the journey of a man to riches and a spiritual destruction made more acute by the fact that he rarely regrets that destruction. Wain's Lumley regards wealth, especially non-inherited wealth, as 'the greatest of all temptations to fully oppress [one's] fellows'. Again more could have been made of their common antipathy to religion, bigotry and all suppression of self-expression. I do not dwell on these aspects of their attack because, in the first place, these writers have nothing new to say on them. This is not to criticise them at all; most of them have wisely disowned the intention of making profound reflections on politics, economics or religion. Their task was emphatically *not* to present blueprints for the Socialist Utopia. Braine goes as far as to say that *Room at the Top* had no critical purpose whatever; and Amis denies that *Lucky Jim* was meant as anything but a comedy with no sociological implications. This is too extreme. Whatever the intentions of the writers, their products are certainly critical. Perhaps, though, Amis and Braine meant, by their denials, no more than that their books are not detailed or constructive answers to technical social problems. The criticism is at a different level. Perhaps John Osborne's statement in *They Call it Cricket* can serve as a banner for them all; 'I am a writer and my contribution to a Socialist society is to demonstrate those values [of justice and equality] in my own medium, not to discover the best ways of implementing them.'

I have not considered these aspects, secondly, since while Socialist and anti-materialistic ideals do show clearly in the books, it is not with these that the books throb. They throb, I believe, with the attacks on superficiality, pettiness and snobbery which I have described.

This too is what gives the books their contemporary feel, something they could not have possessed if their substance had been the traditional campaign against capitalism and injustice. So much the better for the books. The novel or the play is a much better weapon with which to bludgeon pettiness, snobbery and all those aspects which I have summed up in the word 'effeminacy', than the sociological tome. The tome, similarly, is the only way to present a coherent solution to political and economic problems. In recent years there has been no novel or play – and I am not forgetting Brecht – whose theme has been overridingly political or economic and which has been both good art and *coherent* social comment.

So the anger of the novelists and the dramatists was the reaction to 'effeminacy'. Not too much should be made of that word.

But the Angry Young Men *did* use the image of the effeminate to criticise the trappings of the Affluent Society. Their anger was directed at what they regarded as characteristically feminine qualities. Perhaps this attack on effeminacy really distorted what they had to say. Perhaps their anger was wrongly focused. Their view of women was, no doubt, unfair and bordered on caricature. There was also a dangerous ambiguity in their conception of the effeminate society. Technological advances associated with the welfare state had certainly freed women from their hitherto subservient status in society. Was not this to be welcomed by radicals, such as the 'Angries' thought themselves to be? To deplore the changed status of women in the Affluent Society was surely to be angry not because the social structure remained static but because it had changed since the Edwardian era. In this sense, the 'Angries' were looking lovingly back at the past, rather than forward to the future.

Nevertheless, it would perhaps be wrong to look for too much sociological coherence in the work of the 'Angries'. For their conception of the effeminate did succeed in making concrete the object of their anger. It gave their attack force and direction. So if we were to personify society and imagine a creature caricatur-

266

ing all the qualities that the Angry Young Man most despised our natural choice would be a certain sort of woman.

The 'Philosophers'

Colin Wilson is best known for his first book *The Outsider*, written in 1956 when the author was twenty-four. Superlatives abounded. Edith Sitwell proclaimed the advent of a 'truly great writer'. John Connell announced that Wilson had stepped 'immediately into the rank of major writers'. On the other hand, Wolf Mankowitz described the book as 'arrant, inexperienced nonsense'. Some assiduous critic unearthed eighty-two 'major errors' in that one-quarter of the book which is quotation. In the following months 'Colin Wilson' and 'Outsider' became household words. There was even a chic party game, 'Insider or Outsider?' This process was not unaided by Wilson's startling self-confidence and antics. 'I intend to finish as the greatest writer that European civilisation has produced,' he explained. 'Of course!', he casually replied to the question 'Do you think of yourself as a genius?' Notoriety in such diverse forms as suspicion of Fascist leanings, and a whipping from a girl-friend's father boosted fame and sales.

His next book, *Religion and the Rebel*, also aroused extreme opinions – mostly violent attack. Philip Toynbee, a fan of *The Outsider*, condemned the new book as a 'deplorable piece of rubbish', as a 'vulgarising rubbish-bin'. 'He has written in terms appropriate to an audience of apes and spiritual lepers,' wrote Maurice Cranston. Wilson had descended, in quick tempo, from the 'young genius' to 'Comic Personality of the Year', and to *Time* magazine's 'Tohu-Bohu Kid'.[5] After all this hostility, Wilson retired to Mevagissey to write in a less pungent atmosphere. However, his more recent publications have never received the attention of these earliest efforts. There must be no misunderstanding. Such attention, to have been given to a 'philosopher', albeit an untrained one, had been nothing less than phenomenal. Even Sartre was known as a novelist and playwright before the public flocked to his philosophical works. Apart perhaps from Osborne, Colin Wilson was famed as the angriest of the Angry Young Men.

Looking back, the volley of superlatives – pro and con – that greeted *The Outsider* seems unintelligible. For whatever the book professed to be – 'an enquiry into the nature of the sickness of mankind in the mid-twentieth century' – it is little more than a much needed potpourri of the writings of thinkers of a certain ill-defined tradition – the anti-rationalist and nihilist-cum-existentialist-cum-mystical – a tradition broad enough to include Ramakrishna, Swedenborg, Blake, Nietzsche and Sartre. Most of the book consists of quotations from such writers, along with a running commentary on them from Wilson. As such the book leaves much to be desired. It is full of mistakes, and as A. J. Ayer pointed out, Wilson's selection of 'Outsiders' is sometimes hard to follow. It is not clear how Henry James – the man who accepted over one hundred 'high society' dinner invitations in one winter – can sit happily within the same covers as those mentioned above. But whatever its merits or demerits, it is hard to understand why a book lacking in all attempt at originality of thought should have aroused such intense comment. The reviews are more understandable in the case of *Religion and the Rebel*. Here there is rather more of Wilson, and rather less of his heroes.

Moreover *Religion and the Rebel* is an extremely poor book in nearly every way. This is not to deny that in both books Wilson makes the occasional comment that invites reflection. I like his description of Christ as a 'man of action with a distinctly rough side to his tongue. There is no trace in the gospels of "gentle Jesus meek and mild".' But any such statements are more than matched by a mass of silly, mistaken or meaningless ones. It is just a mistake to say that the neurotically craven Spengler 'didn't care' about the Nazis' low opinion of him. Again, only the scantiest reading of Marx could make Wilson believe that Marx denied free will. To say 'all things are discovered by intuition, as the lives of the great mathematicians and scientists prove again and again' is simply stupid. Even worse is this: 'Logical Positivism – I should mention for the uninformed reader – is a kind of Marxist materialism.' This, no doubt, explains Professor Ayer's violent attacks on Marxism *qua* philosophy, and Marxists' no less savage assault on Logical Positivism! Most aggravating of all are such 'deep' statements as 'Truth is Subjectivity; external events are neither true nor untrue, but unimportant'. Left unexplained as it is, this sort of thing really means nothing at all. The books, indeed, are run through with hopelessly muddled logic, and the cant of deservedly forgotten mystics whom Wilson admires and, with much faith, assumes to be profound. Some of his interpretations – of Wittgenstein and Sartre, for example – are quite worthless. On the other hand his thoughts on Dostoevsky are fresh, and I have always suspected that Bernard Shaw, Wilson's prime hero, was more than the hoary old Socialist of present portraiture.

In this vortex of words, reflection, quotation and comment, it is possible, however, to discover argument. Beneath the grotesque logic – Wilson confesses, anyway, to having no respect for logic – there is the bone of a case against our present way of life. What, then, is his contribution to the 'understanding of our deepest predicament' that Philip Toynbee took *The Outsider* to be?

Colin Wilson believes that modern civilisation is seriously sick. Indeed, it has reached its 'moment of crisis'. This malaise, while taking on a social form, is not essentially economic, political or even psychological. That was where Marx, Bakunin and Freud went astray. Rather the problem is a 'metaphysical' one. It is a problem of man's consciousness. Man is sick, in 'despair', because at present his consciousness is limited, and lacks all intensity. Modern man is 'capable of thinking of nothing but personal appetites and ambitions'. While he has the potential to experience a whole keyboard of mental states, he in fact only experiences two or three notes.

This lack of consciousness takes its clearest form in the prevalence of the three dominant outlooks in the

269

West – the 'three mythical goddesses', to use Marx's phrase, of Materialism, Humanism and Rationalism. Materialism is found everywhere – in the adulation of the successful film-star, in the attention to personal appetite and ambition. It means, too, what Kenneth Allsop calls 'the desperate avoidance of thought'. Humanism, in Wilson's sense, is the view that only man's environment need be changed, that men are as high or as low as that environment. It is the belief that man is born free, and that all that we require is to remove the chains. This, for Wilson, ignores the basic need to alter man's consciousness itself, which at present is so degraded. Rationalism is the view that logic and science can answer all questions that are worth asking. For Wilson, it includes that 'most bloodless half-philosophy', the Linguistic Analysis of Austin and Ryle, as well as Logical Positivism, and anything Bertrand Russell has ever said. According to Wilson it fails to realise that the knowledge to be gained from such methods is only a fraction of 'real' knowledge, which requires 'intuition' and 'involvement'. For, worst of all, Rationalism is the view that the thinker should be a mere observer and commentator, not an actor. He quotes with enthusiasm that imbecilic dictum of Spengler's: 'a doctrine that does not attack and affect the life of the period in its inmost depths is no doctrine and had better not be taught'.

In our civilisation, then, man is a humanist-rationalist-materialist. These three attitudes reflect, and prolong, man's spiritual sickness. This is not only bad in itself, representing as it does a limited consciousness and misapprehension of man's potential; it will also result in the breakdown of civilisation. This is bound to happen – here Wilson is supposedly following Arnold Toynbee – where 'the men of genius lose their sense of purpose', where they cannot accept the civilisation in which they live, where they are not utilised. When 'the creative minority' is 'crippled', civilisation 'crashes'.

This creative minority – the renowned 'Outsiders' – are the men who have 'seen too much and too deep', 'for whom the world as most men see it is a lie and a deception'. At first the 'Outsider' – like the hero in

Barbusse's *L'Enfer* or Sartre's *La Nausée* – cannot see why he hates society. Certainly he has no idea of how to deal with what he has seen in such depth. The more advanced 'Outsider' attempts solutions, but these are too one-sided. Like Nijinsky, he may throw himself into physical frenzy, or like Van Gogh into emotional excess. Such behaviour results from the insight into the rottenness of average life, but it is no real remedy. The 'Outsiders' with a real remedy – or something near it – are those 'religious' thinkers considered in the second half of *Religion and the Rebel*, men like Boehme, Swedenborg, Newman and – oddly enough – Shaw and Wittgenstein. These are the men who realise that 'the Outsider's final problem is to become a visionary', that 'man is not complete without a religion'. The problem, it seems, is solved by a mixture of Protestant asceticism and Nietzschean exertions of the Will.

By 'religion', however, Wilson does not mean what most people mean. For him 'religion' is defined as the 'craving for greater intensity of imagination', or in Shaw's phrase, 'a highly developed vital sense, dominating and regulating the mere appetites'. And by 'mystical vision' Wilson does not seem to mean Gautama-like glimpses of Nirvana, but greater awareness of human life. To make things more complicated, this outlook, and the ability to live according to it, is what Wilson means by 'Existentialism'. This will do for men in the twentieth century what Christianity did for the medievals – give him a sense of purpose and spiritual adventure.

How seriously are we meant to take Wilson's talk of 'visions' and 'mysticism'? At times he does seem to accept the genuinely religious, and metaphysical notions of Boehme or Ramakrishna. At other times, when he speaks, as above, of 'greater awareness of human life', his concepts of religion and mysticism seem so watery that nothing is added to his original demand. People lead limited lives, and they should do something about them.

But where now? We can follow Wilson in this demand, but the great question remains, what is to be done? Man perhaps is half dead, but how do we galvanise him? Any answers Wilson gives are rather terrifying. First we are told that 'the "Outsider" must achieve political power over the hogs'. Second – and worse – the masses must be disciplined to work for some great and glorious purpose on the model, supposedly, of medieval Christendom, which was, for Wilson, the only 'healthy' era of our civilisation. Third – and worst of all – this discipline is to be achieved through 'ritual ceremony', through myth and superstition. For the masses would be far too stupid to accept the 'Outsiders'' teachings neat. This, of course, smells of the very worst in Plato's *Republic* – not to mention more sinister propagators of myth for the sake of discipline.

The final verdict on Wilson must be a negative one. Admittedly he has put his finger firmly upon an important aspect of our society; but hardly the first finger, or the firmest. All that he has to say is summed up in Sartre's frightening assessment of modern life: 'There is no adventure.' It is easy enough to see what he is angry about; Governments that preach complacency, genius playing second fiddle to the stars of the moment, the ever decreasing status of intellect and conversation. But this is a complaint as old as society itself. Wilson has not discovered the 'root' of the problems. Or rather, his metaphysical 'roots' are much too deep ever to be dug.

Nor has he picked upon any solution that is either palatable or practicable. Could one really envisage a Cabinet with W. B. Yeats at the Board of Trade and Schopenhauer at the Treasury? I must insist that, despite Wilson's own horror of pragmatism, the impracticability of his solutions, with their Fascist ring, is a serious criticism. For he states time and time again that he is providing genuine solutions. Political thinking, he argues, must always start with 'Outsider premises'. He rejects the accusation that his concept is 'just an intellectual fad with no real relevance to the problems of the world in the twentieth century'.

Yet that is just what it is. Practicality and sense only begin where the mystical athletics of Boehme, Schopenhauer and Swedenborg end. The criticism of Wilson, as of all the heroes that he trots out, is found in Kingsley Amis's simple comment upon *The Outsider* in the

Spectator: 'one is better off with too much reason than with none at all'. Colin Wilson has really done little more than chronicle some of the greatest intellectual comics of the past few centuries, alongside a few of the intellectual giants.

The second member of the 'philosophical Angries' is Stuart Holroyd. I treat him less fully only because his name is less well known that Colin Wilson's, and because, at the level of social criticism, he does little to advance Wilson's arguments. His first book, *Emergence from Chaos*, was published in 1957 when the author was twenty-three. Although younger than Wilson, it was Holroyd who encouraged his friend to go into print. This was perhaps unfortunate for Holroyd, since his own book received very little attention, suffering as it did from the delayed, hostile reaction to *The Outsider*. In fact the book deserved more attention, for although it contains the usual mystical claptrap and misinterpretations, it is more tightly written and more fertile than any of its near relatives.

The title of the book is largely self-explanatory. It is the study of certain poets – the inevitable Yeats, Rilke, Rimbaud and Eliot – with a view to showing how these men, in their lives and writings, 'emerged from the chaos' that modern civilisation displays. In glancing at his argument, I shall be ignoring many of the suggestive points that Holroyd has to make about these poets.

Like Wilson, Holroyd stresses that modern man is sick. In Kierkegaard's sense, man is 'alienated'; that is, there is a 'barrier between his essential self, and his superficial social self'. Man is not in fact what he might, and ought to, be. Holroyd does rather more than Wilson to trace the causes of this state of affairs. First of all, there is the 'humanist-scientist' attitude which, together with a materialistic outlook, encourages a 'flaccid and sentimental way of thinking'. Worse, by glorifying man as he is, this attitude does 'nothing ... to maintain the human ideal at its highest level'. The second cause is democratic and socialistic levelling. This, together with the third cause, the growth of a machine economy, serves to submerge the individual human personality. A final push in this direction is given by the existence

273

of highly organised and huge institutions such as the Church and the welfare state, ruling men's lives.

The cure for this deadly existence is, of course, 'religious', and, as we might expect, 'religious' in an odd sense. 'Religion', says Holroyd, 'is not so much man's attempt to know God ... as to know himself.' It is 'anything that a man can live by, and in being lived it finds its truth'. There is a problem here. For according to these definitions, Marxism, Humanism, even pure Hedonism, are 'religious' – and Holroyd does little or nothing to show that his brand of mysticism is the genuine 'something' that man can live by. When he elaborates, he becomes unintelligible. We must, he tells us, 'experience that sense of mystical identity with all things, that overwhelming sense of the existence of a deep level of ... being, inaccessible to the reasoning intellect'. We must 'penetrate the veil extended between us and reality'.

Holroyd continues to disappoint when we turn to his practical remedies – though, unlike Wilson, he at least seems aware that there is a major problem here. At times, as in his *Declaration* article, 'A Sense of Crisis', Holroyd seems to see the remedy as political in its first stages. 'Government is an art which should be in the hands of an expert minority.' And in *Emergence from Chaos* he sometimes veers towards the views of the philosopher F. H. Bradley – that man's self-realisation consists in his being an active member of a social organisation, and fulfilling the duties that such a station imposes. Nowhere, though, does he go in for the excesses of Wilson's friend and self-confessed genius, Bill Hopkins, with his demand that those who express the 'purity and truth of violence' should take the 'wheel of man's charabanc'. Indeed, at other times Holroyd seems to see the remedy as a purely individualistic one. Rilke, he argues, attained self-realisation in a purely personal, asocial manner. Holroyd claims that 'the problem of man's alienation from himself, from his fellow men, and from God, can only be solved by each individual in his solitude'. This is not weak advice; it is not advice at all.

Holroyd's failure, like Wilson's can be traced back to

274

the very purpose of his book: to see the problems of and remedies for modern civilisation through the eyes of a few poets. He fails to see that such men do not truly reflect or register the problems relevant to the mass of people. Despite his, and Wilson's insistence to the contrary, he fails to see that the 'man of spirit,' like the 'Outsider', is a freak. He is freakly sensitive, freakly neurotic, freakly unworldly. None of this means that poets like Rilke do not offer us much for rumination and appreciation. What it means is that the vast majority of us are not, and could not be, as these men are. It means, secondly, that any 'solutions' these men may find to their personal problems of living, to the question 'How shall I live', will not touch, and should not touch, the 'balanced' man. The personal 'solutions' of Rilke or Rimbaud – perpetual contemplation, or excessive debauchery – are not, fortunately, for the many. When Hopkins tells us that it is fanatics who must rule if the 'Glory of Man' is to be achieved, it is really time to go back to Bentham, Mill and the Government White Papers, however dry.

Causes of the Movement

Many thinkers – Marx is the best example – have assumed that it is a sensible question, with an easy answer, to ask for the causes of literary or cultural movements. This faith has a semblance of sense only when we are considering writers of the distant past, when everything seems so much more clear-cut. In fact, I doubt whether this faith is ever justified. The existence of a literary school is just brute fact. A number of like-minded men wrote a number of like-minded books within a certain period of time. There are, however, closely related questions which are more sensible. We may ask why such books should have attained the popularity they did, what qualities made them chime in such harmony with what the public demanded. We may ask, too, for an explanation of the aspects of society that offended the writers with whom we are dealing.

'Effeminacy', in my sense, only sums up these aspects; it does not explain them.

Let us take a first factor that will illustrate the difference in these questions. Some observers of the 'angry' movement argue that a basic cause was the emergence of a new generation of graduates from the recent redbrick universities, young people who could find a ready-made place in society neither in the traditional university-educated class nor in that class with no university education at all. As an explanation of the origins of the writings themselves, this will not do at all. Amis and Wain went to Oxford, and Holroyd, for a brief time, to University College, London. The other writers had no university education at all. None, then, were disgruntled redbrick graduates. This factor, however, may not be irrelevant to the popularity of the books. In 1956 there were a good number of young men and women who – with a fair stretch of imagination – could identify themselves with disgruntled graduates like Jim Dixon and Jimmy Porter. It may be that these books expressed the problems of a group, liberated by their education, yet still enmeshed by a net of ancient privileges and attitudes that they were now wise enough to assess at their true worth.

A second factor – its weight equally imponderable – must be the widespread *disappointment* that settled in the mid-fifties. This partly must explain the reception of the 'Angries'. First there was disappointment for many that the Tories had returned, and were seemingly entrenched for ever. The optimism of 1945 had changed in the decade to Osborne's sad reflection that 'the old gang are back'. In essence, anger was not political, so we must not exaggerate this purely political fact. It is what the return of the Tories symbolised, rather than the return itself, that created disappointment. The triumphant entry of the pin-striped Etonians into Downing Street was a symbol, like no other, of the apparent immutability of social and political life. The real disappointment was that life had altered so little since 1945. Alison Porter reflects, wisely, upon her husband that what really bothered him was that nothing had changed. The promised equalisation of 1945 had not come to nought – it had not come at all. The idealistic fervour at the end of the war had ebbed quickly, and had been replaced by a selfish inability to accept the rigours of rationing. There was still an Empire; the bulk of industry was still in private hands; Oxford and Cambridge still ruled the roost; church attendance had not declined by much; the British cinema was as bad as ever. In this atmosphere, it was the hopefuls of 1945 that had become the audience for books expressing their own bitterness in 1956.

A further explanation must be – a favourite catch-phrase of the Right – the 'decline in individualism'. By this, I mean the declining ability of any given individual to influence events – in the nation, the factory or the parish – and the consequent frustration. This is one of Colin Wilson's great complaints. 'Our age is essentially unheroic,' he says, since 'heroism is individualism.' This process has, no doubt, made its contribution to the pettiness we have seen condemned. Where men are not able to make themselves felt on the major issues, their impotence will soon turn to lack of interest. Interest in the major issues declining, it will be replaced by interest in the minor and the petty. Real heroism being impossible, petty heroes – film-stars, models – will be invented, and new epic battles will be fought and cheered on the charts of the hit-parade.

Three factors, at least, have contributed to this process. Mechanisation, of course, is one, with the supposed loss of personality this is meant to involve. In Wain's *Declaration* essay, 'Along the Tightrope', he raises the old thunder against the 'worship of the machine', against 'mechanical conformity'. Second, there is the emergence of the welfare state with, supposedly, the same appendix of depersonalisation. The age has become one of 'numbers and labels', says Wilson. Third, we have the growing sphere of governmental power, and within government the growing power of the Cabinet at the expense of Parliament as a whole. This – the inevitable result of Keynesian economics, welfare politics, war-time organisation and H-bomb diplomacy – is meant to imply a divorce between the individual and the organs of decision.

How real is the loss of individuality resulting from these three factors, I do not know. But what matters for our purposes is that people think it is real – and there are enough of these people to provide an eager audience for books complaining of the situation. In actual fact, individuals who have influenced major events during the last hundred years have often been drawn from a very small group only – the intelligentsia. The 'given' individual from any other group has never been in much of a position to influence. Perhaps the massive machinery of industry, and the welfare state, and the receding locus of political power, have made it less possible for the intelligentsia to act – and this is the group who read the books.

A final, obvious, social factor is the number of agencies and agents making for a materialistic outlook that have grown up so rapidly. Advertising, bingo, television, disc-jockeys, football pools, 'we've never had it so good', 'keeping up with the Joneses', Dale Carnegie, women's and now men's fashions, the wages round – we have heard it all before, these materialistic blights. They are very real. Any attack upon them will find a ready audience. Only one aspect of it is worth mentioning.

In his book *The Affluent Society*, Galbraith points out that if a politician describes a certain year as being the best year in history, there is not the least doubt as to his meaning. He means that production has been higher than ever before. The level of production has become the criterion by which to judge governments, and indeed whole societies. As Galbraith puts it, 'production has come to have a goal of pre-eminent importance in our life' – at the expense of all previous social and moral goals, such as the elimination of inequality, or cultural pre-eminence. The point is this: the urge towards more and more wealth, for its own sake, whatever the goods produced, is no longer an evil that exists despite general condemnation of such an ethic. Rather it has become the national ethic of Western countries. It has become the yardstick by which all is judged. When we say that Britain is declining, we mean that the economy is not growing so fast as the German or

French economies – and we would say this even if the increasing wealth of Germany or France consisted solely in the production of drugs, alcohol, comic books, dance-halls, electric guitars and perfumes.

The men who react to this state of affairs are, of course, many. They may object to both the ethic of wealth itself, and to the extraordinary failure to discriminate what this ethic, taken to its extreme, implies. It may be that the 'Angries' failed, in many ways, in their attack on materialism. Yet undoubtedly the considerable hostility to this new ethic is partly responsible for their reception in the 1950s.

A further set of factors explaining this reception is not social, but concerns the state of literature itself in the 1950s. If we are to understand the enthusiasm for John Osborne's *Look Back in Anger*, we cannot ignore the condition of the English theatre before 1956. Of course, the play was heralded as a 'sizzling commentary' on the times we live in, and as an expression of modern youth, and so on. But just as important, it was acknowledged as the *best play* since the war. English playwrights had produced good farce and exciting thrillers, but the Blackpool boarding-house comedy, or the 'who's-for-tennis?' mystery, could hardly satisfy the more intellectual theatregoer. England had no playwright to match Brecht, Sartre, Genet or Beckett. It must be difficult now – after seeing plays by Bolt, Wesker, Pinter, Bowen, Arden and Osborne himself – to realise how much the quality and subject-matter of *Look Back in Anger* must have meant to a starved critical audience in 1956. Nobody had written of the bitter rebel for many years; no one had written anything of the same excellent dramatic effect. A new era in the theatre was proclaimed – and the prediction was fulfilled.

Similarly, when we speak of the social criticism and the irony of *Lucky Jim*, we are apt to forget Lord Snow's observation that it is an 'extraordinarily funny novel'. Once again, the mere literary quality of the book is a fair explanation of its success. It is easy to forget these obvious facts when searching for deep social explanations, a process that the very label 'Angry Young Man' aids. The English novel, admittedly, was not in the same sorry state as the theatre; there was Graham Greene and J. B. Priestley. They were, however, very much in the traditional mould. The literary innovations of Joyce and Lowry had not exerted much influence, despite the attention they received. Nothing new, in content or form, was taking place in the novel. But when Wain wrote *Hurry on Down,* and Braine wrote *Room at the Top,* we were introduced to heroes and settings we had not seen for a long time – men at grips with the real social and personal problems of the day. Lowry had written of dipsomaniacal diplomats in central America; Greene was writing of disturbed intellectuals coming to terms with religion in Africa. The novel that eventually turned to the normal young man trying to find his feet in the materialistic post-war Britain was assured of success, just because it would be the first.

A similar state existed in the sphere of theoretical and philosophical writing. Colin Wilson himself continually charged Logical Positivism and Linguistic Analysis – the dominant philosophies in Britain, according to Wilson – with being 'pseudo-philosophies'. He confesses to 'detesting' Bertrand Russell (who actually belongs to neither school). In fact Wilson's charge is misconceived. The Logical Positivism that Wilson attacks has not been seriously held in Britain for at least twenty years and its 'successor', Linguistic Analysis cannot be dismissed so easily. However, two points must be made. First, Linguistic Philosophy is extraordinarily unavailable to the general public. It really requires a good P.R. man. There are scarcely any textbooks – the nature of this style of philosophy forbids it – introducing the potentially interested reader to the subject. Moreover, the books and journals are rarely written in a style that will appeal. Usually they are minutely and painstakingly written.

The second point is this. Contemporary academic philosophy in Britain confesses to being uninterested in questions dealing with the 'meaning of life'; these are dismissed either as being meaningless, or as the concern of other disciplines or of the individual conscience. For this reason, men who do speculate on such issues

– men like Teilhard de Chardin or Wilson himself – are assured of a reception by the many who always feel a need for metaphysical speculation. Since Linguistic Philosophy is so unavailable, this is the only way in which people can obtain their philosophy.

To this extent, then, despite the different areas of demand and supply, both Osborne and Wilson filled voids. One repaired the deficiencies of the English theatre; the other supplied those with a taste for the transcendental.

A final literary factor must be the demise of the great Titans of social criticism. Shaw was dead, and Laski, Tawney and Cole were no longer the forces they had been. Nobody, it seemed, had been able to replace them in writing those huge but exciting and readable tomes of protest. Nobody had arisen to present such sober and sound sense in such simple prose. So once again there was a void. Each of the writers we have been considering did a little to fill that void. We do not, of course, find the logic of the Titans in *Look Back in Anger* or *Lucky Jim*. Yet, in fictional form, the same role of condemning the absurdities of the society in which we live is performed.

My own view is that the more obvious literary factors, especially the dearth in the theatre and the novel, provide the most important explanation for the reception of the 'Angries'. We must not, of course, ignore the less palatable, but still important, factors: the chic party-game value of *The Outsider*; Colin Wilson's highly effective, if unintentional, publicity campaign; or the shocked delight of audiences at the frank, sometimes coarse, references to sex. Most of all, however, we must not forget the momentum of the movement itself. A young man writes a book; it receives publicity; other young men are encouraged to write in similar vein; their faces appear in the world Press; bright journalistic labels are applied to them; publishers commission mere babes to write for them; another young man writes a book; it receives publicity; other young men are encouraged to write in similar vein....

There were many – and to inquire into these is to inquire into the reasons for the comparatively rapid death of the movement. When I say that Anger is dead, I do not mean that writers no longer produce books of protest, nor that these are unread. I mean that the fuss has gone, the publicity has died, the sales are down, and mostly that the very atmosphere in which these writers could breathe has gone. The psychology of the nation, if you like, is no longer responsive to Anger – or at least that kind of Anger. However, if we are to carry out a post-mortem, we must not forget the obvious fact that the movement become too intense too fast. The audience that greeted Osborne and Wilson in particular was unprecedented. There was a French ring about it. The French are more prone to wreathe their writers. They do not, however, drop the same writers so quickly. Too much was written and said, by and on the 'Angries', in too few weeks. The movement could not settle to a steady, sober and prolonged life. It is, in fact, ironical that the very hero-worship and fashion-mania that the writers condemned should have been responsible for their success, and in some cases their eventual neglect. But this is not the sole reason.

First we should look at the aesthetic limitations. I said that *Hurry on Down* introduced a type of hero we had not seen for a long time. It is, however, a hero seen a thousand times in earlier days. The hero at odds with society, yet who commands the reader's sympathy and so, implicitly, represents a criticism of society, is an old and famous formula. The pages of Turgenev and Dostoevsky, as well as of Sartre, Camus and the early Hemingway, are packed with such heroes. And if we turn to the different type of hero we find in *Room at the Top* – the man who seeks society and, in the process, is ruined spiritually – he again comes from an established stable. The heroes of Balzac's *La Peau de Chagrin*, Stendhal's *Le Rouge et le Noir*, or Maupassant's *Bel-Ami*, are notable pedigrees. The central figures, then, do not break away from old formulas. Nor is there any attempt at innovation in literary

282

form. The form of Osborne's plays (except perhaps for the music-hall device in *The Entertainer*), as of all the novels, is traditional. Essentially they are all *stories* in good, grammatical prose.

None of this is to criticise. But it does help to explain the short life of the movement. For not only have all lasting literary movements made innovations in style and form, but the very defining characteristic of literary movements has usually been a formal one—for example, Symbolism and Naturalism. (An exception, perhaps, is the 'Existentialist' novel.) It was reasonably certain that critical audiences – able to glance at the experimentation across the Channel or the Atlantic – should not long remain satisfied with the simple fare their own writers supplied. More purely aesthetic criteria would be imposed.

Still at the aesthetic level, it is worth noting the amazing similarity of all the novels we have been considering. All contain the party scene which ends with an attempt to humiliate the hero. All have a 'villain' in the form of a well-educated snob, whose vanity serves as a foil to the hero's uninhibited thrusts. All contain a brief portrait of a wealthy, self-made man, serving to bring down appropriately Leftish comments from the hero. All contain the more or less prolonged drunken scene. All begin with the hero about to set out on a new way of life. All end with the hero receiving a fillip in the form of a new job and a girl. Most of these characteristics are repeated a dozen times over in the lesser known Angry productions. Each book of the genre came to have a certain inevitability. One knew what would happen in the next chapter of a new book, or in the chapter after. One knew what comments a certain situation would draw from the hero. The movement rapidly acquired its own bag of clichés. The reader quickly tired.

When we turn to Wilson and Holroyd, we find the same failure to break new ground. I have already remarked upon *The Outsider*'s lack of originality; it is simply a substitute for those who, perhaps wisely, have not taken time off to plough through Schopenhauer and Boehme. Although *Religion and the Rebel* offers us more of Wilson himself, it does not take us beyond the traditional anti-rationalist, mystical tradition. Perhaps fortunately, it lacks the originality of Teilhard de Chardin. Indeed the sole novelty of *Religion and the Rebel* was its composition by an Englishman.

A further severe limitation on the movement was its utter failure to provide any sort of answer to the problems the writers presented. At least the novelists and dramatists had no such intention. What Osborne said in an interview might stand for them all: 'I don't pretend to offer a solution or an alternative. If we create a void, something will fill it.' People like Wilson, though, did set out to provide answers. I have tried to show that these were really quite useless. So the one group never attempts to supply remedies; the other supplies remedies that could never be attempted. Either way there is the void. Admittedly, there was a certain logic in not attempting to supply practical social remedies for the problem, as conceived by the 'Angries', was largely one of people's attitudes. Changes in these could not be engineered with the aid of technology. Yet it is surely too easy to follow Osborne and just create voids. And it is too easy to follow Wilson and supply remedies that nobody could ever set about implementing. That reminds one of the rather pitiful later Tolstoy, whose dreams of complete non-resistance to evil and of universal love blinded him to all real social factors. Anyway, whether the 'Angries' should have provided answers or not, people demanded that they should. Nothing was forthcoming.

There is an even greater limitation. It must be admitted, I think, that the 'Angries' failed to come to grips with the essential problem of the society they attacked. I mentioned as one of the causes of the hearty reception of the writers that, in an age whose national ethic is one of higher and higher productivity, there will be a ready audience for those who present reminders of other ethical questions; who attack inequalities at the economic or social level, or who attack such false idols as the crown or the Church. But while this is so, it does mean that much of the attack is tilting at windmills. For, quite simply, inequality just is not any longer a glaring evil. Again, it just cannot be pretended that the crown and the Church are the sacred cows they once were. People don't really think that all is well in heaven and earth provided the Queen still rides in her carriage, and the Archbishop of Canterbury still preaches. To flay these institutions is really to waste so much time and energy. And their attack on the effeminate veneer of society, fresh and tangy as it is, fails to dig to the root-problems. It was not enough simply to peel off the blighted skin. Wealth is the national ethic, and if it is a bad one, then it is against this that the central attack should have been directed. What the 'Angries' in fact said was: 'Look at the country. People are just trying to make more money. Let's bring them back to some real problems – inequality, the Church, and so on.' What they should have said was: 'Look at the country. People make it a moral end to increase wealth and production. See what this does to people. See what other goods are ignored or by-passed.' They did not. Wain fumed against largely non-existent class divisions, Osborne against already smashed idols, Wilson against the perpetual state of mankind. There is a definite sense in which, despite the up-to-date feel of much of their criticism, their attack was anachronistic. Fact had already answered their criticism.

In fact, the writers need not have brought a frontal assault against the ethic of productivity. Fiction and drama have not generally been very adept at dealing with minor social evils. But they have been adept at a different type of criticism; criticism, not of the deep, underlying social evils, but of the fringe nastiness, the ugly appendices, of society – the little, dirty trimmings of ways of life. Think of Swift on courtly life, Butler on attitudes to criminals in *Erewhon*, Anatole France on high finance in *L'Île des Pingouins*. We find no equivalents in the literature of the 1950s. Yet the ethic of wealth is riddled with a dozen nasty little alleys worth exploring. Why *hasn't* a look been taken – perhaps in humorous vein – at the influence of advertising, or at football pools, or at the unsavoury make-up of the commodity market, at the psychology of marketing executives – at a dozen things. That there was a market for such literature is shown by the satire boom that eventually exploded in the 1960s. If the 'Angries' had really tackled the problem of the ethic of wealth, either centrally or with the sniping shots suggested above, they would have had more to say to us.

Kenneth Allsop argues that the failure of the 'Angries' consisted in their not taking a 'world-wide view'; that is, in not relating their criticisms to the great eternal problems of life and its purpose – unlike, Allsop supposes, Genet, Sartre and Brecht. The fault with the 'Angries' is that their spectrum was too narrow; they did not see across borders and time. It seems to me, however, that their failure is quite the opposite of this. They fail to be sufficiently particular. They attack too much at the same time; they do not delve with sufficient precision; they take too little account of actual conditions; they are blind to the smaller blemishes; they have not even divined the central problem with any accuracy. They are, if you like, limited by their failure to limit themselves. When Osborne moves into action, he leaves nothing untouched, and so touches nothing. When Wilson provides his remedies, they are like the elusive philosopher's stone, a universal panacea, and he is no more successful than the alchemists of old.

Allsop also claims that 'anger' is not the word to describe the attitude of these men; he suggests 'dissentience'. But this is quite wrong. 'Anger' is just the word. Anger is so often pure reaction, often unreasoned, often undirected, a mere feeling. The angry person, just because of his anger, does not look coolly at what offends him. If he did, he would not be *angry*. He does not dissect; he does not perform the required heavy plodding. The mood of the people that accepted the 'Angries' was anger too. That was the trouble; like all moods, anger passes.

Notes

1. The current student movement is certainly an explosion of 'anger', but transatlantic and continental influences have been decisive.

2. *Declaration* (1957), edited by T. Maschler, is a collection of essays by various 'angries', including besides Osborne, John Wain, Colin Wilson and Stuart Holroyd. The tone of the essays, especially the one by Lindsay Anderson, is mainly hysterical.

3. Allsop makes this point in a very lively book, *The Angry Decade* (1958), to which I am much indebted.

4. Or rather, all *were* Socialists in the 1950s. John Braine and Kingsley Amis are now confessed Conservatives. Osborne too seems to be heading in that direction.

5. 'Tohu-Bohu' means 'complete chaos'. It is an expression Wilson uses in *The Outsider*.

9 The Teddy Boy

Paul Rock and Stanley Cohen

THE Teddy Boy is as deserving of a place in a discussion of the fifties as any of his more respectable contemporaries. He was the most visibly 'difficult' of the problems that had become associated with post-war youth. In a stable society, one generation's experience has meaning for its successors. When a society undergoes rapid social change, however, less and less of the traditional wisdom is useful to those who are expected to learn from their elders. When Britain emerged from the war there appeared to be a tendency for the generations to grow apart – for the young to seek guidance from their fellow young. This tendency was increased by the relative economic emancipation of working-class adolescents in the fifties and the establishment of a commercial market reinforcing and creating specifically adolescent desires in consumer goods and services. Colin MacInnes's somewhat stylised 'teenager' personified this new tendency: he says of his elder brother Vernon: 'He's one of the generations that grew up before teenagers existed ... in poor Vernon's era ... there just weren't any: can you believe it? ... In those days, it seems, you were just an overgrown boy, or an undergrown man, life didn't seem to cater for anything else between.'[1]

By no means all adolescents were affluent enough to take on the new glossy teenage image, by no means all were delinquent or even in slight conflict with their elders, but these differences tend to be ignored by the older generation. There was a tendency to perceive all adolescents as members of a problem group. This tendency is not peculiarly British. Friedenberg comments on the American situation:

Only as a customer and, occasionally, as an athlete are adolescents favourably received. Otherwise they are treated as a problem and, potentially, a threatening one. No other social groups except convicted criminals and certified lunatics are subjected to as much restriction.... Willing as they are to trade with him [American adults] have no doubt that the 'teen-ager' is an enemy.... Hostility does not come this easily to the middle class, which prefers to define any nuisance that it wishes to abate, or social situation that it finds threatening or embarrassing, as a problem. Our youth problem is a notable accomplishment. We have made it ourselves, out of little.... Many adults seem to use the terms 'teen-ager' and 'juvenile delinquent' as if they were synonyms.[2]

The trends in Britain, although lagging slightly behind, are parallel. We have had our Beats, Mods and Rockers, and Hippies – all in their turn inevitably labelled problems. The first and greatest of this sequence was the Ted. He seems to stalk like some atavistic monster through much of the otherwise prosaic newspaper reporting of the fifties.

The Teddy Boy emerged without much warning. There was little preparation for his appearance as a fully fledged deviant, i.e. a person defined as a social problem. He had curious parents; one was the upper-class Edwardian dandy, the other the older delinquent subculture of South London. His 'Edwardian' clothes were orginally worn by the middle and upper classes, but this was for only a short period after the war. Indeed, the style was worn throughout the 1950s, but its meaning changed dramatically over the decade. Dress is lent significance by its wearers and by its audiences. When the long jackets and the tight trousers covered the middle class, the fashion was proclaimed a pleasing innovation, but it was rapidly reappraised when it spread to young working-class males in 1953. It seems that these new 'Edwardians' were the lumpenproletarian 'creepers', not the 'respectable' working class. Fyvel says that 'the Edwardian style in its full bloom had utterly unexpectedly transported itself across the Thames to working-class South London.... From all accounts, the first Teds who introduced the fashion south of Waterloo and Vauxhall were a pretty rough lot ... they still had links with the older cloth-capped gangs which in earlier years had dominated areas like the Elephant.'[3]

As a result, the middle class felt that it could no longer share the style with its new adherents. 'It means,' explained a disconsolate young ex-Guardee over a champagne cocktail, 'that absolutely the whole of one's wardrobe IMMEDIATELY becomes UNWEAR-ABLE.'[4] Those who now wore Edwardian dress were described in a vocabulary which derived from former modes of delinquency. Unfavourable social types were summoned forth to define them. They were 'zoot-suiters',[5] 'hooligans'[6] and 'spivs'. The newspapers did not hesitate to award them an unambiguous identity. The clothing was unchanged but its wearers had trans-lated it into a stigma:

> The cosh boys have killed all hopes of men's fashions that *really* are different. For years men have been accused of not being venturesome enough in their appearance, of being content with the same old drab-ness. Then came a change. The Edwardian look came along.... But it's all over now. The cosh boys have moved in. Take the Edwardian look. Three years ago Savile-row tailors got together to push it. They pushed it on the young Mayfair bloods, they pushed it on the Guardees, they pushed it on the Business men. They pushed it so successfully that it became the uniform of the dance hall creepers. Now, very quickly, Savile-row has stopped pushing the Edwardian look, it's out.'[7]

The newspapers deplored the fact that the diffusion of Edwardian dress had denied it to the middle class. But they did not attach any other significance to this phenomenon. The new wearers were not at first recog-nised as a new phenomenon. A person who dressed in Edwardiana was 'really' a familiar actor in an unfamiliar guise. He was an old deviant in new clothes, merely a spiv or a cosh-boy who had taken up a once middle-class fashion.

The Edwardian had not developed a distinctive personality by 1953. In July, for example, a group of Edwardians were involved in the stabbing of a youth near Clapham Common. Although some newspapers mentioned the dress of Michael Davies, the person convicted of the murder, it was not shown to have any symbolic importance. The *Daily Mirror* merely stressed that the convicted man was concerned about his appearance. It did not even specify that he had worn an Edwardian suit:

> Michael Davies, the Clapham Common thug sentenced to die for murder at the Old Bailey yesterday, was crazy about girls. . . . Ever since he was a boy he was out to impress the girls. He took great pains to look like a dandy. Like most of his companions, nearly all his money went on flashy clothes, and just before the murder, he borrowed twelve pounds from his uncle to buy a suit. . . . This man was a born coward beneath his bravado and his 'gay dog' clothes.[8]

Davies was labelled a 'thug' who fortuitously happened to be a dandy. Nevertheless, the link between Edwardian clothes and deviance was to grow. It eventually became so strong that, three years later, the Mayor of Harrogate was unable to determine which was cause and which effect. He stated that 'there would appear to be a very real connection between the action of individuals and the type of dress they wear, and this is nowhere more marked at the present time than in the so-called Edwardian style which is worn by so many of the young hooligans of our country. Is it the outfitter who provides the style, or the hooligans who make the demand on the outfitter?'

In 1953 this link was only gradually becoming established. It was known that the clothes were worn by many disreputable people, but it was assumed that these people would be disreputable with or without Edwardian dress. Tony Parker, who documented the Clapham

Common murder, observed of the Edwardians at the time of the stabbing that 'by those who thought they were better-class they were laughed at, derided, called "Teddy boys". But not with much more than mild amusement, not with hostility in those days, or contempt or fear. That was to come later. After this night particularly, after this night first, and then after other things.'[9] An association between appearance and a delinquent self requires reinforcement by a number of notorious incidents and, in many cases, a dramatic event. The incidents occurred in 1953 and early 1954. The dramatic event took place a little later.

The way in which these incidents were reported itself signified that the style was beginning to symbolise a social problem. Communication about its wearers was to be used to clarify the nature of the problem. In February 1954, for example, the *Sunday Chronicle* stated that the Edwardian suit 'was mortally wounded ... when one of its wearers, described as an Edwardian dandy, attacked a young woman in a suburban train. ... And clothes dealers say that more and more of these suits are being sold to them for give-away prices because they have become the emblem of the spiv and the cosh-boy.'[10] The delinquencies committed were few, but their perpetrators were conspicuous and eminently 'newsworthy'. Unpleasantness caused by Edwardians was eagerly recorded. Four months before this attack, the *Tailor and Cutter* felt constrained to protest that

By a series of vicious coincidences, apparently all the old ladies who have been beaten up lately, all the modest young men who have had their faces slashed and all the poor little pussy cats who have had tin cans attached to their tails have been beset by wicked young dandies in Edwardian clothes.

What a hullabaloo would stir among the nationals if the *Tailor and Cutter* headlined every social transgression with the significant headlines: 'Killer wears tan boots with blue suit', or 'Crepe shoes only worn by footpads'.

Observations published in early 1954 were more interesting as prophecies than as social commentary. As

292

self-fulfilling predictions they may well have precipitated what was to happen later. This was the phase in the natural history of the Teddy Boy when 'society' defined and refined its relation to the new group. Erikson has argued that 'an enormous amount of modern "news" is devoted to reports about deviant behaviour and its punishment ... these items ... constitute our main source of information about the normative contours of society. In a figurative sense, at least, morality and immorality meet at the public scaffold, and it is during this meeting that the community declares where the line should be drawn.'[11] The Edwardian had to be weighed up and assessed. Later on, when he was at his most notorious, the newspapers devoted almost no space to describing him. He was then established as a known outsider.

The basis for this social placement was laid in 1954. Public pronouncements showed what sort of creature an Edwardian was. They construed sartorial uniformity as social uniformity. They imputed a solidarity and an organisation to the Edwardians. The Chairman of the Dartford Juvenile Court proclaimed to some offenders that 'You lads have set yourselves on a path of crime. You have turned yourselves into that very undesirable, horrible type of youth which likes to call itself Edwardian. It is a lot of rubbish. There has never been anything more rubbishy than this Edwardian cult. It will lead to prison or something worse.'[12] Society heard these pronouncements as well as the Edwardians. The reactions of others are of crucial importance in the creation of an identity. Through this ritual denunciation, not only did 'society' resolve an attitude towards the Edwardians, the Edwardians resolved an attitude towards themselves.

This dramatisation of the social implications of dress was likely to have engendered those very traits which were deplored. It seems plausible to suppose that the early Edwardians experienced pressures to become either more 'thuggish' or less 'Edwardian' in appearance. The marginal Edwardian would have been drawn closer to the despised group, or would have left it entirely.

293

Not only was the Edwardian given an identity, he was also given a new name. This renaming of a phenomenon is immensely significant because it announces that a change has taken place in 'society's' attitude towards the phenomenon. 'The direction of activity depends on the particular ways that objects are classified.... The renaming of any object, then, amounts to a reassessment of your relationship to it, and *ipso facto* your behaviour becomes changed along the lines of your reassessment.'[13] 'Teddy Boy' was first displayed in print in March 1954. It seems that the Edwardian could no longer be regarded simply as the old spiv or the old cosh-boy. The old categories or response were inappropriate. New categories had to be invented. The first national newspaper which referred to 'Teddy Boys' provided its readers with an orientation towards them. It described them as 'Teddy boys – young thugs who dress in Edwardian-style clothes....'[14] The Edwardian was renamed because his acts had acquired a dramatic quality which could not be conveniently dealt with in the old terminology. In March, for example, a Camberwell youth centre was wrecked by 'cosh-boys' in Edwardian suits who were armed with razors and knuckledusters. There had been assaults at dances and uproars in cinemas. The Edwardian had to be appreciated as a new type of person.

It may be seen, however, that although the Teddy Boy was now an entity in his own right, he was firmly placed in a galaxy of similar social types – thugs, spivs and so on. His nature was clearly established. In time, like these other social types, he would become a model to be held up before society so that right-thinking people could avoid his behaviour. Just as the first Edwardians had been called cosh-boys and hooligans, so would later anti-social behaviour be labelled 'Teddy Boy'. An eligible person would not have to wear Edwardian clothes. In 1955, for example, the middle class were ironically again associated with Edwardianism. 'University students were warned yesterday: "Stop this Teddy Boy touch attitude".... The reason: hooliganism by university students who run the city's [Birmingham's] annual carnival.'[15]

Spivs and cosh-boys who change their style of dress but remain spivs and cosh-boys have not necessarily become more frightening. A change which is seen to entail a complete metempsychosis *can* be frightening. This was disturbing, but there were other reasons for concern as well. The Teddy Boys were multiplying. They had emerged in South London in 1953. By April 1954 they had spread to the provinces. A child psychiatrist argued that 'the fact that these Edwardian "creepers" are appearing in small country towns should surely convince us it is time to take this phenomenon seriously'. It was now fitting to write of them in terms associated with pathology and epidemiology. Dr Lowenfeld called their proliferation 'an emotional chicken-pox'.

The Teddy Boy was becoming defined as a 'social problem'. A social problem is a thing about which 'something ought to be done'. It is conceivable that almost every social phenomenon has been labelled a 'problem' by at least a few people. A 'traditional' social problem, however, such as crime or prostitution, may be distinguished from behaviour regarded as odd, eccentric or simply different by the fact that the labellers have the power and resources to 'do something about it'.

Fox-hunting is not a social problem, but cock-fighting is. The League against Cruel Sports is not in a position to take action about fox-hunting. As a result, cock-fighters are surreptitious deviants, but fox-hunters are not. If those who promulgate and enforce laws are to classify something as a social problem, it must be brought to their attention.

It may become noticed after a series of minor events, but it is more likely to be noticed if it gives rise to a major happening. Such a happening can be made even more melodramatic by the manner in which it is presented to the community. Indeed, the precipitating event may not have been particularly spectacular. Thus, it could be argued that the Press reporting of the behaviour of the Mods and Rockers at Clacton was largely responsible for their subsequent notoriety. The clashes were actually rather unexciting. Similarly, it was the American Press that rescued the infamous

Hell's Angels motor-cycle club from obscurity. In 1964 the club was unstable and might have dissolved. But publicity and political pressure following a fairly 'conventional' incident led – months later – to the publication by the Attorney-General of California of a lurid and misleading account of the Hell's Angels' depravities: 'The whole scene changed in a flash. One day there was a gang of bums, scratching for any hard dollar ... and twenty-four hours later they were dealing with reporters, photographers, free-lance writers and all kinds of showbiz hustlers talking big money. By the middle of 1965 they were firmly established as all-American bogeymen.'[16]

The Teddy Boy's crisis was not especially distinguished. It could not compete with the events which transformed the Hell's Angels or the Mods and Rockers, but it nevertheless occurred. On 24 April 1954 there was a confrontation between two groups of Teddy Boys at St Mary Cray station in Kent. 'Edwardian gangsters fought on the plafforms.... The battle was on Saturday night when more than 50 youths in Edwardian dandy suits with velveteen collars and drainpipe trousers carried a dance hall feud to the platforms.'[17] Teddy Boy violence was rudely thrust before the non-participating public. Although there had been other incidents in April – a boy had been stabbed, a man and a woman had been chased on Hampstead Heath by a 'gang' of Edwardians – it seems that it was this encounter which triggered off the huge official reaction to the Teddy Boy 'problem'.

Three days later, the first cinema and dance-halls refused entry to those who dressed in Edwardian suits 'because of gang hooliganism'.[18] Four days afterwards, 'Senior Scotland Yard officers have called for reports on all incidents involving gangs of youths wearing Edwardian dress. They are perturbed about the recent series of brawls, fights and outrages by the gangs in the drainpipe trousers and bright waistcoats of the "new Edwardians".'[19] The Teddy Boys were becoming outsiders who required social control. They were subjected to segregation, ostracism and to the campaigns of various agencies. They were 'a grave social evil'.[20]

Exclusion from certain public places led to inevitable friction. At the Palais de Danse in New Cross, there was an encounter between a group of Teddy Boys and the manager who was flanked by his commissionaires. The manager told them: 'You cannot come in. You're not properly dressed – and you know it. You will not be allowed in if you wear velvet lapels, drainpipe trousers, "slim jim" ties or other Teddy Boy outfits.' The iniquities of a few had successfully stamped a whole category of persons as deviant. These encounters between the rejected and the rejectors escalated. It was accepted that the police could now be employed to enforce the edicts of the cinema and dance-hall managers of South London.

Although official agencies had been initially slow to treat the Teddy Boy as a novel figure, they were later anxious to outmanœuvre him. They reacted to him by attempting to repress any growth in the phenomenon. The Member of Parliament for Brighton Kemptown observed that 'something must be done to stop this wave of violence before it gets out of hand'. This sentiment was echoed by many others. People were no longer responding directly to the Teddy Boy; they were organising themselves to deal with the problem as it might become. The *Daily Sketch* reflected this when it suggested in an editorial that 'mistaken, too, is the argument that is being put forward that their eccentric costume need not worry us – that "Edwardian" is not a synonym for "thug". Not yet, perhaps. But it could be, if this curious movement is allowed to spread unchecked.'[21] The Home Secretary, Sir David Maxwell Fyfe, told the House of Commons that the Commissioner of Metropolitan Police had assured him that 'the police are alert to suppress any tendency to hooliganism by "Edwardian gangs" '.[22] Local action was also taken. In Bromley, Kent, emergency police squads now patrolled on Sunday nights. The Mayor of Kingston, Surrey, announced that 'directly these silly young idiots get out of hand then I'm coming on them with a bang. I don't agree with this rot about spoon feeding.' Previously neutral stimuli had suddenly acquired meanings. The appearance of Teddy Boys in an area now signified that the 'wave of violence' would sweep over there too. Hence, within a week of the 'battle' of St Mary Cray, there were repressive measures, antagonistic encounters, and further measures. The Teddy Boy had attracted the attention of those people who were able to 'do something about it'.

Newspapers also encouraged this reaction. An editorial in the *Star* remarked that 'no doubt dozens of young men who like to wear drainpipe trousers and boot-lace ties are law-abiding but their uniform has been disgraced. They should either discard it or share the disgrace.'[23] The critical event had happened and the Teddy Boy was being cast as a villain. Those who wore Edwardian suits now had to realise that they were outsiders – that the suit differentiated 'us' from 'them'. Because it performed this function, it became a target for abuse. A Southend youth counsellor called it 'an ugly badge of violence', and one of his colleagues announced that 'these trouble-makers are now recognisable and club leaders know who to guard against'. 'Our' enemy could be known by his 'uniform'.

The suit was held up for public ridicule. The *Daily Mirror* referred to 'your horrible-looking outfits'.[24] The *Daily Express* observed that 'some of our brighter boys are breaking away from the matching suit rule and are wearing dark trousers and light grey jackets with dark velvet lapels. Ugh!'[25] A Thames Court magistrate informed some Teddy Boys (although they were not wearing Edwardian dress in court) that 'a lot of common or garden people think the clothing you wear is a matter for laughter and jeers'. The suit could be vilified because it was worn by outsiders, and outsiders are not entitled to respect.

Those who controlled clothing shunned everything that suggested the stigmatised Edwardian. A shocked tailoring industry introduced the 'Backward Look' in July. The Secretary of the Men's Fashion Council explained that 'you will find that in all these new styles there is nothing that can be burlesqued by young exhibitionists'. The commanding officer of an Army unit in B.A.O.R. forbade his men to wear black string bow ties 'because such ties are being associated with certain

298

types of juvenile delinquents in Britain'. The Teddy Boy was being thrust further and further beyond the pale. The 'normal' population was anxious to dissociate itself from any resemblance to the deviant. The gulf between the two groups was widening.

Throughout May 1954 the reaction to the Teddy Boy developed its own momentum. The Teddy Boy was depicted in a way which was calculated to disturb the uninformed. The best example of this was provided by the use which was made of the 'gang' concept. All Teddy Boys were described as gang members or 'gangsters' (which is even more threatening). If Teddy Boys came to a district, it was held that gang activity had spread to that area. There is something peculiarly sinister about a 'gang'. It conjures up images of purpose and organisation which lie dormant when the words 'group' or 'clique' or even 'mob' or 'crowd' are used. It justifies vigilant action. It also radically misdirects action. American attempts to deal with it often fail because the gang workers approach the gang of their imagination, not the gang as it exists. This confusion is shared by many others – reporters, police, magistrates and even criminologists. The 'real' delinquent group rarely displays the qualities which are attributed to it. The fact that American working-class youth are even more gang-centred than their English counterparts makes these strictures correspondingly more applicable to the English situation.

Delinquent gangs are in fact extremely uncommon in this country, and even in 1956, the zenith of the Teddy Boy 'movement', they were insignificant. David Downes suggests that the idea of the gang is 'simply a device for registering our lack of understanding'.[26] It is very easy for the middle-class observer to read into working-class groups a 'structure' and a 'hierarchy' which they do not possess; this is a function of the gaps which exist between generations and classes. One Edwardian remarked: 'You see, people talk about "gangs" as though they were something that existed – but they never did really, not in any organised way, nothing really like that at all. You just went around with a group of fellers you knew, that was all there was to it. But there you were, that was it, in the eyes of other people you was a "gang".'[27] Audiences did not react to the Teddy Boy; they reacted to their conception of him. This conception was largely founded on what they had been told by the newspapers and other media. This was true even of those people who had to cope with the problem. The ideas on which they had to act were often simplistic and misleading, and this distortion was sometimes aggravated by the reluctance of officials to wait and see what shape the Teddy Boy problem was going to assume in their area. Thus, in Romford, 'Chief Inspector — has a plan for breaking up gangs as soon as they are formed'.[28] Even if enforcement officials did not share these received definitions of the Teddy Boy, they must often have felt constrained to consider 'public opinion'. 'Public opinion' was again conveyed to them by the Press. The *Daily Herald*, for example, reported that 'war on "Edwardian" hooligans has been declared by a town of 120,000 people [Reading] alarmed by the increase of gangs roaming the streets'.[29] Officials may have felt compelled to put on a display of initiative to reassure a perturbed 'public'. In 1954 there were numerous reports of conferences and campaigns brought about to tackle the Teddy Boy problem. Scotland Yard was often quoted to be asking for reports on gangs; but there were no published results.

Although it is extremely difficult to ascertain what did take place, it seems that many Teddy Boys were associated with territorially based and loosely structured groups. The territory and the group only became important when they were threatened by significant strangers – other Teddy Boys from 'foreign' areas – or when the group itself attacked other territories. Teddy Boys thus organised their social world into groups identified with districts; 'the boys from the Elephant' or the 'Somers Town boys'. They do not seem to have had permanent leaders or clearly defined positions.

Some of the popular attempts to explain the Teddy Boy at this time are most interesting in that they tend to reveal far more about those who explained than about those who were explained. They were presumably thought to be serious pieces which merited consideration. If this is so, they illuminate something of the nature of the reaction to the Teddy Boy. An extreme example of this was given by a 'family doctor' who analysed him for the elucidation of the readers of the *Evening News*. He employed psychology to demonstrate that Teddy Boys are

> all of unsound mind in the sense that they are all suffering from a form of psychosis. Apart from the birch or the rope, depending on the gravity of their crimes, what they need is rehabilitation in a psychopathic institution *(sic)*. . . . But because they had not the mental stamina to be individualists, they had to huddle together in gangs. Not only have these rampageous youngsters developed a degree of paranoia, with an inferiority complex, they are also *inferior* specimens apart from their disease. . . . It is the desire to do evil, not the lack of comprehension, which forces them into crime. This is the real reason why they carry lethal weapons.[30]

The community did not receive any information to correct these impressions. Throughout the period, the Teddy Boy somehow escaped the attention of those who had the expertise to clarify what was happening.

It was undoubtedly true that the Teddy Boy was violent; that in the early fifties he was becoming more violent; and that he did present a problem. Teddy Boys fought one another, they attacked solitary individuals, they slashed cinema seats. But their depravity was raised to a greater prominence through a distorting screen which upset its audience even more.

May 1954 was an extraordinary month. A month before, the Teddy Boy had been seen as a somewhat disturbing figure. Now some newspapers could present southern England as an arena in which a conflict was taking place between 'society' and a malevolent and threatening group. Indeed, this interaction sometimes assumed an almost Manichaean scale. The *Daily Herald*'s account of the declaration of war by Reading has already been cited. The report continues:

POLICE of Reading will 'combat very rigorously attempts to create disturbances' said Superintendent — the deputy Chief Constable.... THE MAGIS-TRATE fined three youths yesterday.... Dance hall owners may take united action. Said one owner: 'The time has come to ban from all dance halls in the town any Edwardian youths and their Edwardian girl friends.' But the trouble is not so much in the dance halls as in the streets. Councillor — is to ask Reading's Watch Committee what is being done to safeguard the public.[31]

Similar accounts were published of other towns.

The reporting of Teddy Boys assumed more and more that the public was familiar with their 'character-istics'—their 'gang' activity, their vandalism and their violence. May, then, saw the making of the Teddy Boy. He was given a form and a substance. He had become a 'menace'. He was not only introduced to the public, he was introduced to himself. He learned that, because he wore Edwardian suits, he must be a certain type of person. His suit led to differential treatment. He could not pretend that he was a member of 'normal' society because people did not treat him as one. He was re-jected from more and more public places; in some areas only the cafés and the streets were open to him. He thus became even more conspicuous and menacing. Above all, he learned that he shared common enemies and common allies with those who dressed like him. 'I go after jobs and don't get them. I go to dance halls and I'm told to leave. I go to cinemas and they won't admit me. I talk on street corners and the police move me on. Why? Because I am a Teddy Boy. A boy who wears a suit which labels him as a trouble-maker, a hooli-gan....'[32]

May established the pattern which was to be fol-lowed throughout the year. The Teddy Boys became more violent. There were 'gang' fights at Welling and Sidcup. Policemen were assaulted. In July there were further incidents in cinemas. The community became increasingly hostile. Fyvel claims that 'no group of young people in modern England has found itself the target of quite so much concentrated dislike'.[33]

Wherever they appeared, the Teddy Boys were greeted with suspicion and, if they offended, were sanctioned severely. Thus, after 'gang' fights in Newcastle upon Tyne, the chairman of a magistrates' court said that 'we are going to stamp this out in Northumberland. You are going to get as much punishment as we can give you.' The sanctions were not only penal. Teddy Boys were banned from cinemas and dance-halls in most of the large English cities. The definition of a Teddy Boy had, in some cases, become elastic enough to encompass anyone who dressed in an 'offensive' manner. In Blackpool, for example, a cinema manager declared that 'I'm the one who decides whether a youth is wearing Edwardian dress or not. My decision is final.'

The pattern which had earlier developed in South London accompanied the spread of the Teddy Boy to other areas. Local police forces organised campaigns against him. In Kingston, Surrey, the police initiated 'Operation Teddy Boy' in July. Special patrols, reinforced by a dog team, conducted a 'big drive on hooliganism'.[34] The police had accepted the 'social problem' definition of the Teddy Boy, and were prepared to anticipate any encounters by taking special measures. A typical sequence of events had developed in Brighton:

Terrorism by 'Edwardian' thugs in exaggerated jackets and drainpipe trousers has broken out again in Brighton. Trouble, brewing since early this year, came to a head a week ago, when three men were stabbed and slashed in the Regent Dance Hall, one of the largest on the South Coast. Several months ago, the *Sunday Chronicle* revealed that teenaged gangsters from other South Coast towns and from London were menacing the town. . . . This weekend police will be watching all dance-halls in Brighton, including the Regent, where the manager has now banned all dancers wearing Edwardian clothes.[35]

Other dance-hall and cinema managers deliberately

made their entertainment unattractive to Teddy Boys. They showed unexciting films, and dispensed with the 'ultra-modern dances of high tempo'. The 'normal' world started to reassert itself in 1954. The Edwardians were discouraged, punished and thrown more and more into their own world. The 'acceptable' adolescents were those who observed the conventions of adult society. Appeals were made to the outsiders to return. The act required the symbolic renunciation of the Edwardian suit – the 'cause' of the Teddy Boy menace. The Chairman of the Acton Magistrates' Court urged an offender to 'get rid of that suit and try to become a decent member of society'. The offender's father said that 'he was never in trouble before he bought an Edwardian suit'. Similarly, a North London magistrate told a Teddy Boy who had been the *victim* of an attack: 'Don't make yourself so odd in appearance by your sideboards and clothes. Conform to the usual pattern of dress and you will not be regarded as an oddity.'[36]

1954 had provided the reaction to the Teddy boy. In 1955 something of a reaction to the reaction took place. Perhaps the community's response had been too monolithic to be quite acceptable to all its members. In 1954 the Teddy Boy had been cast as a villain; in the next year some doubts were raised about whether all Teddy Boys were always villains. When the Teen Canteen – an experimental youth club in a café setting – was opened at the Elephant and Castle in June, the M.P. for Southwark admitted that there were 'some damn nice lads in Edwardian clothes'. Similarly, a Lewes councillor in the same month opposed a recommendation to ban Teddy Boys from the Saturday night dances in the Town Hall. He said that 'there are plenty of respectable men who wear Edwardian costume. If I were to dress up in this way and present myself at the Town Hall, I should feel put out if I were not admitted.' This type of hesitation could be seen in the protracted controversy over the attitude of the armed forces to the wearing of Teddy Boy suits by recruits who were off duty. There had been a number of clashes involving National Servicemen, particularly those in the R.A.F., who had descended on market towns and fought with the native population. In July, Western Command forbade soldiers to walk out when off duty in civilian clothes of 'unorthodox' styles – particularly Teddy Boy suits. The Royal Engineers cancelled walking-out passes for those who wore Teddy Boy clothes. These actions gave birth to a heated debate about individual rights and discrimination. An M.P., who intended to raise the issue in the Commons, claimed that it was 'no business of Army officers to decide whether one man's trousers are too tight or another man's coat too long'.

These doubts were ineffectual. Those who manned the 'public scaffold' continued to pronounce judgment on the clothing and on its wearers. As a result, there were clear indications that for most people the symbol was taking on clearly unambiguous qualities. It was seen not only to accompany but also to *cause* forms of undesirable behaviour. In January, a Barnet magistrate told a boy to take his Teddy Boy suit home and burn it. In June, one father in Brentford and another in Bath told courts that they would return home and tear up their sons' suits. In November, a Bristol parent hacked his son's suit to pieces, telling a reporter that 'since my son bought this thing a year ago his personality has changed'.

The archetypal reaction to the deviant – segregation and exclusion – gained strength. Boys wearing Edwardian clothes were banned from more youth clubs, dance-halls, cinemas, cafés and, in one town, even from the fish-and-chip shops. Some idea of the impotent rage which was now being channelled into such forms of social control can be gauged from a headline in the *Sunday Dispatch*: 'Dance Halls, Cinemas, Police and Public Join Forces to Wage WAR ON THE TEDDY BOYS. Menace in the Streets of Britain Being Cleared up at Last'.[37] The article described measures taken throughout the country to combat the 'thugs in Edwardian dress ... who have terrorised peace-loving citizens for two years'. Vigilante squads in country villages; policewomen in 'tight skirts and sloppy Joe shoes' mingling with the crowds in Merseyside dance-halls; security guards in London cinemas; police-dog teams patrolling along the Thames; and so on.

Besides being hopelessly wrong about the 'menace' being cleared up (it had hardly started), the reports were fundamentally misleading in their presentation of a picture of concerted social action instead of what really took place – *ad hoc* and desperate local efforts. Throughout the fifties, the organised social response to the Teddy Boy was always out of step, either one step behind (not recognising the significance of changes in fashion, for example) or one step ahead (by anticipating non-existent dangers). The frequent announcements of 'special reports' on the Teddy Boys by the Home Office or the Metropolitan Police Commissioners served only to reassure the public that 'something was being done' and had the unintended consequence of giving the 'menace' a structure which it never had.

A crucial process in the spread of such phenomena as the Teddy Boy is the interpretation and reporting of neutral or ambiguous stimuli as *necessary* manifestations of the phenomenon. This process was becoming established in 1955. Although many incidents of hooliganism, violence and rowdyism were reported at their face value, there was enough reclassification of these events to crystallise further the process whereby all such behaviour was automatically regarded as Teddy Boy symptoms. The Press coverage of a murder that took place in May provides an instructive example of the role played by the mass media in the spread of ideas. A sixty-year-old Cypriot was killed by one of a group of four youths in a road in Camden Town. He was returning home with his wife when he saw one of the boys jump at a girl who was walking along the road. The wife shouted at the boy to leave the girl alone, but he merely swore at her. When the Cypriot reproved the boy for swearing and went to help the girl, he was punched in the face, knocked to the ground, and kicked as he lay on the pavement. There was nothing about this unpleasant killing which indicated the 'typical' Teddy Boy crime; yet almost all the newspapers which appeared on the following morning referred to the killer as a 'Teddy Boy'. There were reports of police investigations of Teddy Boy activity in Camden Town, and a detective superintendent was widely quoted as sending out a message to his men to 'see the Teddy Boys, go into the pubs and dance-halls – bring in the boys of that gang'. (When, a month later, a twenty-one-year-old was arrested and sent for trial, the same detective superintendent said at the preliminary hearing that the boy had an 'excellent' character and was not a Teddy Boy. There was no evidence that he had been a member of a gang.)

The *Daily Express* report of the crime nicely captures the allegorical uses to which such incidents are put: 'Along Parkway came vivacious 22-year-old Greek-born — —, her high heels clicking on the wet pavement. She was going home after her Thursday night piano accordion lesson. As she crossed the road she was noticed by four sallow-faced Teddy Boys lounging in the shadows of the corner baker's shop....' The accuracy of this description is not at issue – although it would be interesting to know how the reporter learned of the boys' complexions – but its message was devastatingly simple: in contrast to the 'vivacious' girl, the Teddy Boys were evil personified.

The effect of such messages was to introduce the Teddy Boy into the gallery of folk devils and villains. There were first signs in 1955 of the term being used as a general epithet of abuse. One minister referred in a sermon to 'the Teddy Boys of the business World'. A few years later, John Osborne was labelled 'an intellectual Teddy Boy'. The term could be used – at first metaphorically and in inverted commas, but later literally – to describe juvenile misbehaviour in entirely different cultural contexts: 'Four American "Teddy Boys" last night tried to assassinate a judge who recently jailed several teenagers.'[38]

What in fact was happening was that the label was no longer just a label. The label became the person. The assumption that the Teddy Boy was an identifiable psychological (and even biological) type was captured beautifully in the reporting of the claim by two American doctors that a drug, chlorpromazine, could help 'cure' juvenile crime. 'They say it soothes Teddy Boys and makes them co-operative for treatment.'[39] Soon, a person could not lose his identity by the mere act of shedding his clothes, although he had been able to earlier on. In 1956 a local councillor, commenting on the delinquencies of some National Servicemen, observed that 'some of these soldiers here are just Teddy Boys in Army uniform'.[40]

1955 also witnessed actual changes in the pattern of delinquent behaviour. Although there were no outstanding dramatic incidents, the statistics of crimes of violence showed a large increase and there was a growth in the behaviour which was typically labelled as hooliganism or rowdyism. Loose groups, which were based on nothing more cohesive than a tenuous territorial loyalty, expanded and either brawled in dance-halls or marched down streets in line knocking over strangers. The groups who indulged in cinema rowdyism became larger, and some London cinemas hired professional wrestlers to keep the peace.

As the phenomenon spread from London, incidents were reported from more and more seaside resorts and provincial towns. There were attacks on policemen who attempted to break up fights. Isolated cases of robbery and vandalism – where the identity of the offender was dubious – were being blamed on the Teddy Boys. There were also reports of violence being triggered off by affronts which seemed trivial to the outside observer. In December, a boy who refused to pay for his ticket in a London underground station threatened an official with a knife.

The fashion was changing. There is only an apparent paradox in the fact that it was just at the time when the public began to regard the Teddy Boys as a serious threat that the fashion started to lose its popularity. The very identification of the extreme Teddy Boy outfit with deviant values – the 'badge of shame' – rendered it more and more esoteric, and it even underwent modification itself to become the less extreme 'Drape' style. As early as April 1955 there were reports of second-hand Edwardian suits being sold in an open market in Hertfordshire. Other sections of working-class youth had initiated or imitated new fashions. They flirted with the 'Bohemian' style and, above all, with the 'Italian' style which was the precursor of the Modernist. By 1957–8 the Italian style was normal 'smart' dress for a substantial number of working-class adolescents. By 1958–9 the 'real' Teds were only to be found in the provinces. In London they had become a very much submerged minority.

In 1956 there was a consolidation of the pattern of violence which had been apparent in the previous years. There were mass fights in some London suburbs. In Tooting, for example, groups of sixty or seventy were involved. There was a particularly vicious encounter in Scotland where a group of Teddy Boys from Fife fought a pitched battle with some sailors. As usual, these clashes were described as 'gang fights', although the groups possessed few of the characteristics of gangs. They were accompanied by vast pre-publicity. In April, the 'King' of Fife's Teddy Boys was photographed and he outlined in an interview his plans for the fight which was to take place the following weekend.[41]

Nevertheless, towards the end of the year the larger groups appeared to be losing their already nebulous identity, and the typical event became not so much an internecine feud but an attack by a small group on a solitary stranger. The range of weapons was extended to include such items as potatoes which concealed razor blades. Although the number of these attacks was never great, it is hard to exaggerate their sheer brutality and apparent senselessness ('apparent' because the label 'senseless' is too often used by the outside, middle-class observer to denote a cultural pattern which he cannot understand). In Nottingham some Teddy Boys flung a dog into a deep rubbish-pit, pelted it with bricks, and left it there all night. In July, Liverpool Teddy Boys were reported to be playing a new game. They tied a rope to a cat's tail, swung the cat round and round and then released it. The object was to see whose half-strangled cat travelled furthest. In 1957, a thirteen-year-old Clapton boy was pinioned to the ground by two Teddy Boys who had ignited a firework inside his shirt and then watched it burn. His chest and stomach were painfully seared.

1956 also saw the eruption of a particular type of behaviour which gained the Teddy Boys a great deal of publicity. It also gave another adolescent activity a bad name. This was the so-called 'rock 'n' roll riot' in cinemas. There had been incidents of hooliganism in cinemas before, but they had not involved large groups and, what was more important, they were not widely publicised. During the peak years of the riots, the disturbances seemed to occur in distinct phases and were clearly fanned by publicity. The phases were associated with the showings of particular films, the most notorious being *Rock Around the Clock*. An analysis of the riots which stemmed from the showing of this film in the week following 28 August 1956 demonstrates how this process developed.

On that night, the film was shown at the Prince of Wales Cinema in the Harrow Road, Paddington, which was the home territory of many of the early Teds. People started jiving in the aisles and the manager was attacked when he protested. A number of seats were torn and ten policemen were eventually called. On the next night, the cinema was protected by twenty men – ex-soldiers and ex-boxers – who had been recruited from the A.B.C. cinemas of North London. Policemen were placed at exits outside the cinemas. In the next week there was a wave of disturbances at showings of the film at various London cinemas. There were at least eight separate incidents recorded in the London area. When the film went on wider circuit, there were further manifestations of what had now become regarded as the typical 'rock 'n' roll' riot: fighting, slashing of seats, and other types of vandalism. Between 1955 and 1957 these riots – associated with rock 'n' roll films or the 'live' appearances of such people as Bill Haley – took place in a number of European capitals. The West Berlin police reports of a peak period, between April 1956 and December 1957, recorded 108 incidents which had involved ten or more participants. Four of these had involved over a thousand persons.

The proliferation of these riots can be described in terms of a particular feedback sequence in which an initial departure from valued norms is followed by a punitive reaction by the community. This reaction is more likely to take place when there is a gross lack of information about the potential deviant group and its behaviour (as is the case with drug taking) and when the group is already regarded with suspicion and hostility by the community (as is the case with adolescents). This reaction in turn may lead to the segregation of groups and their identification as deviant, together with the development of a deviant self-concept and behaviour appropriate to this self. In turn, this may lead to a further punitive reaction. In this manner the behaviour is amplified.[42] The sociologist, Lemert, has used the terms 'primary' and 'secondary' deviation to distinguish between the initial breach of the rules and the way in which the deviant then responds to the society's reaction to his behaviour. These concepts – slightly adapted – fit the feedback sequence in the rock 'n' roll riots.

The primary deviation is the response to the music or the performance which follows upon a vast publicity campaign aimed at stressing its sensational nature. This response involved the clapping of hands, dancing in the aisles, the banging of feet on the floor, chanting, singing and so on. This behaviour typically led to punitive social control measures. Cinema managers attempted to evict people; the police were summoned and 'trouble-makers' were segregated. This again may produce types of secondary deviation – seat slashing, fighting, objects being thrown at the screen, fire buckets being torn from the walls and hosepipes being turned on. All these behaviour patterns were made more 'contagious' and were encouraged by the semi-darkness, the crowded and confined space, and the probable presence of a few 'trouble-makers' who in any riot situation are likely to respond at a lower threshold to perceived provocation and discrimination.

In the communication about these incidents the focus was placed on the secondary deviation, and this prepared the next stage of the amplification sequence. The potentially deviant group immediately adopted the secondary adjustment pattern because it felt that this was what was expected of it in the situation. This expectation was often justified by the presence of television cameras, police, reporters and security guards. The controller acted upon the assumption that it was secondary deviation which he had to tackle or that any primary deviation would *inevitably* become secondary. This was also reasonable, because the self-fulfilling prophecy had been set in motion.

Not all incidents went through the complete sequence. The following report shows that social control does sometimes 'work' (it also shows that 'excitement' could now be defined as deviant behaviour): 'At Romford, police were called to the Gaumont when several youths and girls became excited by the music. The young people left without any unruly scenes.'[43]

1957 was a year of little interest. Press reports show a steady increase in incidents now looked on as typical of the Teddy Boys: disturbances at cinemas (which were mainly in the provinces), gang fights (in August there was one which was described by the *Daily Mail* as the largest in London for years), and attacks on bus crews and café owners. The identification of an offender as a Teddy Boy was frequently somewhat tenuous. In July, for example, a boy who had been assaulted and thrown into the Thames claimed that his assailants were Teds because they wore 'black Edwardian trousers and open-necked white shirts'. There were very few public attempts to improve the Teddy Boy image. In the only reported speech of its kind during the year, Sir Edward Boyle defended the current fashions as sartorial extravagances which made their wearers cleaner and tidier. But on the whole the adult reaction was one of fear or surly suspicion. In a review of a television play, Maurice Richardson explained his terror by saying that 'I see the Teddy as a kind of existential storm-trooper in the age-war; he is coming for you as sure as Death'.[44] In July, Tom Harrisson, who was labelled an explorer and anthropologist, returned from Borneo. He was asked by an *Evening Standard* reporter about what had impressed him most on his return to Britain. 'It's this new terror that stalks the land, the Teddy-Boy. The first time I went out in Hampstead I was so frightened that I nearly took off again for

Borneo and the comparative security of head hunting.'[45]. The accuracy of these melodramatic hyperboles is not important, they may be quite unrepresentative, but the fact that they could be expressed and reported at all indicates something of the climate of the time.

Although there were increasing references to adolescent violence, delinquency and, for the first time, sexual misbehaviour in 1958, these references were couched in general terms and were not often reports of actual events. In fact, there was more of a reaction than anything to react to, and this was especially true of the old style of London Teds. Laurie describes this period well: 'Even with the reports and comments before one, it is difficult to recapture the aura of social catastrophe that enveloped the teenager at the end of the fifties. By then the Teddy Boys had reached and passed their peak of influence but in the public mind their image had just jelled.'[46]

The violence had not quite evaporated. In the provinces the traditional Teddy Boy pattern was being re-enacted with the ferocity characteristic of a beaten army in its last stand. Fashions tend to take on a corrupted formalism when they reach their last potential consumers. 'Gang' fights were reported in Cornish villages, in towns like Weston-super-Mare and particularly in Bristol. The Lord Mayor announced in May that 'Teddy Boys are becoming a menace to this city'. In London and the larger cities, Teddy Boys occasionally displayed 'typical' behaviour by creating disturbances in cinemas. The films were now *Jailhouse Rock*, *King Creole* and *Disc Jockey Jamboree*.

Crimes of violence were now committed mainly by solitary offenders. Society was disturbed about a vanishing group. In February, a Private Member's Bill was introduced in the Commons to enable a fine of £10 to be imposed in London for threatening, abusive or insulting words or behaviour in any thoroughfare or public place'. During the Third Reading of the Bill, an M.P. suggested that Teddy Boys' suits should be impounded and their curls kept cropped until the fines were paid. These new sanctions were unnecessary; the Teddy Boy was dying.

But if he was going to die in 1958, he was not going to die with a whimper. The Notting Hill riots at the end of the year and two highly publicised dance-hall killings a little later were his last dull bangs.

The most interesting feature of the Notting Hill riots was the active role taken by a group clearly identifiable as 'yobbos', 'hooligans' or Teds. Although, as the riots progressed, other elements – extremist political groups, curious onlookers, etc. – were attracted and eventually outnumbered the Teds, there was always a hard core of violent adolescents who were instrumental in provoking incidents. This behaviour could be expected from a group drawn from a sector of society predisposed to xenophobia and more susceptible to extremist propaganda[47] and who were also more likely to resort to physical violence. Moreover, this was a group already labelled, segregated and excluded not only from adult society but from their own peer group. The new teenage image had swamped them, just as the Rockers were later on to be swamped by the Mods and driven to violent retaliation. There was enough latent hostility to make the object of the Teds' aggression irrelevant; as it happened, the object – a coloured racial minority group – was visible and very relevant. The Teds in turn could serve as a scapegoat for respectable British society to cover up its own failures and prejudices in dealing with its immigrant population.

The more publicised of the two dance-hall killings – the Marwood case – was important for symbolic reasons. The reaction was intensified by the fact that the victim was a policeman and Marwood (who ended on the scaffold after a protracted campaign to have the death penalty lifted) was held up, as it were, as evidence that the Teddy Boy gangs were not yet dead. But dead they were, and ironically Marwood had no connection at all with either of the gangs involved in the brawl that led to the stabbing of the policeman.

One of the most common reasons given for the Teddy Boy phenomenon was the effect of the war. This explanation was given credibility by the Home Office Research Unit Report of 1960 which suggested that children aged about five were more likely to be disturbed by war or other forms of social upheaval than children of any other age. Nevertheless, the generation who had lived through the war during their critical first years displayed even more delinquency than this hypothesis alone could predict. Clearly – as Wilkins, the author of the report, has himself pointed out – some other factor which was peculiarly conducive to delinquency had begun to operate in the early fifties. Wilkins speculates that this 'other factor' was the assumption of a 'communication symbol' by youths who were already candidates for delinquency. The symbol was the Teddy Boy suit. It functioned for this group – as communication symbols do for all minority groups – as a means of maintaining the group and preserving its identity. Scarves worn by university students play the same role. Because such symbols can be recognised by people outside the group, the application of social control is made easier. The group may become rejected, segregated and punished. Such treatment could simply shatter the group, or else increase its solidarity and self-awareness; thus, as Wilkins puts it, 'the delinquents become more delinquent'.

It docs not much matter that the symbol was the Teddy Boy suit. Clothing styles are neutral until they are given significance by others. Indeed, the Edwardian suit was once favourably defined. It does not really matter how the suit was adopted in 1953.[48] But the fact that the suit became so clearly associated with delinquency *is* important. When the first working-class Edwardian appeared in 1953, there was enough of an expectancy of violence, and a latent hostility towards the strange animal, to create an atmosphere which was ripe for one or two dramatic incidents to confirm the fears and consolidate the stereotypes. In any society there are always a number of people who are prepared to react to any signs of incipient deviance in terms of the 'thin end of the wedge' argument – who call for it to be 'clamped down on' before 'it's too late'.

We have already discussed the 'deviance amplification' system which centred round the Teddy Boy. We have not yet touched upon why he was delinquent, why his delinquency assumed the form it took, and why it was he, and not his middle-class peer, who became the 'menace'. The audience who helped to fashion the Teddy Boy did not conjure up his deviance from the void. The Ted was not a completely innocent target for the hostility of an outraged adult world.

David Downes has suggested a framework for explaining delinquency which we believe is applicable to the Teddy Boy.[49] He argues that many working-class adolescents are dissociated from the system of school and work. They are not interested in the middle-class standards which dominate the school. They also lack occupational aspiration – in the conventional middle-class sense of 'ambition' – and they do not question the social system which has allocated them to their roles. They are thus devoid of any aspirations towards achievement in school or at work, and also of the idealism which appeals to their middle-class counterparts – for example, political involvement or community service. In a low-ceilinged market, they drift through a series of dull, undemanding jobs which hold out no future.

Leisure, therefore, becomes extremely important, and they seek from it the excitement, self-respect and autonomy which are so conspicuously absent from work. It is at this point that the teenage culture becomes important – not because it is in itself delinquent, but because it generates precisely the values 'missing' elsewhere – excitement, autonomy and so on. In the fifties this took place at a time when the wages of adolescents were, for the first time, rising significantly faster than those for other age groups. They were thus given a new-found economic independence from their parents and were open to the attractions of the teenage culture. There was, moreover, a certain continuity between this subculture and the larger, traditional working-class subculture in which the Teddy Boy and his successors were raised. The 'focal concerns' of the lower working-class world, which have been suggested as the logical antecedents of delinquent values, are in fact very similar to the concerns of the teenage culture. Preoccupations with toughness, excitement, fate, autonomy and status are found in both cultures, and so the Teddy Boy was not only estranged from middle-class values, but was also involved in the lower-class culture and its adolescent variant. Although *all* adolescents are in a position of subservience to adult society and thus use the leisure culture to achieve some independence, the dependence on this culture by the working-class adolescent is much more intense and comprehensive.

Yet it was precisely in the area of leisure that he found his opportunities for satisfaction blocked. The conventional youth service had little to offer. With rare exceptions, such as the Teen Canteen and the Leicester experiment,[50] the adult response to the Teddy Boys – when it was not simply punitive – was well-meaning but drearily predictable and unimaginative. As Gosling and many others have pointed out, it was just this well-meaning and patronising attitude by responsible adults which made the youth service so stiflingly unattractive. The town had just as little to offer. Fyvel has vividly portrayed the drabness and the uniformity of the commercial 'entertainment' of that time – the caffs, the cinema, the occasional dance, bingo and the amusement arcade. These settings were hardly capable of fostering a sense of self-respect, and they were not particularly exciting. There were, of course, other forms of leisure which *were* attractive; but these required contacts, knowledge or the acceptance of the forms as appealing, which were all foreign to the working-class adolescent. Moreover, he was eventually denied many of those legitimate pleasures which *were* accessible to him:

> You started just by being noisy and a bit of a show-off when you were with the others, you used a bit of bad language and had one or two fights amongst yourselves, and before you knew where you was the lot of you'd been told not to come around that place any more – a café p'raps, or a cinema, something like that. Then you found people were even telling you not to come in to places before you'd ever been near them, they'd say if they saw you and your mates around they'd send for the Law straight off. The one

317

place we could never get barred from was the Common. . . .[51]

Thus to those who demanded the most of leisure, the least was offered. Delinquency arose from this type of discontinuity and frustration. It was the response to the setting of impossibly high leisure aspirations which arose from the previous dissociation from work and school achievements. Although the delinquent solution takes place in the field of leisure, the problem it solves goes further back into the social structure.

When the Teddy Boys manufactured their own excitement, it was their clothing which distinguished them to those who wielded social control. It was the encounter between these two groups which branded the Teddy Boys as folk devils. Just as social types are created and branded by the community, on the individual level too the very forces which attempt to arrest the delinquent's career may have the opposite effect:

The process of making the criminal, therefore, is a process of tagging, defining, identifying, segregating, describing, emphasising, making conscious and self-conscious; it becomes a way of stimulating, suggesting, emphasising, and evoking the very traits that are complained of. If the theory of relation of response to stimulus has any meaning, the entire process of dealing with the young delinquent is mischievous in so far as it identifies him to himself or to the environment as a delinquent person. The person becomes the thing he is described as being.[52]

Early in 1961, the director of a costume museum advertised for a Teddy Boy suit to add to his collection. Thus do the tags, definitions and social types change, to be embalmed in the folklore. When the Teddy Boy ungracefully left the stage, there were other nameless horrors to replace him and play out their own scenes.

Notes

1. Colin MacInnes, *Absolute Beginners* (1959).
2. Edgar Friedenberg, 'Adolescence as a Social Problem', in Howard S. Becker (ed.), *Social Problems: A Modern Approach* (New York, 1966) pp. 37–8.
3. T. R. Fyvel, *The Insecure Offenders* (1961) pp. 49–50.
4. *Daily Mirror*, 17 November 1953.
5. *Daily Sketch*, 14 November 1953
6. *Daily Herald*, 14 November 1953.
7. *Daily Sketch*, 9 December 1953.
8. *Daily Mirror*, 23 October 1953.
9. Tony Parker, *The Ploughboy* (1965) pp. 20–1.
10. *Sunday Chronicle*, 28 February 1954.
11. Kai T. Erikson, 'Notes on the Sociology of Deviance', in Howard S. Becker (ed.), *The Other Side: Perspectives on Deviance* (Glencoe, Ill., 1964) p. 14.
12. *Evening Standard*, 24 February 1954.
13. Anselm Strauss, *Mirrors and Masks* (Glencoe, Ill., 1959) pp. 21–2.
14. *Daily Sketch*, 22 March 1954.
15. *Daily Express*, 17 November 1955.
16. Hunter S. Thompson, *Hell's Angels: A Strange and Terrible Saga* (New York, 1966) p. 40.
17. *Daily Mail*, 26 April 1954.
18. Ibid., 27 April 1954.
19. *News Chronicle*, 1 May 1954.
20. *Reynolds News*, 1 May 1954.
21. *Daily Sketch*, 7 May 1954.
22. *Star*, 7 May 1954.
23. Ibid., 8 May 1954.
24. *Daily Mirror*, 26 June 1954.
25. *Daily Express*, 19 July 1954.
26. David Downes, 'The Gang Myth', *The Listener*, 14 April 1966.
27. Tony Parker, *The Ploughboy*, pp. 24–5.
28. *Evening Standard*, 2 June 1954.
29. *Daily Herald*, 23 May 1954.
30. *Evening News*, 12 May 1954.
31. *Daily Herald*, 23 May 1954.

32. *Daily Sketch*, 7 May 1954.

33. Fyvel, *The Insecure Offenders*, p. 50.

34. *Evening News*, 17 July 1954.

35. *Sunday Chronicle*, 21 November 1954.

36. *Evening Standard*, 2 October 1954.

37. *Sunday Dispatch*, 27 June 1955.

38. *Daily Express*, 1 July 1957.

39. Ibid., 7 June 1955.

40. *News Chronicle*, 10 December 1956.

41. In the period 1956–9 we traced reports of at least eight self-styled 'Kings' of the Teddy Boys. Such reports – the products of melodramatic crime reporting or sheer gullibility – have the effect of giving the amorphous 'near-group' a bogus structure.

42. Suggested by L. T. Wilkins, *Social Deviance* (1964).

43. *Daily Telegraph*, 3 September 1956.

44. *Observer*, 31 March 1957.

45. *Evening Standard*, 27 July 1957.

46. P. Laurie, *The Teenage Revolution* (1965).

47. See, for example, J. Robb, *Working Class Anti-Semite* (1954).

48. Fyvel believes that the suit was first seen and emulated by working-class visitors to the West End and Soho.

49. David Downes, *The Delinquent Solution* (1966).

50. See Ray Gosling's autobiography *Sum Total* (1963).

51. Tony Parker, *The Ploughboy*, p. 27.

52. Frank Tannenbaum, *Crime and the Community* (New York, 1938) pp. 19–20.

10 Fifties Children: Sixties People

Anthony Bicât

POPULAR songs provide the images that define an age, not for the critics and analysts of that age, but for the people who live in it. That old cliché and joke, 'Listen, darling, they're playing our song', is merely an expression of the way in which it is songs that are often the landmarks in our emotional lives. My generation grew up to the songs of the Beatles, the Stones and Bob Dylan, as an earlier generation had grown up to the songs of Porter, Hart, Coward and Anderson.

The popular song is the lyric evocation of the collective dream. In its nostalgia and its myth-making it provides people with something much nearer their real spiritual needs than does conventional poetry. Its very need to be popular, the way it is tied to commercialism, ensures its relevance. It is a debased currency, but it is a genuine one. The same could not be said of the poetry of our time.

In the fifties the whole character of popular music changed completely. People were getting bored with the large swing orchestras and the soupy balladeers. The young in many cases turned towards the less refined dance music of trad. This was a copy, in some cases efficient, in some reverential, of the old Negro jazz, Dixieland. The musical papers started listing not the top twenty sales of sheet music but the top twenty sales of records, thereby reflecting the change in emphasis and the increasing sales of records. More people had money, more people had gramophones, more people bought records.

The emphasis shifted from large orchestras of as many as twenty pieces to small groups of five or six. This change is very important. Though the reason for it was largely economic, the effect was to break down the structure of pop music and to create units that were efficient to run and also, perhaps more important, units that it was possible to identify with. It is very hard to have a large fan following for a group of twenty people, but with six this becomes possible. This is true of all branches of music.

Pop music, which hitherto had been jazz or swing music, finally broke down into its component parts. Firstly there was trad, small-group copy of the original Dixieland jazz. Then there was dance music, the old-fashioned swing music which steadily lost its popularity but today seems to have found its audience and settled down with a staunch but small following. Finally there was music specifically designed for the young, and it is with this music that I propose to deal.

The old-style pop music had been, and still is, music specifically designed for adults. The image it projected was one of affluent sophistication – the great white myth of style. Men in white dinner-jackets sung to ladies in evening gowns on romantically lit terraces or the first-class decks of ocean liners. It was the projection of a dream of affluence. The possession of wealth would give one grace, style and beauty. The sad songs were not songs of disillusionment with society, but with love. Their misery was a well-fed alcoholic haze of sentimentality, where sex was a memory and passion a lost thing that stalked in the streetlight, empty as a shadow and as solid as the last martini:

> In the wee small hours of the morning,
> When the whole wide world is fast asleep,
> You lie awake and think about the girl
> And never even think of counting sheep.
> When your lonely heart has learned its lesson,
> You'd be hers if only she would call,
> In the wee small hours of the morning
> That's the time you miss her most of all.
> (Dave Mann/Bob Hilliard)

It is a twilight world of lamplight and memory, and the nostalgia is not really for a lost love but, it seems to me, also for a lost age, the lost age of style, the thirties – which was by any standards a golden age of song. By the fifties the lyric strength of the old standards had been watered down to a hideous parody. Cole Porter and especially Lorenz Hart, whatever their sentiments, had possessed a wit that made them able to deal with even the most cloyingly sentimental without creating nausea:

> *Is your figure less than Greek?*
> *Is your mouth a little weak?*
> *When you open it to speak*
> *Are you smart?*

> (Lorenz Hart)

By the fifties we were getting songs of the order of 'Love and Marriage':

> *Love and marriage, love and marriage,*
> *Just go together like a horse and carriage.*
> *This I tell you, brother,*
> *You can't have one without the other.*

The change was gradual, and even today songs of this type linger on, but one of the good things about the teenage market was that it meant a distinct cutdown in songs like 'Love and Marriage', and by implication all that they stood for.

The change is best illustrated by quoting two Top of the Pops top tens, both from the *Melody Maker*. The first is for May 1956:

1. 'No Other Love'/Ronnie Hilton
2. 'Rock and Roll Waltz'/Kay Starr
3. 'Poor People of Paris'/Winifred Atwell
4. 'A Tear Fell'/Teresa Brewer
5. 'My September Love'/David Whitfield
6. 'I'll be Home'/Pat Boone
7. 'It's Almost Tomorrow'/Dream Weavers
8. 'Only You'/Hilltoppers

9. 'Main Title' ('Man with the Golden Arm')/
   Billy May
10. 'Lost John'/Lonnie Donnegan

The second is for May 1959:

1. 'Living Doll'/Cliff Richard
2. 'Dream Lover'/Bobby Darin
3. 'Battle of New Orleans'/Lonnie Donnegan
4. 'Lipstick on Your Collar'/Connie Francis
5. 'A Big Hunk of Love'/Elvis Presley
6. 'A Teenager in Love'/Marty Wilde
7. 'Lonely Boy'/Paul Anka
8. 'Roulette'/Russ Conway
9. 'Ragtime Cowboy Joe'/David Seville
10. 'The Heart of a Man'/Frankie Vaughan

It is quite easy to see that by 1959 the hit parade was totally dominated by the teenage market. And with various minor fluctuations it has remained so. Both the singers and the songs were now being moulded to capture this new public.

The most obvious result of this swing was rock 'n' roll. Rock 'n' roll was music specifically designed for the teenage market. From its outset, rock 'n' roll as played by Bill Haley and his Comets was associated with violence and rioting. In Essen in 1958, 8,000 teenagers rioted at a Bill Haley concert. All the seats were ripped out and hoses were turned on the rioters outside.

In England many towns banned the showing of Bill Haley's film *Rock Around the Clock* for fear of violence. In 1956 the *Melody Maker* reported that rock 'n' roll riots didn't scare Bill Haley, who said that he'd played a hundred and fifty rock 'n' roll gigs in America and there had never been any trouble. However, in Manchester, after the showing of *Rock Around the Clock*, ten youths were fined for insulting behaviour when they left the cinema. 'Rhythm-crazed' youngsters, after they had seen the film, held up traffic for half an hour and trampled on the flower beds in the municipal garden. In Blackburn the Watch Committee banned the film; in Preston the Chief Constable and the Mayor wanted to ban the film and cinema managers were advised not to show it. In Croydon the police cleared the Davis Theatre on Sunday of jiving youngsters, but during the second performance a fresh crowd stamped and chanted 'We want rock 'n' roll! We want rock 'n' roll!' Clergymen thundered from the pulpit that rock 'n' roll was devil's music, and comparisons were made with the Black Mass. On 9 February 1957, *Melody Maker* announced with considerable surprise: 'Bill Haley opens and no riots'.

The image of the idols, too, began to change. The idols of the forties, Frank Sinatra and Bing Crosby, were replaced by young singers like Elvis Presley and Cliff Richard. The older idols had been suave and sophisticated, stylistically impeccable as in Crosby's case, or coolly passionate as in Sinatra's. The young ones with their greased-back hair and raucous music refused to stand still on stage, and indeed the pelvic gyrations of Cliff and Elvis became for many another symptom of moral decline.

There was a continuous breakdown throughout the fifties in the impeccable exterior of music. Performance became more relaxed in its technique if more frantic in its movements. There was less attempt to polish a performance. The music eventually became so simple that almost anybody with any musical ability at all could play it. The craze for skiffle, which was a do-it-yourself form of music, was the ultimate result of this.

Anybody could play skiffle. All you needed was three chords on a guitar, a washboard and an old tea-chest, with string and broom. The remoteness of the swing bands, with their intricate and demanding reed and brass playing, was finally conquered. Musicians complained about the decline in the standard of sax playing; and the saxophone, which had been a fashionable instrument for thirty years, began to lose its precedence to the electric guitar.

The new music was loud and raucous and for the most part diabolical. Its great virtue was that it was a music that generated a spontaneous liberation in its young listeners. Years of frustration at a music which said nothing to them expressed itself in tearing up cinema seats and trampling the municipal flower beds. But *it was* liberating. It had ceased to be a mystic thing practised by men in white dinner-jackets on high bandstands, and become something that anyone with a fiver for a guitar and a minimal amount of intelligence could have a go at.

In 1959 teenagers had £830 million to spend. Of this, the largest proportion went on records. This spending-power controlled over 40 per cent of the record market. Whereas the old music had been spread over all ages and all strata of society, the new music had a special public, for the teenager developed a taste and a style of his own. So although teenagers do not in fact buy more records than anybody else, they are the largest single identifiable market. This explains their continued domination of the record industry.

In 1955 Johnnie Ray talked about the rhythm and blues fad in America. He said that though it was a fad that wouldn't last, it was the only music made 'by Americans for Americans'. Johnnie 'Cry' Ray was a kind of transitional idol. He was neither the old sophisticated idol of the days of Sinatra nor the young idol of the Elvis period. His stage act involved breaking down into tears of emotion at the sadness of his songs, thereby causing screams of adulation. A number of women in the audience would faint.

Rhythm and blues spread across the Atlantic and injected a measure of fire into the veins of pop. It was the urban equivalent of the old country blues, e.g. 'Slave Hollers of the City'. It was raw, crude music and its words reflected, with little or no subtlety, the pain and frustration of the urban American Negro.

It is significant that the early influences on the Beatles were singers like Mary Wells and Chuck Berry who came from this background. It was, however, the Rolling Stones who were to take over rhythm and blues and use the medium to express the frustration of British youth. The Rolling Stones are, indeed, the most obvious example of the young turning against the values of a whole society in their music. They represent very clearly the reactions of young people brought up in the Age of Affluence.

To a large extent, the songs of the forties and fifties portrayed a yearning for conventional prosperity and respectability – 'Love and Marriage' which went together like a horse and carriage. The songs of the thirties had projected an image of affluence and, above all, style. The achievement of what was called affluence in the fifties led, however, to people finding out that it was not the stylish sophisticated veneer that they had expected – that this affluence had no solidity at all. The young, sensing this, revolted directly against the pursuit of such standards. All the tearing-up of cinema seats was an extreme expression of this disillusionment with the goals of the adult world.

The Rolling Stones carried this disgust to its logical conclusion. They were scruffy and dirty. Their abilities as musicians were at best minimal, at worst non-existent. And yet they were one of the most exciting acts to watch. They created an enormous sensation whenever they appeared. Their revolt was much more obvious than that of the Beatles, and though in the long run their songs were not so revolutionary, Mick Jagger's words were the most striking expressions of hatred for the Affluent Society that have ever appeared in any medium whatsoever.

Mick Jagger really was an Angry Young Man, beside whom the writers and dramatists who had caused such a big splash in such a small puddle in the fifties dwindled into insignificance. After all they never actually tried to put John Osborne in gaol. Although it was not a very reasonable response, the adult world seemed to hold Mick Jagger in abject terror. He was a challenge to all that parents held sacred. Every mother who saw him realised that he was the one who would come in to steal her housekeeping, seduce her daughter, and light his cigarette, probably drugged, with the latest article by Godfrey Winn. He seemed to hold nothing sacred. He even appeared on the Ed Sullivan show in his tee-shirt.

It was as if the English language had gained a new swear word. 'Bloody Mick Jagger! Bloody Mick Jagger!' made the pop song a battlefield between the young and the old, between them and us. Wealth and position were seen as destructive forces that ruined young lives:

> *Your mother who neglected you*
> *Owed a million dollars tax.*
> *Your father's still perfecting ways*
> *Of making sealing wax.*
> *You'd better stop, look around,*
> *Here it comes,*
> *Here comes your nineteenth nervous breakdown.*

The situation is often of the poor boy and the rich girl whose position he wishes to break through and degrade:

> *She's very wealthy it's true,*
> *So in that she is one up on you.*
> *She dresses all in red, white and blue*
> *And she always knows more than you do.*
> *She's well protected,*
> *Cool, calm, collected.*

The mums were right to be frightened. It was positively inciting the young to acts of Jimmy Porterism.

In songs like 'Mother's Little Helper' he lashed out at the corruption of the adult world. The attack is on the suburban pill-taking of women who take any one of the numerous pick-me-ups on the market to keep them going. It is ironic that it was for the possession of just such pills that Jagger himself was later arrested:

> *Kids are different today*
> *I hear every Mother say.*
> *Mother needs something today to calm her down.*
> *So though she's not really ill*
> *There's a little yellow pill.*
> *She goes running to the shelter*
> *Of her mother's little helper*
> *And it helps her on her way,*
> *Gets her through her busy day.*

328

But the song is not really about this sort of pro-
scribed addiction; it is, like many of Jagger's other
songs, about the general emptiness of the affluent life.
The song goes on to take in the growing tastelessness
of pre-prepared food, the lazy way to a comfortable
life that, as the song shows, rebounds on the people
who use it:

> Things are different today
> I hear every Mother say.
> To cook fresh food for her husband's just a drag.
> So she buys an instant cake
> And she burns a frozen steak
> And goes running to the shelter
> Of her mother's little helper.

The song goes on to include the sexual life of the
couple: 'Men just don't appreciate that you get tired
... You can tranquillise your man...', etc. The song
ends with a note of warning:

> And if you take more of those
> You will get an overdose.
> No more running to the shelter
> Of your mother's little helper
> Just to help you on your way
> Through your busy dying day.

The condemnation is explicit and runs through all
the Stones' songs, and it is this that made them so
popular with the young and so unpopular with the old.
The early songs of the Beatles were lyrically very
simple. The words were entirely subservient to the
music. The good thing about the songs was the absence
of the old imagery. Although they were simple and
banal, they made no attempt to ape the style and sophistication of a previous generation of songwriters:

> I'll call you on the phone
> And you'll come running home.
> Yeh that's all I've gotta do...

It was a straight teenage world pictured in everyday language.

In the film *Help*, John Lennon sang the song

> Here I stand head in hand
> Turn my face to the wall.
> Now you've gone
> I can't go on
> Feeling two foot small ...

This song was a kind of parody of Bob Dylan, and was sung in the film with Lennon in the familiar Dylan cap and to a simple guitar accompaniment. After this time, whether it was due to the influence of Bob Dylan or not, they began to write much more complex songs. However, they stuck to writing songs from an immediately referrable contemporary experience – their own – but the songs were much more complicated and the situations that they described were similarly much more fraught:

> I once had a girl,
> Or should I say
> She once had me.

'Norwegian Wood' is a song for the Affluent Society if ever there was one. The situation is of the poor boy and the rich sophisticated career girl. They spend a loveless night of love together, and when she has gone off to work in the morning the boy burns her furniture – her 'Norwegian Wood':

> So I lit the fire,
> Isn't it good
> Norwegian Wood?

As in the songs of the Stones, the contempt is for the children of affluence and the trappings of a habitat-furnitured society. The difference between the Beatles and the Stones is that the Beatles are always more detached than the Stones. For them the indignation is contained within the song; for Jagger, the indignation is the song. Because they are less obvious they are less offensive, and the demands of an ever increasing musical sophistication tend to push the words into the background and make them less important than in the songs of the Stones.

The Beatles have always had a very strong sense of what money means, and it has provided them with the theme, and occasionally with the images, for songs:

> *The best things in life are free,*
> *But you can keep them for the birds and bees.*
> *Give me money – That's what I want.*
> *Give me money – That's what I want.*
> *Money Money That's what I want.*

And in the same vein:

> *Your lovin' gives me a thrill,*
> *But your lovin' don't pay the bill.*
> *Give me money – That's what I want.*

The Bradford/Gordy blues 'Money' was a typical example of a number of rhythm and blues songs that became popular in the early sixties. The children of the Affluent Society were identifying, and still are, with the American Negroes, their poverty and their music. The Negroes' poverty and suffering were striking and still strike a responsive chord in children of a society that, in the words of its leader, had 'never had it so good'.

Yet the attitude to money remains ambiguous. It has not altered the reality of 'us' and 'them':

> *People standing round*
> *Who'll screw you in the ground*

'Taxman' by George Harrison has in it some of the best ironical lines the Beatles ever wrote:

> *And my advice to those who die:*
> *Declare the pennies in your eyes.*

331

In John Lennon's songs the note of jeering is even more pronounced:

> *How does it feel to be one of the Beautiful people?*
> *Now that you know who you are*
> *What do you want to be?*

He uses the 'things' that so obsess our society as part of the vocabulary of his songs.

> *When your prized possessions start to get you down,*
> *Look in my direction, I'll be rou 1, I'll be round.*

The obvious conclusion – that mo   isn't everything after all – foreshadows the hippies:

> *Make love all day long*
> *Make love singing songs.*

The contradictions in these songs echo the confused response of their audience to the arrival of affluence. The children of Affluence have everything, yet they have nothing. There is no analysis, that would be expecting too much; what remains is a feeling of confusion, of bewilderment. In the work of John Lennon, the simple 'story' song collapses into absurdity. He has invented several completely new sorts of song – the altercation song in 'She said, She Said', the poster song in 'For the Benefit of Mr Kite', and a sort of composite abstract song which musically and lyrically is built up to an anarchic sound picture that defies analysis but creates an atmosphere of zany abandon. An example of this is 'I am the Walrus':

> *I am he as you are he as you are me*
> *And we are all together.*

The nearest thing to it in literature is Alfred Jarry: a desire to shock by the absurdity of juxtaposition – a desire to show that the component parts of literature can be put together, totally haphazardly, to reflect a new kind of absurdity.

> *Semolina pilchard climbing up the Eiffel*
>   *Tower.*
> *Elementary penguin, singing Hare Krishna.*
>   *Man you should*
> *Have seen them kicking Edgar Allan Poe.*
> *I am the eggman, they are eggmen, I am the*
>   *Walrus,*
> *GOO GOO GOO JOOB GOO GOO GOO*
>   *JOOB, etc.*

Paul McCartney, on the other hand, has written some superb examples of the story song which, though the Beatles didn't invent it, they at least made fashionable. One of the best of the Beatles' songs is 'For No One', which was written by McCartney. The situation of this song is that of a couple who find love has died between them. The situation is imagined dramatically; it is a real situation evoked in simple language:

> *Your day breaks, your mind aches.*
> *You find that all her words of kindness linger*
>   *on.*
> *When she no longer needs you.*
>
> *She wakes up, she makes up,*
> *She takes her time and doesn't feel she has to*
>   *hurry.*
> *She no longer needs you*
> *And in her eyes you see nothing,*
> *No sign of love behind the tears cried for no*
>   *one:*
> *A love that should have lasted years.*

McCartney's songs always manage to have a superb economy of language, the sort of unaffected simplicity that made the Beatles write in one of their earlier songs:

> *When I get home tonight I'm going to hold*
>   *her tight,*
> *I'm going to love her till the cows come home.*

333

This simplicity of language arises, I think, from the fact that for him the music is more important than the words. The reverse of this is true for Lennon, and that is why they make such a good songwriting team.

The effect that serious songs such as 'Eleanor Rigby' and 'She's Leaving Home' had upon the teenage public was immense; there followed upon the heels of the serious songs an enormous quantity of similar story songs, most of which, because they were created in the image rather than in the essential feeling of the Beatles' songs, failed miserably.

The most powerful influence upon the pop song in the sixties is Bob Dylan. His influence has pervaded all spheres of life, and he remains for the young the symbol of what they mean and what they hope for.

Bob Dylan started off as a folk singer, that is, a singer with a fairly modest audience of devotees. His early songs are a personal version of the Negro blues and white hillbilly music. He still remains one of the few white men who can sing the blues well. He manages to do this, not by aping the style and intonation of the Negro blues singers, but by getting inside the lyrics of these songs, in some cases actually rewriting them, and in this way making them exclusively his own. The paradox is that, by doing this, he remains much more faithful to the blues than the singers who try and copy them as a musical form. He realises that the blues are primarily a literary form; the simplicity of their musical make-up makes the listeners' attention fall naturally upon the words. The simplicity of the form allows for a lot of natural freedom in the actual structure of the verse. This makes it possible, and indeed fairly easy, to improvise lyrics within the chord sequence. Dylan made free use of this freedom and captured the stance of the blues poets rather than any actual 'sound'.

Many of his early songs, which gained enormous currency, if not actual popularity, in terms of record sales, were protest songs. His protest was always well defined, often bitterly humorous, as in the last verse of his 'Talking World War Three Blues'. This is, as the title suggests, a 'talking' blues, that is a blues where the words are chanted over a chorded base, sometimes rhyming, sometimes not, but always with a free-ranging verse feel to them. The song concerns Dylan who goes to his doctor and tells him he's been having a recurring dream about being the only person left after World War Three. The doctor tells him it's 'a bad dream' and that he has been having a similar dream, but that the only difference is, he says, 'I dreamt the only person left alive was me'. The last verse is typical of the Dylan songs of the period; the humour is knife-edge:

> *Well now time passed and now it seems*
> *Everybody has been having these dreams,*
> *Everybody sees theirself walkin' around with*
> *   no one else.*
> *Half of the people can be part right all of the*
> *   time,*
> *Some of the people can be all right part of the*
> *   time,*
> *But all the people can't be all right all of the*
> *   time.*
> *I think Abe Lincoln said that.*
> *I'll let you be in my dream if I can be in yours*
> *I said that.*

Dylan also paved the way for a new kind of love song, or song about love. These were altogether more realistic than the songs of any previous age. An example of this is the unsentimental 'Don't Think Twice'. The singer is leaving his girl, but in the place of the self-pitying nostalgia we are used to, we get:

> *It ain't no use to sit and wonder why babe,*
> *It doesn't matter any how.*
> *An' it ain't no use to sit and wonder why*
> *   babe,*
> *If you don't know by now.*
> *When the rooster crows at the break of dawn*
> *Look out your window and I'll be gone.*
> *You're the reason I'm travellin' on.*
> *Don't think twice it's alright.*

It was a song much more relevant to contemporary experience than, say, 'Sealed with a Kiss', a song of the period which consisted predominantly of lines like 'I'll send you all my love every day in a letter, sealed with a kiss'. The effect of 'Don't Think Twice' and other similar songs like 'It Ain't Me Babe' and the later 'It's All Over Now Baby Blue', which contains lines like

> Your lover who has walked out the door
> Has taken all his blankets from the floor.
> Strike another match, let's start anew,
> For it's all over now baby blue.

was prodigious. People no longer felt at ease writing the nostalgic pseudo-thirties love songs; and the young certainly tended to stop buying them.

In 1965 Dylan invented something that came to be called folk rock. This was basically folk music with rock 'n' roll instrumentation. When he first performed this sort of music at the Newport Folk Festival many of the 'folkniks' booed, and to this day many of them still accuse Dylan of betraying the people. This musical change corresponded to a change in the theme of his lyrics. He simply abandoned his commitment. The new songs were strange and desperately beautiful symbolist poems with genuine surrealist overtones. They became even more popular than the old songs and created a whole new audience for Dylan, an audience that put him among the really big record sellers. These songs, too, had a corresponding effect upon the general shape of songs. It became obvious to the record producers that people were buying songs for the words, and the bandwagon was dutifully jumped upon. The most important song of this period was 'Desolation Row'.

'Desolation Row' is the imaginative re-creation of a letter, as the poet explains in the last verse:

> Yes I received your letter yesterday
> About the time the doorknob broke
> When you asked me how I was doing.
> Was that some kind of joke?

> *All these people that you mention*
> *Yes I know them, they are quite lame.*
> *I had to rearrange their faces*
> *And give them all another name.*
> *Right now I don't read too good.*
> *Don't send me no more letters, no,*
> *Not unless you mail them from Desolation Row.*

Desolation Row itself is an imaginary landscape after the manner of Dali, or more precisely Hieronymus Bosch. It is peopled with characters from fact and fiction, all mixed up together and all unified in the status of bums and clowns and in their location — Desolation Row. It is a vision of Hell, but a Hell on earth, a Hell that is preparing for the carnival:

> *And the good Samaritan he's dressing,*
> *He's getting ready for the show,*
> *He's going to the carnival tonight on Desolation*
> *Row.*

The ambulances have gone, the riot squad is restless; it is both the crime and the punishment of a sick world. Characters like Cinderella, Romeo, Casanova, Ophelia, the Phantom of the Opera, T. S. Eliot and Ezra Pound rub shoulders with each other in the gutter; there are no gods, no more heroes.

The personification of the heights of human intellect is depicted in the following manner:

> *Einstein disguised as Robin Hood,*
> *With his memories in a truck,*
> *Passed this way an hour ago*
> *With his friend a jealous monk.*
> *He looked so immaculately frightful*
> *As he bummed a cigarette,*
> *And he went off sniffing drainpipes*
> *And reciting the alphabet.*
> *You would not think to look at him*
> *That he was famous long ago*
> *For playing electric violin on Desolation Row.*

Einstein is a derelict busker and Ezra Pound and T. S.
Eliot are engaged in a brawl on a doomed ship, the
Titanic.

In this song Dylan reduces the cultural heritage that
is depicted in the letter to a cultural heritage of hobos
and tramps – the world that Woody Guthrie sings
about. And this is precisely what Dylan does in his
poetry; he has rejected the traditional literary heritage
for one that he believes is healthier. He is sick unto
death of the society and the culture that it offers him.
In his latest record 'John Wesley Hardin' he has gone
further back still and is imaginatively re-creating the
Old West as a kind of morality play of the present age.
Dylan provides a savage indictment of the age, and his
ever increasing popularity, especially in this country
as it models itself more and more upon America, cannot but be significant.

So we are left with a 'new song'; it is as uniquely part
of the age as is possible. It is the accurate poetic
evocation of the feelings of the children who grew up
in the Age of Affluence – fifties children who were
sixties people, who have everything and lack everything, as the song says:

> *Too much of nothing*
> *Can make a man feel ill at ease.*
> *One man's temper might rise*
> *While another man's temper might freeze.*
> *In the days of long confessions*
> *You cannot mark a soul,*
> *But when there's too much of nothing no one*
> *   has control.*

Suggested Reading

J. K. Galbraith, *The Affluent Society* (Hamish Hamilton, 1958).

Hugh Thomas (ed.), *The Establishment* (Anthony Blond, 1959).

Anthony Hartley, *A State of England* (Hutchinson, 1963).

Harold Macmillan, Autobiography, vol. 1: *Winds of Change* (Macmillan, 1966); vol. 2: *The Blast of War* (Macmillan, 1967); vol. 3: *Tides of Fortune* (Macmillan, 1969).

Anthony Sampson, *Macmillan: A Study in Ambiguity* (Penguin Press, 1967).

R. T. McKenzie, *British Political Parties*, rev. ed. (Mercury, 1963).

Samuel Beer, *Modern British Politics* (Faber, 1965).

C. A. R. Crosland, *The Future of Socialism* (Cape, 1956).

R. H. S. Crossman, *Planning for Freedom* (Hamish Hamilton, 1965).

Stephen Haseler, *The Gaitskellites* (Macmillan, 1969).

Andrew Shonfield, *British Economic Policy since the War*, 2nd ed. (Penguin, 1959).

Samuel Brittan, *Steering the Economy* (Secker & Warburg, 1969).

W. P. Snyder, *The Politics of British Defence Policy, 1945–1962* (Benn, 1964).

Hugh Thomas, *The Suez Affair* (Weidenfeld & Nicolson, 1967).

Anthony Moncrieff (ed.), *Suez: Ten Years After* (B.B.C. Publications, 1967).

Christopher Driver, *The Disarmers* (Hodder & Stoughton, 1964).

Frank Parkin, *Middle-Class Radicalism* (Manchester U.P., 1968).

Kenneth Allsop, *The Angry Decade*, 3rd imp. (Peter Owen, 1964).

Colin Wilson, *The Outsider* (Gollancz, 1956).

John Osborne, *Look Back in Anger* (Faber, 1957).

John Russell Taylor, *Anger and After* (Methuen, 1962).

T. R. Fyvel, *The Insecure Offenders*, 2nd ed. (Penguin, 1963).

J. B. Mays, *The Young Pretenders* (Michael Joseph, 1965).

S. Hall and P. Whannel, *The Popular Arts* (Hutchinson, 1964).

Colin MacInnes, *England, Half English* (MacGibbon & Kee, 1961).

A List of Contributors

ANTHONY BICÂT is director of the leading experimental theatre group, 'Portable Theatre', which travels the country, presenting new plays to young audiences.

VERNON BOGDANOR was born in 1943 and educated at Bishopshalt School and Queen's and Nuffield Colleges, Oxford. At present he is a Fellow in Politics at Brasenose College, Oxford. He is writing a book on British political ideas in the twentieth century.

STANLEY COHEN was educated at Witwatersrand University and the London School of Economics. He has published a number of articles on juvenile delinquency, and is now Lecturer in Criminology at Durham University.

D. E. COOPER has been a lecturer in Philosophy at Pembroke and Jesus Colleges, Oxford. He has contributed several articles to philosophical journals in the fields of semantics and ethics, and is currently engaged in writing two books on these topics.

PETER OPPENHEIMER was born in 1938 and educated at Haberdashers' Aske's School and The Queen's College, Oxford. From 1961 to 1964 he worked as an economist with the Bank for International Settlements in Basle. He returned to Oxford as a Research Fellow of Nuffield College in 1964, and in 1967 was elected a Student (i.e. Tutorial Fellow) of Christ Church, Oxford. His special interests are in international economics and public policy, and he has published a number of articles in these areas.

MICHAEL PINTO-DUSCHINSKY was born in 1943 and educated at the City of London School, the Sorbonne, Pembroke College, Oxford, Cornell University and Nuffield College, Oxford. He is at present a Research Fellow of Merton College, Oxford.

PAUL ROCK was born in 1943 and graduated from the London School of Economics in 1964. He then went to

Nuffield College from 1964 to 1967, and is at present an Assistant Lecturer in Sociology at the London School of Economics.

L. A. SIEDENTOP was educated at Harvard and Magdalen College, Oxford. At Oxford he wrote a D.Phil. thesis on the French critics of the Enlightenment and Revolution, and from 1965 to 1968 was a Research Fellow of Nuffield College. He is now writing *The Life and Thought of Alexis de Tocqueville*.

ROBERT SKIDELSKY was born in 1939 and educated at Brighton College and Jesus College, Oxford. He was a Research Fellow of Nuffield College, Oxford, from 1965 to 1968, and is the author of *Politicians and the Slump* (1967) and *English Progressive Schools* (1969).

ROBERT TAYLOR was born in 1943 and educated at St Bees School, Cumberland, and Wadham College, Oxford. He was a Research Student at Nuffeld College, Oxford, and was Lecturer in Modern History at the University of Lancaster. He is now a political correspondent with *The Economist*.

WILLIAM WALLACE was educated at Westminster Abbey Choir School and St Edward's School, Oxford, where he won the school debating prize in 1958 with a speech attacking the Government's defence policy. He read history at King's College, Cambridge, and was then at Cornell University for three years, where he obtained a Ph.D. in Politics and International Relations. Since 1967 he has been a Lecturer in the Department of Government at Manchester University.

Index

343

347

Morel, E. D., 230
Morrison, Herbert, 20, 53 n., 81, 83, 86, 89, 114; and Suez, *see under* Suez crisis
Mosley, Sir Oswald, 19, 53 n.
municipalisation, 92
Murdoch, Iris, 254
Murphy, Robert, 20–1; *Diplomat among Warriors*, 20
Must Labour Lose?, 70

Nahas Pasha, 187
Nassau Agreement (1962), 9, 218, 239, 249
Nasser, President, 168, 172–90 *passim*; *Philosophy of Revolution*, 172
National Board for Prices and Incomes, 141
National Campaign for the Abolition of Capital Punishment, 224–5, 232
National Coal Board, 66
National Committee for the Abolition of Nuclear Weapon Tests (N.C.A.N.W.T.), 222, 224
National Economic Development Council, *see* N.E.D.C.
National Government, 19
National Health Service, 56, 72
National Incomes Commission (N.I.C.), 141
National Plan, 153
National Service, 196–7, 202–3; ending of, 144, 193, 204–5, 209, 211, 212. *See also* conscription
National Union of Mineworkers and the Amalgamated Engineering Union, 233, 235
National Union of Railwaymen, 236, 240
Nationalised Industries, Financial and Economic Obligations of, 133
nationalised industries, prices in, 131
nationalised industries, Select Committee on, 132
nationalised industries, social obligations of, 133
nationalisation: Conservatives reverse, 132; Crossman and, 92; Labour Party and, 10, 71–2, 76, 78, 81–4, 86–91, 103, 113; and 'the scientific revolution', 106. *See also* Labour Party Constitution: Clause 4
NATO (North Atlantic Treaty Organisation): and C.N.D., 229, 234, 236–7, 239, 249; and defence policy, 184–5, 204, 210, 212, 218
N.E.D.C. ('Neddy'/National Economic Development Council), 152–3
Negro music, 321
Neguib, General, 174, 176, 187
Neild, R. R., 166 n.

neutralism, 91
'never had it so good', 38–9, 120,
New Fabian Essays, 87, 89, 111, 230
New Left, 12, 15, 222
New Left Review, 232
New Outlook, 19
New Party (Mosley's), 19
New Statesman, 79, 82, 223–4, 227, 228, 232, 237, 239–40
Newcastle upon Tyne, 303
Newman, Cardinal, 271
News of the World, 262
Next Five Years Group, 18–19
N.I.C., *see* National Incomes Commission
Nicholas, Herbert, 170
Nicholls, Sir Harmar, 59
Nicholson, R. J., 167 n.
Nicolson, Sir Harold, 53 n., 54 n
Nicolson, Nigel, 54 n.
Nietzsche, Friedrich, 262
Nigeria, 36
Nijinsky, Vaslav, 271
non-nuclear club, 235
Northern Ireland, unemployment rates in, 138
Notting Hill Riots (1958), 314
novels and Angry Young Men, 256–67
nuclear blackmail, 206
nuclear deterrent, 193, 200, 204, 211, 213, 215, 217–18, 229, 234, 248. *See also* atom bomb; hydrogen bomb; unilateralism
nuclear test-ban treaty (July 1963), 36
nuclear weapons, 198, 201; China and, 250; France and, 249; U.K. and, *see* atom bomb; hydrogen bomb; unilateralism
N.U.G.M.W. (National Union of General and Manual Workers), 233, 235
Nuri es-Said, 174
Nutting, Anthony, 172; *No End of a Lesson*, 168–9

O.E.E.C. (Organisation for European Economic Co-operation), 123, 141. *See also* European Economic Community
Operation Robot, 125
opinion polls, 71
Oppenheimer, Peter, 117, 162 n.
Orpington 1962 by-election, 70
O.S.A. (overseas Sterling Area), 124–5, 127, 145
Osborne, John, 226, 242, 254–6, 260–2, 276, 283, 284–6, 287 n., 307, 340; *Declaration*, 256, 262–3; *Entertainer, The*, 260, 262–3, 282; *Epitaph for George Dillon*, 264; *Look Back in Anger*,